Managing Quality and Human Resources

A Guide to Continuous Improvement

Barrie Dale, Cary Cooper and Adrian Wilkinson

BLACKWELL
Business

First published 1997

2 4 6 8 10 9 7 5 3 1

Blackwell Publishers Ltd
108 Cowley Road
Oxford OX4 1JF
UK

Blackwell Publishers Inc.
350 Main Street
Malden, Massachusetts 02148
USA

British Library Cataloguing in Publication Data

A CIP catalogue record for this book is available from the British Library.

Library of Congress Cataloguing in Publication Data has been applied for.

ISBN 0-631-20024X

Commissioning Editor: Tim Goodfellow
Desk Editor: Linda Auld
Production Manager/Controller: Lisa Parker

Typeset in 11/13pt Garamond
by Photoprint, Torquay, Devon
Printed in Great Britain by T. J. International Ltd, Padstow, Cornwall

This book is printed on acid-free paper

Managing Quality and Human Resources

Contents

List of Tables and Figures

Tables

Figures

Preface

We felt it was time to build on the success of the first edition, called *Total Quality and Human Resources,* and have written this new edition, called *Managing Quality and Human Resources.* It has been completely updated and revised to reflect new study and developments in TQM as well as the new interest in continuous improvement. MBA and MSc students, and those studying for postgraduate diplomas in TQM and other professional qualifications that involve considerations of quality management, should find the book of particular interest as will the increasing number of academics in universities, business schools and colleges of further education with research and/or teaching interest in TQM.

As well as being used by students, we envisage that the second edition will be a practical guide for senior managers and, it is hoped, will provide them with answers to the quality challenges being faced on both internal and external fronts by their organizations. The material in the book is based to a large extent on involvements with CEOs and senior managers during the course of the UMIST TQM research, operation of a TQM Multi-Company Teaching Company Programme and TQM training and advisory work undertaken during the last sixteen or so years by the UMIST Quality Management Centre. This is supplemented by the specific research carried out by Professor Cary Cooper and his colleagues in the field of industrial organizational psychology and that of Dr Wilkinson in the human resource components of TQM.

We believe that the collaboration of specialists in quality management, human resources and industrial organizational psychology gives the book an added dimension providing additional insights into TQM and the improvement process not covered by more traditional texts of the subject of total quality management.

How this Edition Differs from the First

A number of chapters of the first edition tended to focus more on the implications of organizational psychology in TQM, rather than on the soft and behavioural issues. This has been changed in the second edition. The material has been reconfigured to reflect current thinking in the soft issues of TQM. An additional chapter has been included dealing with the main approaches to TQM, covering issues such as the received wisdom on the subject, self-assessment and quality award models.

Specifically, this book aims to:

1   provide an insight into the issues involved with continuous improvement;

2   describe the role of senior managers in TQM and tell them what they should be doing;

3   explore some common failings in relation to this role;

4   examine some of the key issues in the introduction, development and advancement of TQM;

5   highlight the so-called soft issues of TQM and its behavioural implications and say what senior management should do to encourage developments in these areas;

6   stress the dependency of technical and behavioural issues of TQM and the need for everyone to work together in the introduction and development of TQM in order to help to realize its full potential.

Finally, in preparation of the text we have increased our knowledge of each other's disciplines and their importance to TQM. We hope that you, the readers, will benefit from our multidisciplined effort.

Barrie Dale, Cary Cooper, Adrian Wilkinson
Manchester School of Management
University of Manchester Institute of Science and Technology

Acknowledgements

In the preparation of this book the authors have drawn upon the findings from a number of research projects. They acknowledge the support of the Engineering and Physical Sciences Research Council, the Economic and Social Sciences Research Council, the Institute of Personnel and Development and the Institute of Management.

The authors also wish to thank the companies that allowed their factories to be used as research laboratories and gave permission for material to be used as examples in the text. Adrian Wilkinson would also like to thank Queensland University of Technology for providing him with a visiting fellowship, which gave him the opportunity to write some of this material. In addition, the authors acknowledge the comments made on drafts of the chapters by a number of directors from a range of organizations.

Adrian Wilkinson would like to thank his parents Brian and Margaret Wilkinson for their support over the years.

List of Abbreviations

AQL	acceptable quality level
ASQC	American Society for Quality Control
BPR	business process re-engineering
BS	British Standards
BSI	British Standards Institution
CBI	continuous business improvement
CEO	chief executive officer
Cpk	process capability index
CQAD	corporate quality assurance department
CWQC	company-wide quality control
DTI	Department of Trade and Industry
EFQM	European Foundation for Quality Management
EI	employee involvement
EIF	error identification form
EOQ	European Organisation for Quality
EPSRC	Engineering and Physical Sciences Research Council
FMEA	failure mode and effects analysis
EQA	European Quality Award
FTA	fault tree analysis
HR	human resources
HRM	human resources management
IPM	Institute of Personnel Management
ISO	International Organization for Standardization
JIT	just in time
JUSE	Union of the Japanese Scientists and Engineers
MBNQA	Malcolm Baldridge National Quality Award

MD	Managing Director
MITI	Ministry of International Trade and Industry
NIST	National Institute of Standards and Technology
OD	organizational development
PDCA	plan–do–check–act
PIMS	profit impact of market strategy
QC	quality circle
QCD	quality, cost and delivery
QFD	quality function deployment
QM	quality management
R&D	research and development
RPQ	relative perceived quality
SMED	single minute exchange of die
SMPC	statistical process control
STA	success tree analysis
SWOT	strengths, weaknesses, opportunities and threats
TQC	total quality control
TQM	total quality management
TUC	Trade Union Congress
UMIST	University of Manchester Institute of Science and Technology

1 Total Quality Management: An Introduction

Introduction

In today's global competitive market-place, the demands of customers are forever increasing as they require improved quality of products and services but are prepared to pay less for their requirements. Continuous improvement in total business activities with a focus on the customer throughout the entire organization is one of the main means by which companies meet these demands. This is why quality and its management, the focus of this chapter, are looked upon by many organizations as the means by which they can gain and maintain a competitive edge over their rivals. This chapter introduces the reader to Total Quality Management (TQM). Many of the themes outlined are explored later in the book.

This chapter opens by examining the different interpretations that are placed on the word 'quality'. It then goes on to outline why quality has grown in importance during the last decade or so. The evolution of quality management is described through the stages of inspection, quality control and quality assurance, to TQM. In presenting this evolution the drawbacks of a detection-based approach to quality are compared to the recommended approach of prevention. The elements of TQM are explored along with its perceived benefits from a senior management perspective.

What is Quality?

'Quality' is now a familiar word; however, a variety of interpretations are placed on its use and meaning. Today and in a variety of situations it is perhaps an overused word. For example, when a case is being made for extra funding and resources, to prevent a reduction in funding, to keep a unit in operation, or to try to emphasize excellence, just count the number of times the word 'quality' is used in the ensuing argument/presentation.

Many people say that they know what is meant by quality; they typically claim, 'I know it when I see it' (i.e. quality by feel, taste, instinct and/or smell). This simple statement, and the interpretations of quality made by lay people, masks the need to define quality in an operational manner. In fact, quality as a concept is quite difficult for many people to grasp and understand, and much confusion and myth surround it.

In a linguistic sense, quality originates from the Latin word *qualis*, which means 'such as the thing really is'. There is an international definition of quality: 'Totality of characteristics of an entity that bears on its ability to satisfy stated and implied needs' (BS EN ISO 8402, 1995).

In today's business world there is no single accepted definition of quality. However, irrespective of the context in which it is used, it is usually meant to distinguish one organization, institution, event, product, service, process, person, result, action or communication from another. For the word to have the desired effect as intended by the user and to prevent any form of misunderstanding in the communication, the following points need to be considered:

- The person using the word must have a clear and full understanding of its meaning.

- The people/audience to whom the communication is directed should have a similar understanding of quality as the person making the communication

- Within an organization, to prevent confusion and to ensure that everyone in each department and function is focused on the same objectives, there should be an agreed definition of quality. For example Betz Dearborn Ltd defines quality as 'that which gives complete customer satisfaction', and Rank Xerox (UK) as 'providing our customers, internal and external, with products and services that fully satisfy their negotiated requirements'.

There are a number of ways or senses in which quality may be defined, some being broader than others. These different definitions are now examined.

QUALITATIVE

When the term 'quality' is used in this way, it is usually in a non-technical situation. BS EN ISO 8402 (1995) refers to it as relative quality, where entities are ranked on a relative basis in the degree of excellence or 'comparative sense'. The following are some examples of this:

- In advertising slogans to assist in building an image: Esso – Quality at Work, Hayfield Textiles – Committed to Quality, Kenco – Superior Quality, Philips Whirlpool – Brings Quality to Life, Thomson Tour Operators – Thomson Quality Makes the World of Difference.

- By television and radio commentators (a quality player, a quality goal, a quality try).

- By directors and managers (quality performance, quality of communication).

- By people, in general (quality product, top quality, high quality, original quality, quality of communications, quality person, loss of quality, German quality and 100% quality).

It is frequently found that in such cases the context in which the word quality is used is highly subjective, and the word in its strictest sense is being misused. For example, there is more than one shop called 'Quality Seconds', and there is even a shop that trades under the banner of 'Top Quality Seconds'. A van was recently spotted with the advertising slogan 'Quality Part Worn Tyres'.

QUANTITATIVE

In BS EN ISO 8402 (1995) the terms 'quality level' and 'quality measure' are used where precise technical evaluations are carried out in a 'quantitative sense'.

The traditional quantitative term, which is still used in some business environments, is Acceptable Quality Level (AQL), in particular when used in the context of acceptance sampling. This is defined in BS 4778: Part 2 (1991) as: 'when a continuing series of lots is considered, a quality level which for the purposes of sampling inspection is the limit of a satisfactory process'. This is when the product and/or production quality is paradoxically defined in terms of non-conforming parts per hundred (i.e. some defined degree of imperfection).

An AQL is often imposed by a customer on its supplier in relation to a particular contract. The customer will then inspect the incoming batch according to the appropriate sampling scheme. If more than the allowed number of defects are found in the sample the entire batch is returned to the supplier, or the supplier can, at the request of the customer, sort out conforming from non-conforming product on the customer's site. The employment of an AQL is also adopted by some companies under the mistaken belief that trying to eliminate all defects is too costly.

The setting of an AQL by a company tends to work against a 'right first time' mentality in its people because it appears to condone the production and delivery of non-conforming parts or services, suggesting that errors are acceptable to the organization. It is tantamount to planning for failure. For example, consider a final product that is made up of 3000 parts. If the standard set is 1 per cent AQL, this would mean that the product is planned to contain thirty non-conforming parts. In all reality it is likely to be many more because of the vagaries of the sampling used in the plan or scheme, whereby acceptance or rejection of the batch of product is decided. This is clearly an unacceptable situation in today's business environment, and represents a non-survival performance.

UNIFORMITY OF THE PRODUCT CHARACTERISTICS OR DELIVERY OF A SERVICE AROUND A NOMINAL OR TARGET VALUE

In a manufacturing situation if a product's dimensions are within the design specification or tolerance limits it is considered acceptable; conversely, if the dimensions are outside the specification it is not acceptable (figure 1.1). The difference between what is judged to be

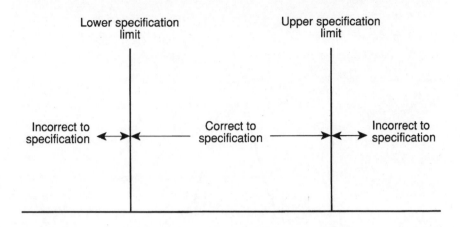

Figure 1.1   The inside/outside specification dilemma

just inside or just outside the specification is marginal. It may also be questioned whether this step change between pass and fail has any scientific basis and validity.

Designers often establish specification limits without sufficient knowledge of the process by which the product or service is to be produced or delivered or of its capability. It is often the case that designers cannot agree among themselves about the tolerances/ specification to be allocated and it is not uncommon to find outdated reasoning being used. They also tend to define and establish a tight tolerance to provide safeguards and protect themselves, taking the view that production and operations personnel will find the tolerance too tight and the part difficult to make, and will ask to have the tolerance increased. In many situations there is inadequate communication on this matter between the design and manufacturing functions. Fortunately, this is changing with the increasing use of simultaneous or concurrent engineering.

The problem with working to the specification limits is that it frequently leads to tolerance stack-up and parts not fitting together correctly at the assembly stage. This is especially the case when one part that is just inside the lower specification limit is assembled to one that is just inside the upper specification. If the process is controlled such that a part is produced around the nominal or a target dimension (figure 1. 2), this problem does not occur and the

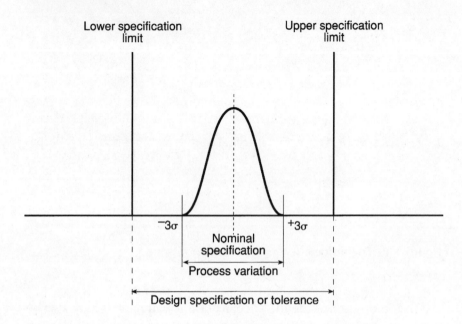

Figure 1.2 Design tolerance and process variation relationship

goodness of fit and smooth operation of the final assembly and/or end product are enhanced.

The idea of reducing the variation of part characteristics and process parameters so that they are centred around a target value can be attributed to Taguchi (1986). He wrote that 'the quality of a product is the (minimum) loss imparted by the product to the society from the time the product is shipped'. This is defined by a quadratic loss curve. Among the losses he included consumers' dissatisfaction, warranty costs, loss of reputation and, ultimately, loss of market share.

The relationship of design specification and variation of the manufacturing and/or production process can be quantified by a capability index, for example, Cp, which is an indication of the process potential:

$$Cp = \frac{\text{Total specification width}}{\text{Process variation width}}$$

CONFORMANCE TO AGREED AND FULLY UNDERSTOOD REQUIREMENTS

This definition of quality is attributed to Crosby (1979). He believes that quality is not comparative and that there is no such thing as high quality or low quality, or quality in terms of goodness, feel, excellence and luxury. A product or service either conforms to requirements or it does not. In other words, quality is an attribute (a characteristic that, by comparison to a standard or reference point, is judged to be correct or incorrect), not a variable (a characteristic that is measurable). Crosby makes the point that the requirements are all the actions needed to produce a product and/or deliver a service that meets the customers' expectations, and that it is the responsibility of management to ensure that adequate requirements are created and specified within the organization.

Some products are highly sophisticated in terms of their design but are poor in terms of conformance to requirements. On the other hand, some products are simple in terms of their design but exhibit high levels of conformance to requirements. The 'quality of design' (the degree to which the design of the product and/or service achieves its purpose) can be confused with the 'quality of conformance' (how well the product and/or service conforms to the design). Stemming from this confusion about design and conformance can be a tendency to believe that 'better' quality means high costs. This view results from the confusion between quality and grade. Grade represents the addition of features and characteristics to satisfy the additional needs of customers, and this clearly requires extra monies, but grade can be seen as different to quality. A high-grade product or service may not conform to requirements, and thus may result in customer dissatisfaction.

FITNESS FOR PURPOSE/USE

This is a standard definition of quality, first used by Juran (1988). Juran classified 'fitness for purpose/use' into the categories of quality of design, quality of conformance, abilities and field service. Focusing on fitness for use helps to prevent the over-specification of products. Over-specification can add greatly to the manufacturing costs and tends to militate against a 'right first time' performance.

How fit a product or service is for use has obviously to be judged by the purchaser, customer or user.

SATISFYING CUSTOMERS' EXPECTATIONS AND UNDERSTANDING THEIR NEEDS AND FUTURE REQUIREMENTS

A typical definition that reflects this sentiment is given by Betz Dearborn: 'the attributes of a product and/or service which, as perceived by the customer, makes the product/service attractive to them and gives them satisfaction'. The focus of the definition is adding value to the product and/or service.

This is the crux of TQM, which concerns itself with effective and efficient management and having customers who are totally satisfied and who come back for more of the same product or service. The customer is the major reason for an organization's existence, and customer loyalty and retention are perhaps (in the long term) the only measures of organizational success. In most situations customers have a choice; they need not place future orders with a supplier who does not perform as they expect. They will certainly not jeopardize their own business interest out of loyalty to a supplier whose products and services fail to perform in the expected manner. The aim of the superior performing companies is to become the supplier of choice of their customers, to 'lock themselves' into their customers' mode of operation by becoming the sole supplier, and to add value to their customers' business by process improvement. The report of the European Foundation for Quality Management (EFQM) Customer Loyalty Team (1996) explores a range of issues on the importance of customer loyalty, making the point that 'in highly competitive and rapidly changing markets, with reduced product differentiation, satisfying customers or even delighting them may not be enough to guarantee business growth and profitability'. The report explores the definition of loyalty, loyalty drivers and measurements, and describes how to improve loyalty.

The process of continuous improvement is all about customer orientation, and many company missions are based entirely on satisfying customer perceptions. The superior performing organizations go beyond satisfying their customers; they emphasize the need to delight customers by giving them more than what is required in the contract; they also now talk about winning customers and 'cuddling' customers – some, in fact, talk of everyone in the organization being 'infatuated' with their customers. The importance of this can be seen by considering situations where more than what was expected has been received from a supplier (e.g. an extra glass of wine on an aircraft, or sales assistants going out of their way to be courteous, being helpful, and providing very detailed information) and the positive perception produced by this type of action.

This class of organization also devotes considerable effort to anticipating the future expectations of its customers and, by working with them in long-term relationships, helping them to define their future needs and expectations. Such organizations listen very closely to their customers and 'real' users of the product or service, in order to gain a clearer perspective of customer experiences. They aim to build quality into the product, service, system and/or process as upstream as is practicable.

Those companies intent on satisfying their customer needs and expectations will have in place a mechanism of facilitating a continuous two-way flow of information between themselves and their customers. This is essential to the process of continuous improvement. There is a need for a system to handle this flow of information. For example, banks until recently did not have a mechanism or system for collecting customer complaints. Complaints went to the branches, which often could not deal with problems originating within the system. But complaints were not funnelled through to head office. There are a variety of means available to companies for them to assess issues such as:

- how well they are meeting their customer expectations,

- what the customers' chief causes of concern are,

- what the main complaints are,

- what suggestions the customers might have for improvements,

- how they might add value to the product or service,

- how well they act on what the customer says, and

- the best means of differentiating themselves in the marketplace.

The trend is for increasing the level of contact with the customer. These 'moments of truth' (Carlzon, 1987) occur far more frequently in commerce, public organizations, the civil service and service type situations than in manufacturing organizations. The means include:

- customer workshops,
- panels and clinics,
- focus groups,
- customer interviews,
- market research,
- dealer information,
- questionnaire surveys,
- product reports,
- trailing the service or product,
- trade shows, and
- using 'test' consumers and mystery shoppers.

Having listened to 'customer voices', an organization should put into place appropriate strategy and corrective actions for making the necessary changes and improvements. It is also important to clarify and identify the elements and characteristics of the product or service that the customer finds attractive. This customer-required quality (that is, customers' wants) should be translated into the language of internal needs and driven back through all levels in the organizational hierarchy. It is important that the requirements are put into terms that are measurable, realistic and achievable; Quality Function Deployment (QFD) is useful in this respect. This is central to the issue of total customer satisfaction. Customer needs and requirements are forever changing, and organizations have to live up to their customer expectations and these are never satisfied, even though the supplying organization may think they are.

Why is Quality Important?

To answer this question just consider the unsatisfactory examples of product and/or service that you have experienced, the bad feelings they gave, the resulting actions taken and the people you told about the experience and the outcome. The following customer service information, from statistics compiled by Mattson and Associates from US service sector companies (CMC partnership Ltd, 1991), provides some quantitative detail about this:

Customer Service Facts – Did You Know That . . .

1   If 20 customers are dissatisfied with your service, 19 won't tell you. 14 of the 20 will take their business elsewhere.

2   Dissatisfied customers tell an average of 10 other people about their bad experience; 12 per cent tell up to 20 people.

3   Satisfied customers will tell an average of 5 people about their positive experiences.

4   It costs five times more money to attract a new customer than to keep an existing one.

5   Up to 90 per cent of dissatisfied customers will not buy from you again, and they won't tell you why.

6   In many industries, quality of service is one of the few variables that can distinguish a business from its competition.

7   Providing high quality service can save your business money. The same skills that lead to increased customer satisfaction also lead to increased employee productivity.

8   Customers are willing to pay more to receive better service.

9   95 per cent of dissatisfied customers will become loyal customers again if their complaints are handled well and quickly.

The following are examples of data from surveys that have focused on the perceived importance of product and service quality.

PUBLIC PERCEPTIONS OF PRODUCT AND SERVICE QUALITY

In 1988 the American Society for Quality Control (ASQC) commissioned the Gallup organization to survey public perceptions on a variety of quality-related issues. This survey was the fourth in a series which began in 1985; the 1985 and 1988 surveys focused on US customers and the 1986 and 1987 studies surveyed attitudes of company executives. The 1988 study was done by conducting telephone interviews with 1005 adults in the United States during the summer of 1988. A selection of results, as reported by Ryan (1988) and Hutchens (1989), is outlined below:

- The following is a ranking of factors that people consider important when they purchase a product:
  - performance,
  - durability,
  - ease of repair, service availability, warranty, and ease of use (these four factors were ranked about the same),
  - price,
  - appearance,
  - brand name.

- People will pay a premium to get what they perceive to be higher quality.

- Consumers are willing to pay substantially more for better intrinsic quality in a product.

- According to the respondents, the following are the factors that make for 'higher' quality in services:
  - courtesy,
  - promptness,
  - a basic sense that one's needs are being satisfied,
  - attitudes of the service provider.

- When consumers do experience a problem with the product, they appear reluctant to take positive action with the manufacturer. The 1987 survey revealed that executives regard customer complaints, suggestions and enquiries as key indicators of product and service quality; this feedback gap clearly needs to be bridged.

An ASQC-Gallup survey was conducted in 1991 (Gallup Organization/ASQC, 1991) to survey the attitudes and opinions of consumers in Japan, Germany and the United States in relation to questions such as 'What does quality really mean to them?', 'How do they define it and does it influence their buying behaviour?', 'What is their perception of the quality from other parts of the world?', and 'What are the dynamics underlying a consumer's reasons for buying or not buying something produced in a foreign country?'. On a number of issues, this survey updates American attitudes expressed in the 1988 survey. Over 1000 people in each country were questioned. A selection of summary highlights from the report are outlined below:

Consumers in the US, Japan and West Germany in many respects are alike in terms of the attributes they consider important in determining the quality of the products they buy. For example, approximately one in five look to the brand name of a product. Durability is also important to at least 10% of the consumers in each of the countries surveyed.

Asked what factors are most important in influencing their decision to buy a product, price is the leading response in West Germany (64%) and in the US (31%). Performance (40%) is most important among Japanese consumers, followed by price (36%).

Compared to the 1988 survey, US consumers are now more likely to rate American-made products higher for quality (55% rating them an '8', '9' or '10' versus 48% who did so in 1988).

A majority (61%) of US consumers believe it is very important to US workers to produce high quality products or service.

Price and quality are the reasons given most frequently by American consumers for buying a product made in Japan or Germany.

VIEWS AND ROLES OF SENIOR MANAGEMENT

In 1992 ASQC commissioned the Gallup organization to study the nature of leadership for quality within American business organizations of senior management in both large and small organizations. The objective was to explore their views concerning quality improvement and the role of directors with regard to quality. Some 684 executives were interviewed. The following is a summary of the main findings extracted from Gallup organization/ASQC (1992).

At least six in ten executives report that they have a great deal of personal leadership impact on customer focus and satisfaction, strategic quality planning, quality and operational results and financial results.

On average, executives rate American-made products 7.0 on a ten-point scale for quality. Thirty-three per cent give American products a rating of '8' or better.

Most executives believe management plays a greater role than the board in determining quality policy within their company.

More than four in ten (45%) report their board does discuss quality frequently.

Four in ten (43%) executives report their board reports on consumer satisfaction frequently, and almost as many (38%) report the board reviews reports on customer retention or loyalty frequently'.

The European Foundation for Quality Management (EFQM) contracted McKinsey and Company to survey the CEOs of the top 500 Western European corporations in relation to quality performance and the management of quality; 150 CEOs responded to the survey. The following are some of the main findings as reported by McKinsey and Company (1989):

- Over 90% of CEO's consider quality performance to be 'critical' for their Corporation.

- 60% of CEO's said that quality performance had become a lot more important than before (late 70's)

- The four main reasons why quality is perceived to be important are:
  - primary buying argument for the ultimate customer
  - major means of reducing costs
  - major means for improving flexibility/responsiveness
  - major means for reducing throughout time

- The feasible improvement in gross margin on sales through improved quality performance was rated at an average of 17%

- More than 85% of the leading CEO's in Europe consider the management of quality to be one of the top priorities for their corporations.

Lascelles and Dale (1990), reporting on a survey they carried out of 74 UK CEOs, say that 'almost all the respondents believe that product and service quality is an important factor in international competitiveness. More than half have come to this conclusion within the past four years'.

QUALITY IS NOT NEGOTIABLE

An order, contract or customer lost on the grounds of non-conforming product and/or service quality is much harder to regain than one lost on price or delivery. In a number of cases the customer could be lost forever; in simple terms the organization has been outsold by the competition.

If you have any doubt about the truth of this statement just consider the number of organizations that have gone out of business or lost a significant share of the market, and consider the reported reasons for them getting into that position. Quality is one of the factors that is not negotiable; in today's business world the penalties for unsatisfactory product quality and poor service are likely to be punitive.

QUALITY IS ALL PERVASIVE

There are a number of single-focus business initiatives that an organization may deploy to increase profit. However, with the improvements made by companies of their mode of operation, reduction in monopolies, government legislation, deregulation, changes in market share, mergers, takeovers, and collaborative joint ventures, there is less distinction between companies than there was some years ago. TQM is a much broader concept than previous initiatives, encompassing not only product, service and process improvements but also those relating to costs, productivity, people involvement and development. It also has the added advantage that it is focused on satisfying customer needs, something with which few people can disagree.

QUALITY AND PRODUCTIVITY

Cost, productivity and quality improvements are complementary, and not alternative, objectives. Managers sometimes say that they do not have the time and resources to ensure that product and/or service quality is done right the first time. They go on to argue that if their people concentrate on planning for quality then they will be losing valuable production and operating time, and as a consequence output will be lost and costs will rise. Despite this argument, management and their staff will make the time to rework product and service a second or even a third time, and spend considerable time and organizational resources on corrective action, and on placing customers who have been affected by the non-conformances.

QUALITY AND PERFORMANCE IN THE MARKET-PLACE

The Profit Impact of Market Strategy (PIMS), conducted under the Strategic Planning Institute in Cambridge (Massachusetts), has a database containing over 3000 records of detailed business performance. The Institute is a cooperative run by its members. The database allows a detailed analysis of the parameters that influence business performance. A key PIMS concept is that of Relative Perceived Quality (RPQ); this is the product and service offering as perceived by the customer. It has been established that the factors having most leverage on return on investment are RPQ and relative market share, and that companies with large market shares are those whose quality is relatively high, whereas companies with small market shares are those whose quality is relatively low. It was also found that customer-perceived quality helps low- and medium-share businesses gain market share and helps high-share business defend their position (see Buzzell and Gale, 1987).

QUALITY AND IMPROVED BUSINESS PERFORMANCE

Kano et al. (1983) carried out an examination of twenty-six companies that had won the Deming Application Prize (a prize awarded to companies for their effective implementation of company-wide quality control) between 1961 and 1980. They found that the financial performance of these companies in terms of earning rate, productivity, growth rate, liquidity and net worth was above the average for their industries.

A report published by the US General Accounting Office (1991) focused on the top twenty scorers of the Malcolm Baldrige National Quality Award (MBNQA) in the period 1988–9. Using a combination of questionnaire and interview methods, the report asked companies to provide information on four broad classes of performance measures – employee-related indicators, operating indicators, customer satisfaction indicators and business performance indicators. Improvements were claimed in all of these indicators (for example, in market share, sales per employee, return on assets, and return on sales). Useful information on financial performance was obtained from fifteen of the twenty companies, which experienced the following annual average increases:

- Market share: 13.7 per cent

- Sales per employee: 8.6 per cent

- Return on assets: 1.3 per cent

- Return on Sales: 0.4 per cent

Larry (1993) reports on a study carried out on the winners of the MBNQA and found that they 'yielded a cumulative 89% gain, whereas the same investment in the Standard and Poor 500-Stock Index delivered only 33.1%'. Wisner and Eakins (1994) also carried out an operational and financial review of the MBNQA winners, 1988–93. One of the conclusions reached was that the winners appeared to be performing financially as well or better than their competitions.

The US Commerce Department's National Institute of Standards and Technology (NIST) invested a hypothetical $1000 in each of the five publicly traded whole company MBNQA winners and the parent companies of seven subsidiary winners, and also made the same investment in the Standard and Poor 500. It was found that the twelve winning companies outperformed the Standard and Poor 500 by almost three to one. In addition, NIST invested a hypothetical $1000 in a group of 32 companies receiving MBNQA site visits; these companies outperformed the Standard and Poor 500 companies by two to one. Curt Reimann (1995; then director of the MBNQA programme), commenting on the results, said 'this review adds to the mounting evidence that, done right, quality management can lead to outstanding returns in many business areas, including financial performance, satisfied customers, and improved market share'.

The Aeroquip Corporation, which is a Trinova company, involved in aerospace, automotive and industrial markets, has 9000 employees in twelve countries and on forty manufacturing sites. It has developed its own version of the MBNQA, called Aeroquip Quality Plus (AQ+). Each of its operating sites is required to obtain a score of 700 of 1000 points to attain an AQ+ award. The following are the details of the 1994 performance of the nine sites that have attained the award compared to those sites that are still working towards it:

- 64 per cent of Aeroquip operating income is generated from 31 per cent of sales.

- 15.1 per cent return on sales against 3.9 per cent for the remainder to the Aeroquip companies.

- 21 per cent sales growth against 5.0 per cent for the remainder of the Aeroquip companies.

- 31 per cent income growth against a 3.2 per cent decrease for the remainder of the Aeroquip companies.

A study has been carried out by Zairi et al. (1994) on the impact of quality on the business performance of 29 UK companies, which were chosen for their perceived knowledge and application of TQM. Data from these companies for eight performance indicators was analysed over a five-year period. It was reported that for these indicators a high proportion of the companies exhibited above-average industry performance.

The most extensive study of the impact on TQM on corporate performance was provided by Easton and Jarrell (1996). They studied the impact of TQM on the performance of a sample of 108 firms that began serious efforts to implement TQM between 1981 and 1991. It was concluded that 'performance, measured by profit margin, return on assets, asset use efficiency, and excess stock returns, is improved for the sample of firms that adopted TQM'.

Although there are methodological problems with most of these studies, the broad picture emerging is of the benefits of quality management competence in terms of competitive advantage and business performance.

THE COST OF NON-QUALITY IS HIGH

Based on a variety of companies, industries and situations, the cost of quality (or to be more precise, the cost of not getting it right the first time) ranges from 5 to 25 per cent of an organization's annual sales turnover (see Chapter 4 and Dale and Plunkett (1995) for details). An organization should compare its profit to sales turnover ratio to that of its quality costs to sales turnover, in order to gain an indication of the importance of product and service quality to corporate profitability.

PRODUCT LIABILITY

The 1987 Consumer Protection Act and the 1988 legislation on strict product liability has resulted in:

- CEOs and senior managers becoming more aware of the importance of having a recognized quality system which meets the requirements of the ISO 9000 series of quality management system standards. Registration to this series of standards is seen by many executives as some defence against any product liability claims.

- Organizations:
  - being able to trace batches of work that were produced some time in the past,
  - keeping detailed records of actions taken, and
  - engaging in advanced quality planning using techniques such as Failure Mode and Effects Analysis (FMEA) to pinpoint, early on in the planning of the design and operating processes, potential modes of failure.

CUSTOMER IS KING

In today's markets, customers' requirements are becoming increasingly more rigorous and their expectations of the product and/or service in terms of conformance, reliability, dependability, durability, interchangeability, performance, features, appearance, serviceability, user friendliness, safety and environmental friendliness are also increasing. These days many superior performing companies talk in terms of being 'customer obsessed'. At the same time, it is likely that the competition will also be improving and, in addition, new and low-cost competitors may emerge in the market-place. Consequently, there is a need for the process of improvement to be continuous and to involve everyone in the company. The organization that claims to have achieved TQM will be overtaken by the competition. Once the process of continuous improvement has been halted, under the mistaken belief that TQM has been achieved, it is much harder to re-start and gain the initiative on the competition (figure 1.3). This is why TQM should always be referred to as a process and not as a programme. Those people who frequently refer to TQM as a programme do not understand the fundamentals of continuous improvement. An organization committed to product and service quality needs quality of working life of its people in terms of participation, involvement and development, and quality of its systems, processes and products. A combination of all of these features lays the base for a quality organization.

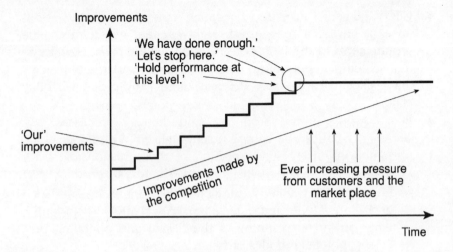

Figure 1.3 Quality improvement is a continuous process

The Evolution of Quality Management

Systems for improving and managing quality have evolved rapidly in recent years. During the past two decades or so, simple inspection activities have been replaced or supplemented by quality control, quality assurance has been developed and refined, and now most companies are working towards TQM. In this progression, four fairly discrete stages can be identified: inspection, quality control, quality assurance, and Total Quality Management, (figure 1.4). British and International Standards definition of these terms are given to provide the reader with some understanding of the general meaning, but the discussion and examination is not restricted by these definitions.

INSPECTION

Activity such as measuring, examining, testing or gauging one or more characteristics of an entity and comparing the results with specified requirements in order to establish whether conformity is achieved for each characteristic. (BS EN ISO 8402, 1995).

At one time inspection was thought to be the only way of ensuring quality. Under a simple inspection-based system, one or more characteristics of a product, service or activity is examined, measured, tested or assessed and compared with specified requirements to assess conformity. In a manufacturing environment the system is applied to incoming goods, manufactured components and assemblies at appropriate points in the process and before passing finished goods into the warehouse. In service- and commercial-type situations the system is also applied at key points, sometimes called appraisal points, in the producing and delivery processes. The inspection activity can be carried out by staff employed specifically for the purpose or by self-inspection of those responsible for a process. Materials, components, paperwork, forms, products and goods that do not conform to specification may be scrapped, reworked, modified or passed on concession. In some cases inspection is used to grade the finished product (for example, the production of cultured pearls). The system is an after-the-event screening process with no prevention content other than, perhaps, identification of suppliers, operators or workers who are producing non-conforming products/services. Simple inspection-based systems are usually wholly in-house and suppliers or customers are not directly involved in the activity.

QUALITY CONTROL

Operational techniques and activities that are used to fulfil requirements for quality. (BS EN ISO 8402, 1995)

Under a system of quality control one might expect, for example, to find in place a paperwork and procedures control system raw material and intermediate stage product testing, logging of elementary process performance data, and feedback information to appropriate personnel. With quality control there will have been some development from the basic inspection activity in terms of sophistication of methods and systems and the tools and techniques employed. While the main mechanism of preventing off-specification products and services from being delivered to a customer is again screening inspection, quality control measures lead to greater process control and a lower incidence of non-conformance.

Those organizations whose approach to the management of product and service quality is based on inspection and quality control are operating in a detection-type mode (that is, finding and fixing mistakes).

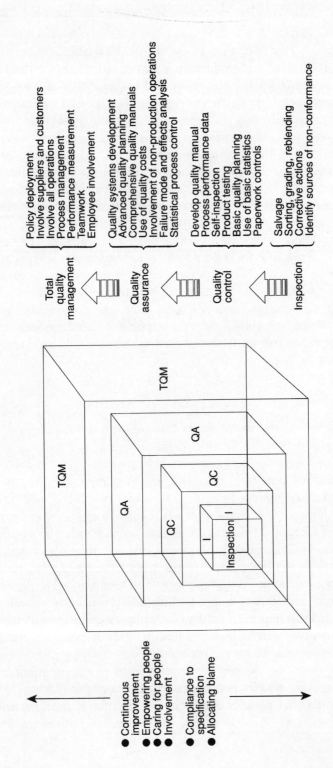

Policy deployment
Involve suppliers and customers
Involve all operations
Process management
Performance measurement
Teamwork
Employee involvement

Quality systems development
Advanced quality planning
Comprehensive quality manuals
Use of quality costs
Involvement of non-production operations
Failure mode and effects analysis
Statistical process control

Develop quality manual
Process performance data
Self-inspection
Product testing
Basic quality planning
Use of basic statistics
Paperwork controls

Salvage
Sorting, grading, reblending
Corrective actions
Identify sources of non-conformance

Total quality management

Quality assurance

Quality control

Inspection

● Continuous improvement
● Empowering people
● Caring for people
● Involvement
● Compliance to specification
● Allocating blame

TQM

TQM

QA

QA

QC

QC

Inspection

I

I

Figure 1.4 The four levels in the evolution of total quality management
Source: Developed from Dale (1994).

QUALITY ASSURANCE

Finding and solving a problem after a non-conformance has been created is not an effective route towards eliminating the root cause of the problem. A lasting and continuous improvement in quality can only be achieved by directing organizational efforts towards planning and preventing problems occurring at source. This concept leads to the third stage of quality management development, which is quality assurance:

> All the planned and systematic activities implemented within the quality system and demonstrated as needed to provide adequate confidence that an entity will fulfil given requirements for quality. (BS EN ISO 8402, 1995).

Examples of additional features acquired when progressing from quality control to quality assurance are, for example, a comprehensive quality management system to increase uniformity and conformity, use of the seven quality control tools (histogram, check sheet, Pareto analysis, cause and effect diagram, graphs, scatter diagram and control chart), Statistical Process Control (SPC), FMEA and the gathering and use of quality costs. Above all, one would expect to see a shift in emphasis from mere detection towards prevention of non-conformances. In short, more emphasis is placed on advanced quality planning, improving the design of the product, process and service, improving control over the process, and involving and motivating people.

TOTAL QUALITY MANAGEMENT

The fourth and highest level, that of TQM, involves the application of quality management principles to all aspects of the business, including customers and suppliers. TQM requires that the principles of quality management should be applied in every branch at every level in the organization. It is a company-wide approach to quality, with improvements undertaken on a continuous basis by everyone in the organization. Individual systems, procedures and requirements may be no higher than for a quality assurance level of quality management, but they will pervade every person, activity and function of the organization. It will, however, require a broadening of outlook and skills and an increase in creative activities from that required at the quality assurance level. The spread of the TQM philosophy would also be expected to be accompanied by greater sophistication in the application of tools and techniques and increased emphasis on people (the so-called soft aspects of TQM). The process will also extend beyond the organization to include partnerships with suppliers and customers. Activities will be reoriented to focus on the customer, internal and external.

There are may interpretations and definitions of TQM, but to take an international definition of the term, it is the:

> Management approach of an organization centred on quality, based on the participation of all its members and aiming at long-term success through customer satisfaction, and benefits to all members of the organization and to society. (BS EN ISO 8402, 1995)

Put simply, TQM is the cooperation of everyone in an organization and associated business processes to produce products and services that meet the needs and expectations of customers. TQM is both a philosophy and a set of guiding principles for managing an organization.

Prevention versus Detection

In tracing the development of quality management from inspection to TQM, it was said that inspection and quality control are basically detection-type activities while quality assurance and TQM are prevention-based. The point was made of the need to switch resources from detection to prevention. The key differences between detection and prevention are now examined.

In a detection or 'fire-fighting' environment, the emphasis is on the product, procedures and/or service deliverables and the downstream producing and delivery processes. Considerable effort is expended on after-the-event inspecting, checking, screening and testing of the product and/or service and on providing reactive 'quick fixes' in a bid to ensure that only conforming products and services are delivered to the customer. In this approach, there is a lack of creative and systematic work activators, with planning and improvements being neglected. Detection will not improve quality but only highlight when it is not present; sometimes it does not even manage to do this. Problems in the process are not removed, but contained.

Inspection is the primary means of control in a 'policeman' or 'goalkeeper' type role, and a 'producing' versus 'checking' situation is thereby encouraged, leading to confusion over people's responsibilities for quality: 'Can I, the producer, get my deliverables past the checker?' It leads to the beliefs that non-conformances are due to the product/service not being inspected enough and also that operators are the sole cause of the problem, not the system.

A question that organizations operating in this mode must answer is: does the checking of work by inspectors affect an operator's pride in the job and responsibility for his or her own quality assurance? The production–inspection relationship is vividly described by McKenzie (1989).

With a detection approach to quality, non-conforming 'products' (products are considered in their widest sense) are culled, sorted and graded, and decisions made on concessions, rework, reblending, repair, downgrading, scrap and disposal. It is not unusual to find products going through this cycle more than once. While a detection-type system may prevent non-conforming products, services and paperwork being delivered to the customer (internal or external), it does not stop them being made. Indeed, it is questionable whether such a system does in fact cull all of the non-conforming products and services. Physical and mental fatigue decreases the efficiency of inspection, and it is commonly claimed that, at best, 100 per cent inspection is only 80 per cent effective. It is often found that with a detection approach the customer also inspects the incoming product or service, thus the customer becomes a part of the organization's quality control system.

In this type of approach a non-conforming product must be made and a service delivered before the process can be adjusted, and this is inherently inefficient in that it creates waste in all its various forms; all of the action is 'after-the-event' and backward looking. The emphasis is on 'today's events', with little attempt to learn from the lessons of the current problem or crisis. It should not be forgotten that the scrap, rework, retesting and reblending are extra efforts, and represent costs over and above what has been budgeted and which ultimately will result in a reduction of bottom-line profit. Figure 1.5, taken from the Ford Motor Company three-day SPC training course (1985), is a schematic illustration of a detection-type system.

An environment in which the emphasis is on making good the non-conformance, rather than on preventing it arising in the first

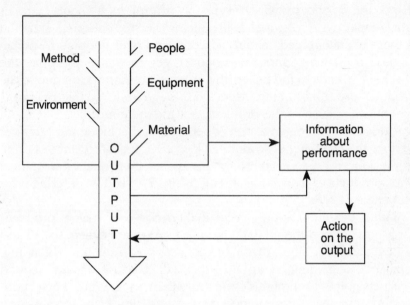

Figure 1.5 A detection-based quality system
Source: Ford Motor Company (1985).

place, is not ideal for engineering team spirit, cooperation and a good climate for work. The focus tends to be on switching the blame to others; people making themselves 'fireproof', not being prepared to accept responsibility and ownership, and taking disciplinary action against people who make mistakes. In general, this behaviour and attitude emanates from middle management and quickly spreads downwards through all levels of the organization hierarchy.

Quality assurance is a prevention-based system which improves product and service quality, and increases productivity by placing the emphasis on product, service and process design. By concentrating on source activities, it stops non-conforming products being produced or non-conforming services being delivered. This is a proactive approach compared with detection, which is reactive. There is a clear change of emphasis from the downstream to the upstream processes and from product to process (figure 1.6). This change of emphasis can also be considered in terms of the Plan–Do–Check–Act (PDCA) cycle. In the detection approach the act part of the cycle is limited, resulting in an incomplete activity, whereas with prevention it is an essential part of individuals' and

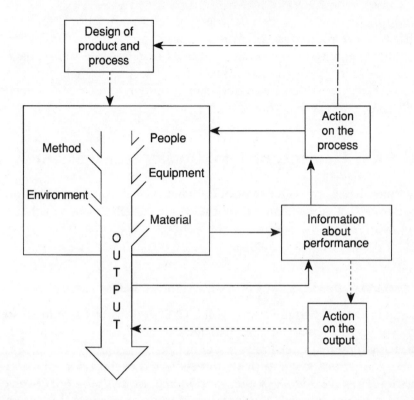

Figure 1.6 A prevention-based quality system
Source: Ford Motor Company (1985).

teams' striving for continuous improvement as part of their everyday work activities.

Quality is created in the design stage and not in the control stage. The majority of quality-related problems are caused by poor or unsuitable designs of products and processes. In the prevention approach, there is a recognition of the process as defined by its input of people, machines, materials, method, management and environment. It also brings a clearer and deeper sense of responsibility for quality to those actually producing and delivering the product or service.

Changing from detection to prevention requires not just the use of a set of tools and techniques, but the development of a new operating philosophy and approach, which requires a change in management style and way of thinking. It requires the various departments and functions to work and act together in cross-functional teams to discover the root cause of problems and pursue their elimination. Quality planning and improvement truly begins when top management includes prevention as opposed to detection in their organizational policy and objectives and start to integrate the improvement efforts of various departments.

The Key Elements of Total Quality Management

Despite the divergence of views on what constitutes TQM, there are a number of key elements in the various definitions, which are summarized in the following subsections. Other chapters provide more detail of these elements.

COMMITMENT AND LEADERSHIP OF SENIOR MANAGEMENT

Without the total commitment of the CEO and his or her immediate executives and other senior managers, nothing much will happen and anything that does happen will not be permanent. They have to take charge personally, provide direction and exercise forceful leadership. However, while some specific actions are required to give TQM a focus, as quickly as possible it must be seen as the natural way of operating a business.

PLANNING AND ORGANIZATION

Planning and organization in a number of facets of the quality improvement process, including:

- Developing a clear, long-term approach for TQM, which is integrated with other strategies such as information technology, production/operations, human resources and the business plans of the organization.

- Building product and service quality into designs and processes.

- Developing prevention-based activities (for example, mistake-proofing devices).

- Putting quality assurance procedures into place that facilitate closed-loop corrective action.

- Planning the approach to be taken towards the effective use of quality systems, procedures and tools and techniques, in the context of the overall strategy.

- Developing the organization and infrastructure to support the improvement activities. While it is recommended to set up some form of Steering Committee and make people responsible for coordinating, facilitating and championing improvement, the infrastructure should not be seen as separate from the management structure.

- Pursuing standardization, systematization and simplification of work instructions, procedures and systems.

USING QUALITY MANAGEMENT TOOLS AND TECHNIQUES

To support and develop a process of continuous improvement, an organization will need to use a selection of tools and techniques. Without the effective employment and mix of tools and techniques it will be difficult to solve problems. The tools and techniques should be used to facilitate improvement and should be integrated into the routine operation of the business. The organization should develop a 'route map' for the tools and techniques that it intends to apply. The use of tools and techniques helps to get the process of improvement started – employees using them feel involved and that they are making a contribution, quality awareness is enhanced, behaviour and attitude change starts to happen, and projects are brought to a successful conclusion.

EDUCATION AND TRAINING

Employees should be provided with a level of education and training to ensure that their general awareness of quality management concepts, their skills and their attitudes are appropriate and suited to the continuous improvement philosophy; education and training also provides a common language throughout the business. A formal programme of education and training needs to be planned and provided on a timely and regular basis to enable people to cope with increasingly complex problems. It should suit the operational conditions of the business (for example, is training done in a cascade mode, where everyone is given the same basic training within a set time frame, or is an infusion mode – consisting of training by team/function on a gradual progression basis – more suitable?). The training programme should be viewed as an investment in developing the ability and knowledge of people and helping them to realize their potential. Without training it is difficult to solve problems, and without education, behaviour and attitude change will not take place. The training programme must also focus on helping managers think through what improvements are achievable in their areas of responsibility. It also has to be recognized that not all employees will have received and acquired adequate levels of education. The structure of the training programme may incorporate some updating of basic educational skills in numeracy and literacy, but it must promote continuing education and self-development. In this way, the latent potential of many employees will be released.

INVOLVEMENT

There must be a commitment to the development of employees, with recognition that they represent an asset that will appreciate over time. All available means, from suggestion schemes to various forms to teamwork, must be considered for achieving broad employee interest, participation and contribution in the process of continuous improvement; management must be prepared to share some of their powers and responsibilities. This also involves seeking and listening carefully to the views of employees and acting upon their suggestions. Part of the approach to TQM is to ensure that everyone has a clear understanding of what is required of them and how their processes relate to the business as a whole. The more people who understand the business and what is going on around then, the greater the role they can play in continuous improvement. People must be encouraged to control, manage and improve the processes that are within their sphere of responsibility.

TEAMWORK

Teamwork needs to be practised in a number of forms. Consideration needs to be given to the operating characteristics of the team(s) employed, how they fit into the organizational structure and the roles of member, team leader, sponsor and facilitator. Teamwork is one of the key features of involvement, and without it difficulty will be found in gaining the commitment and participation of people throughout the organization.

There is also a need to recognize positive performance and achievement and to celebrate and reward success. People must see the results of their activities and understand that the improvements made really do count. This needs to be constantly encouraged through active communication. If TQM is to be successful it is essential that communication is effective and widespread. Sometimes managers are good talkers but poor communicators.

MEASUREMENT AND FEEDBACK

Measurement needs to be made continually against a series of key results indicators, both internal and external. The latter are the most important because they relate to customer perceptions of product and/or service improvement. The indicators should be developed from existing business measures, and external (competitive, functional and generic) and internal benchmarking, as well as from customer surveys and other means of external input. This enables progress and feedback to be assessed against a road map or checkpoints. From these measurements, action plans must be developed to meet objectives and bridge gaps.

WORKING TOGETHER

It is necessary to create an organizational environment that is conducive to continuous improvement and in which everyone can participate and work together. Quality assurance also needs to be integrated into all of an organization's processes and functions. This requires changing people's behaviour, attitudes and working practices in a number of ways. For example:

- Everyone in the organization must be involved in 'improving' the processes under their control on a continuous basis and must take personal responsibility for their own quality assurance.

- Employees must be inspecting their own work.

- Defects must not be passed, in whatever form, to the next process. The internal customer–supplier relationship (everyone for whom you perform a task or service or to whom you provide information is a customer) must be recognized.

● Each person must be committed to satisfying his or her customers, both internal and external.

● External suppliers and customers must be integrated into the improvement process.

● Mistakes must be viewed as an improvement opportunity. In the words of the Japanese, every mistake is a pearl to be cherished.

Changing people's behaviour and attitudes is one of the most difficult tasks facing management, and thus considerable thought needs to be given to facilitating and managing these types of change.

What Are the Benefits of Total Quality Management?

The various benefits of TQM are mentioned by most of those writing on the subject. Indeed, in the early discussion of the importance of quality, some of the benefits were aired. In drawing to a close this introductory chapter, the benefits of TQM, as outlined in different ways by four CEOs from diverse business institutions and with differing lengths of TQM experiences, are now summarized.

P. F. Monk, chief executive, RHP Bearings Ltd   The company is a European manufacturer of bearings to the general industrial, automotive, machine tool and aerospace industries.

> Total quality has been the major catalyst which has united the management and workforce in the common pursuit of profitable growth of the company. The key areas of success have been:
>
> *People*
>
> ● An acceleration of continuous improvement through teamwork across all levels of the organization,
>
> ● Development of a learning culture evidenced through a significantly increased number of employees undertaking further education,

- Employee surveys have indicated a substantial improvement of employee satisfaction and morale,

- A flatter organization plus a more participative, less autocratic management style.

Customer satisfaction

- Customer complaints halved in one year,

- Customer surveys: in 1994 RHP were seen as better than the competition in five out of ten most critical requirements; in 1995 this had improved to being better in eight out of ten most critical requirements.

Better results

- In 1995 RHP returned to profit after three years of loss, a result of three consecutive years of improvement,

- A 20 per cent improvement in productivity in both 1994 and 1995,

- Reduction in scrap material of 50 per cent in both 1994 and 1995.

In recent years the company achievements have been recognized by the following:

- Ford Motor Company Q1 Award

- Perkins Quality Award

- IIP Award

D. Green, executive chairman, UK Utility Division, United Utilities The company is involved with electricity, water and wastewater services.

Our actions to improve the services we deliver to our customers, and each other, have had a significant positive impact on our business. We have used our business improvement process to provide an objective view on where, and in what way, to focus our attention. This focus has enabled us to improve what we do and how we do it. This in turn has led to major bottom line benefits. In the past year:

- We have saved over £1m from just one of our critical process benchmarking projects,

- We have ensured that over half of our entire workforce have been involved in business improvement activity that has enabled us to reduce our operating costs by 1 per cent,

- We have implemented innovative programmes of investment that are targeted at 'delighting' our customers (and differentiating ourselves within the utility sector),

- We have increased the number of employees who believe that we are a Quality Company from 40 to 70 per cent.

This process of improvement has also aided our ability to respond to changing operating conditions and a tough economic environment:

- We have improved everyone's understanding of what we are doing and why we are doing it,

- We have improved everyone's awareness of the wider context within which our business has to operate.

Overall we believe that a quality approach to doing business will be a cornerstone of our drive to maintain our 'licence to operate' in what can only be described as turbulent times.

H. Grainger, managing director, Rexam Corrugated, Heavy Duty   The company is a supplier of heavy duty corrugated board.

We started down the road of TQM some seven years ago. During that time it has evolved through the concept of Total Quality Performance to emerge in the form of Continuous Business Improvement (CBI). It is a journey without end and, as on many great journeys, there are times when you feel footsore and weary and others when your step has a real spring.

Over the time we have been pursuing TQM/CBI:

1 Sales and profits have more than doubled.

2 Productivity has increased annually.

3 Training budget has grown by 400 per cent.

In short, our approach to quality is consistently being reviewed but our most persistent themes remain those of 'training' and 'communication'. Our belief is that the development of teamwork across a flat organizational structure is vital for our ongoing success. In striving for this, our company has experienced and is still in the process of absorbing a major change in corporate leadership. Total Quality has been the catalyst, when footsore, for survival and when in buoyant mood for real progress along the road to success.

R. D. Polson, managing director – Manchester Circuits Ltd   The company is a supplier of advanced technology printed circuits to the defence and aerospace industries.

TQM has brought into sharp focus the ultimate importance of customer satisfaction as it is consistently and ruthlessly measured in the areas of delivery performance, internal remakes and customer returns. While our performance remains the subject of continual improvement, we are getting better and, most importantly, it is being recognized by our customers. This is of vital importance in the relationship with our blue chip customer base. Recognition of the company's progress has been in the form of:

● Costs down,

● Smiths Industries Quality Award (Bronze),

● Ship to stock status with GEC-Marconi,

● Operational benefits,

● Formal collaboration partnership with British Aerospace Defence.

Summary

This chapter has explored the various ways in which quality is defined. In relation to this, the point is made that an organization must develop for itself its own definition of quality. The importance of quality in today's business environment was explored and it is concluded that, despite the various surveys that are less than enthusiastic about TQM, the experience from the business world is that a process of continuous improvement is vital to take cost out of the organization in order to stave off the competition. These organizations are ignoring the noise and just carrying on driving their improvement process forward. The views from a number of CEOs on the benefits of TQM provide an insight into this. The chapter has also traced the development of quality management, from inspection, quality control and quality assurance to TQM. The drawbacks of a detection-based approach were outlined and the need for a more preventive-based approach was emphasized.

References

BS 4778 1991: *Quality Vocabulary*, Part 2: *Quality Concepts and Related Definitions*. London: British Standards Institution.

BS EN ISO 8402 1995: *Quality Management and Quality Assurance*. London: British Standards Institution.

Buzzell, R. D. and Gale, B. T. 1987: *The Profit Impact of Marketing Strategy: linking strategy to performance*. New York: Free Press.

Carlzon, J. 1987: *The Moments of Truth*. Cambridge, Mass.: Ballinger.

CMC Partnership Ltd 1991: *Attitudes within British Business to Quality Management Systems*. Buckingham: CMC Partnership.

Crosby, P. B. 1979: *Quality is Free*. New York: McGraw-Hill.

Dale, B. G. (ed.) 1994: *Managing Quality*, 2nd edn. London: Prentice Hall.

Dale, B. G. and Plunkett, J. J. 1995: *Quality Costing*, 2nd edn. London: Chapman & Hall.

Easton, G. S. and Jarrell, S. L. 1996: The effects of total quality management on corporate performance: an empirical investigation. *Journal of Business*, 14(4), 16–31.

European Foundation for Quality Management 1996: *Customer Loyalty; a key to business growth and profitability*, EFQM Customer Loyalty Team, March. Brussels: EFQM.

Ford Motor Company 1985: Three-day statistical process control notes, Ford Motor Company, Brentwood, Essex.

Gallup Organization/ASQC 1991: *An American Survey of Consumers' Perceptions of Product and Service Quality*. Milwaukee, Wis.: American Society for Quality Control.

—— 1992: *An ASQC/Gallup Survey on Quality Leadership Roles of Corporate Executives and Directors*. Milwaukee, Wis.: American Society for Quality Control.

Hutchens, S. 1989: What customers want: results of ASQC/Gallup survey. *Quality Progress*, February, 33–6.

Juran, J. M. (ed.) 1988: *Quality Control Handbook*, 3rd edn. New York: McGraw-Hill.

Kano, N., Tanaka, H. and Yamaga, Y. 1983: *The TQM Activity of Deming Prize Recipients and its Economic Impact*. Tokyo: Union of Japanese Scientists and Engineers.

Larry, L. 1993: Betting to win on the Baldrige winners. *Business Week*, 18 October, 16–17.

Lascelles, D. M. and Dale, B. G. 1990: Quality management: the chief executive's perception and role. *European Management Journal*, 8(1), 67–75.

McKenzie, R. M,. 1989: *The Production–Inspection Relationship*. Edinburgh/London: Scottish Academic Press.

McKinsey and Company 1989: Management of quality: the single most important challenge for Europe, European Quality Management Forum, 19 October, Montreux, Switzerland.

Reimann, C. 1995: Quality management proves to be a good investment. *US Department of Commerce News*, 3 February.

Ryan, J. 1988: Consumers see little change in product quality. *Quality Progress*, December, 16–20.

Taguchi, G. 1986: *Introduction to Quality Engineering*. Dearborn, Mich.: Asian Productivity Organization.

US General Accounting Office 1991: Management practices: US companies improve performance through quality efforts, report to the Honorable Donald Ritter. Washington, DC: House of Representatives, May.

Wisner, J. D. and Eakins, S. G. 1994: Competitive assessment of the Baldrige winners, *International Journal of Quality and Reliability Management*, 11(2), 8–25.

Zairi, M., Leitza, S. R. and Oakland, J. S. 1994: Does TQM impact bottom-line results? *The TQM Magazine*, 6(1), 38–43.

2 Approaches to Total Quality Management

Introduction

Each writer on the subject of TQM develops and outlines an approach reflecting his or her own background and experience. These approaches include: (a) a listing of TQM principles and practices, which are presented in the form of a generic plan for the implementation of TQM along with a set of guidelines, (b) prescriptive step-by-step approaches, (c) methods outlining the wisdom, philosophies and recommendations of the internationally respected experts on the subject, such as Crosby (1979), Deming (1986), Feigenbaum (1983) and Juran (1988), (d) self-assessment methods such as the Malcolm Baldrige National Quality Award (MBNQA) and the European Foundation for Quality Management (EFQM) Model for Business Excellence, and (e) non-prescriptive methods in the form of a framework or model. With all these available sources of advice and prescriptions it is not surprising, then, that there is sometimes inertia on the part of senior management teams who are faced with the task of introducing a formal process of continuous improvement in their organizations.

There are a number of ways to get started and it is up to each organization to identify the approach that best suits its needs and business operation. Indeed, it is not unusual for an organization to find that its TQM approach is not working out as planned and to switch to another approach. Some of the main ways of starting TQM are now examined. In addition, this chapter summarizes the basics of self-assessment and the main quality awards, and also explores the difficulties in sustaining TQM.

Applying the Wisdom of the Quality Management Experts

The writings and teachings of Crosby (1979), Deming (1986), Feigenbaum (1991) and Juran (1988) are a sensible starting point for any organization introducing TQM. These four writers have had a considerable influence on the development of TQM in organizations throughout the world. The usual approach is for an organization to adopt the teachings of one of these quality management experts and attempt to follow his programme. The argument for this is that each expert has a package that works – the package gives some form of security, it provides a coherent framework, gives discipline to the process, and provides a common language, understanding and method of communication. To facilitate this, some companies have purposely opted for the simplest package. The approach of Crosby is generally recognized as being the easiest to follow, Dale (1991). He also found that Crosby followed by Juran and then Deming were the most frequently used experts. Observations of organizations setting out to employ the methods advocated by one of these gurus suggest that sooner of later they will start to pull into their improvement process the ideas of other quality management experts. This is understandable because none of these experts has all of the answers to the problems facing an organization, despite the claims made about the exclusivity of approach.

Whichever programme or approach is being followed, it should be used as the mechanism to focus on the improvement process, not treated as an end to itself.

CROSBY

Philip Crosby's audience is primarily top management. He sells his approach to top management and stresses increasing profitability through quality improvement. His argument is that higher quality reduces costs and raises profits. He defines quality as conformance to requirements. Crosby's quality improvement programme has fourteen steps (Crosby, 1979) that focus on how to change the organization and tend to be a specific action plan for implementation:

1 Management commitment

2 Quality improvement team

3 Quality measurement

4 Cost of quality evaluation

5 Quality awareness

6 Corrective action

7 Establish an ad hoc committee for the zero defects programme

8 Supervisor training

9 Zero defects day

10 Goal setting

11 Error cause removal

12 Recognition

13 Quality controls

14 Do it over again

Crosby's approach is based on four absolutes of quality management:

1 Quality means conformance, not elegance

2 It is always cheaper to do the job right the first time

3 The only performance indicator is the cost of quality

4 The only performance standard is zero

Crosby has also produced a 'quality vaccine', comprising twenty-one areas divided into the five categories of integrity, systems, communications, operations and policies, which he treats as preventative medicine for poor quality.

He does not accept the 'optimal quality level' concept because he believes that higher quality always reduces cost and raises profits. Cost of quality is used as a tool to help achieve that goal. With respect to cost of quality, he produced the first serious alternative to the 'prevention, appraisal, failure' categorization, with the price of conformance and price of non-conformance model. In terms of employee roles, Crosby allocates a moderate amount of responsibility to the quality professional. Top management has an important role, and the hourly workforce has a role that is limited to reporting problems to management. One way in which Crosby measures quality achievement is with a matrix, the quality management maturity grid, which charts the stages that management goes through from ignorance to enlightenment.

In summary, Crosby is acknowledged as a great motivator of senior management in helping to get the improvement process started. His approach is generally regarded as simple and easy to follow, which leads his critics to claim that his work lacks substance in giving detailed guidance on how to apply quality management principles, tools, techniques and systems.

DEMING

W. Edwards Deming's argument is that quality through a reduction in statistical variation improves productivity and competitive position. He defines quality in terms of quality of design, quality of conformance, and quality of the sales and service function. Deming aims to improve quality and productivity, improve jobs, ensure long-term survival of the firm, and improve competitive position. He does not accept the trade-off shown in the 'economic cost of quality' models and says that there is no way of calculating the cost of delivering defective products to customers, which he believes is the major quality cost.

Deming advocates the measurement of quality by direct statistical measures of manufacturing performance against specification. While all production processes exhibit variation, the goal of quality improvement is to reduce variation. Deming's approach is highly statistical and he believes that every employee should be trained in statistical quality techniques. A fourteen-point approach (Deming, 1986) summarizes his management philosophy for improving quality:

1 Create constancy of purpose towards improvement of product and service, with the aims of becoming competitive, staying in business and providing jobs.

2 Adopt the new philosophy – we are in a new economic age. Western management must awaken to the challenge, learn from their responsibilities and take on leadership for future change.

3 Cease dependence on inspection to achieve quality. Eliminate the need for inspection on a mass basis by building quality into the product in the first place.

4 End the practice of awarding business on the basis of price tag. Instead, minimize total cost. Move toward a single supplier for any one item on a long-term relationship of loyalty and trust.

5 Improve constantly and forever the system of production and service, to improve quality and productivity, and thus constantly decrease costs.

6 Institute training on the job.

7 Institute leadership (see point 12): the aim of supervision should be to help people, machines and gadgets to do a better job. Supervision of management, as well as supervision of production workers, is in need of overhaul.

8 Drive out fear, so that everyone may work effectively for the company.

9 Break down barriers between departments, people in research, design, sales and production must work as a team, to foresee problems in production and problems in use that may be encountered with the product or service.

10 Eliminate slogans, exhortations and targets for the workforce that ask for zero defects and new levels of productivity. Such exhortations only create adversarial relationships, as the bulk of the causes of low quality and low productivity belong to the system and thus lie beyond the power of the workforce.

11 (a) Eliminate work standards (quotas) on the factory floor; substitute leadership instead.
   (b) Eliminate management by objectives, by numbers and by numerical goals; substitute leadership instead.

12 (a) Remove barriers that rob the hourly worker of his or her right to pride of workmanship. The responsibility of supervisors must be changed from sheer numbers to quality.
   (b) Remove barriers that rob people in management and in engineering of their right to pride of workmanship. This

means, *inter alia*, abolishment of the annual or merit rating and of management by objectives.

13 Institute a vigorous programme of education and self-improvement.

14 Put everybody in the company to work to accomplish the transformation. The transformation is everybody's job.

Deming's view is that quality management and improvement are the responsibility of all of the firm's employees: top management must adopt the 'new religion' of quality, lead the drive for improvement and be involved in all stages of the process. Hourly workers should be trained and encouraged to prevent defects and improve quality, and be given challenging and rewarding jobs. Quality professionals should educate other managers in statistical techniques and concentrate on improving the methods of defect prevention. Finally, statisticians should consult with all areas of the company.

Other contributions of Deming include the PDCA (Plan–Do–Check–Act) cycle of continuous improvement, which Deming himself termed the Shewhart cycle after the father of statistical quality control, and the pinpointing of the seven 'Deadly Diseases' (1, lack of consistency of purpose; 2, emphasis on short-term profits; 3, evaluation of performance, merit rating or annual review; 4, mobility of management; 5, running a company on visible figures alone; 6, excessive medical costs; 7, excessive cost of liability), which he used to criticize Western management and organizational practices.

In summary, Deming expects the managers to change – to develop a partnership with those at the operating level of the business and to manage quality with direct statistical measures without cost-of-quality measures. Deming's approach, particularly his insistence on the need for management to change the organizational culture, is closely aligned with Japanese practice. This is not surprising in view of the assistance he gave to the Japanese after the Second World War.

A number of Deming user Groups and Associations have been formed, which are dedicated to facilitating awareness and understanding of his work and helping companies to introduce his ideas. Also, a number of authors have produced books explaining Deming's approach and ideas (e.g. Aguayo, 1990; Kilian, 1992; Scherkenbach, 1991; Yoshida, 1995).

FEIGENBAUM

Armand V,. Feigenbaum was General Electric's worldwide chief of manufacturing operations for a decade until the late 1960s. He is now president of an engineering consultancy firm, General Systems Co., that designs and installs operational systems in corporations around the world. Feigenbaum was the originator of the term 'Total Quality Control', defined in the first edition of *Total Quality Control* (1961) as:

> an effective system for integrating the quality-development, quality-maintenance, and quality-improvement efforts of the various groups in an organization so as to enable marketing, engineering, production, and service at the most economical levels which allow for full customer satisfaction.

Feigenbaum does not so much try to create managerial awareness of quality as to help a plant or company design its own system. To him, quality is a way of managing a business organization. Significant continuous improvement can only be achieved in a company through the participation of everyone in the workforce, who must, therefore, have a good understanding of what management is trying to do. Fire-fighting quality problems has to be replaced with a very clear, customer-oriented quality management process that people can understand and commit themselves to.

Senior management's understanding of the issues surrounding continuous improvement and commitment to incorporating quality into their management practice are crucial to the successful installation of Feigenbaum's total quality system. They must abandon short-term motivational programmes that yield no long-lasting improvement. Management must also realize that quality does not mean only that customer problems have to be fixed faster. Quality leadership is essential to a company's success in the market-place.

Feigenbaum takes a very serious financial approach to the management of quality. He believes that the effective installation and management of a continuous improvement process represent the best return-on-investment for many companies in today's competitive environment.

Feigenbaum's major contribution to the subject of cost of quality was the recognition that quality costs must be categorized if they are to be managed. He identified three major categories: appraisal costs, prevention costs and failure costs. Total quality cost is the sum of these costs. He was also the first of the international experts to identify the folly of regarding quality professionals as being solely responsible for an organization's quality activities.

According to Feigenbaum, the goal of continuous improvement is to reduce the total cost of quality from the often quoted 25–30 per cent of annual sales of cost of operations to as low a percentage as possible. Therefore, developing cost of quality data and tracking it on an ongoing basis are integral parts of the process.

Feigenbaum says that management must commit themselves to:

- Strengthening the quality improvement process itself
- Making sure that quality improvement becomes a habit
- Managing quality and cost as complementary objectives

In summary, although he does not espouse fourteen points or steps like Deming or Crosby, it is obvious that his approach is not significantly different; it simply boils down to managerial know-how. He does, however, identify the following benchmarks for success with TQM:

1 Quality is a company-wide process
2 Quality is what the customer says it is
3 Quality and cost are a sum, not a difference
4 Quality requires both individual and team zealotry
5 Quality is a way of managing
6 Quality and innovation are mutually dependent
7 Quality is an ethic
8 Quality requires continuous improvement
9 Quality is the most cost-effective, least capital-intensive route to productivity
10 Quality is implemented with a total system connected with customers and suppliers

JURAN

Joseph Juran has made perhaps a greater contribution to the quality management literature than any other quality professional. Like

Deming, he has had an influence on the development of quality management in Japanese companies. While Deming provided advice on statistical methods to technical specialists from the late 1940s onward, Juran, in the mid-1950s, focused on the role of senior people in quality management.

Part of his argument is that companies must reduce the cost of quality. This is dramatically different from Deming's approach. Deming ignores the cost of quality, while Juran, like Crosby and Feigenbaum, claims that reducing it is a key objective of any business. A ten-point plan summarises his approach:

1   Build awareness of the need and opportunity for improvement

2   Set goals for improvement

3   Organize to reach the goals

4   Provide training

5   Carry out projects to solve problems

6   Report progress

7   Give recognition

8   Communicate results

9   Keep the score

10 Maintain momentum by making annual improvement part of the regular system and processes of the company

Juran defines quality as 'fitness for use', which he breaks down into quality of design, quality of conformance, availability and field service. The goals of Juran's approach to continuous improvement are increased conformance and decreased cost of quality, and yearly goals are established in the objective-setting phase of the programme. He developed a quality trilogy comprising quality planning, quality control and quality improvement. Basically, his approach focuses on three segments: a programme to attack sporadic problems, one to attack chronic problems, and an annual quality programme, in which top management participates, to develop or refine policies. Juran defines two major kinds of quality management – breakthrough (encouraging the occurrences of good things), which attacks chronic problems, and control (preventing the occurrence of bad things), which attacks sporadic problems. He views the improvement process as taking two journeys – from symptom to cause (diagnosis) and from cause to remedy (from diagnosis to solution).

Juran also allocates responsibility among the workforce differently from Deming. He puts the primary responsibility on quality professionals (who serve as consultants to top management and employees). The quality professionals design and develop the programme, and do most of the work. While granting the importance of top management support, Juran places more of the quality leadership responsibility on middle management and quality professionals. The role of the workforce is mainly involvement in quality improvement teams.

In summary, Juran emphasizes the cost of quality, because the language of top management is money, and he recommends cost of quality for identifying quality improvement projects and opportunities, and developing a quality cost scoreboard to measure quality costs. Juran's approach is more consistent with American management practices – he takes the existing management culture as a starting point and builds a continuous improvement process from that baseline.

Applying a Consultancy Package

Some companies (usually large concerns) decide to adopt the programme of one of the major management consultancies on the grounds that it is a self-contained package that can be suitably customized for application in their organization. Some companies are very comfortable with consultants, others not so. It should also be noted that most of the 'gurus' have their own consultancy activities to help organizations to implement their ideas and principles.

It is important for a company to understand that the use of a consultant organization does not relieve the senior management team of their own responsibilities or TQM (for example, demonstrating commitment and giving direction to the improvement process). Executives should never allow the consultant to become the 'TQM champion' or the company expert on TQM. A key part of consultancy is transfer of skills and knowledge, and when the project is complete the training and guidance provided by the consultant must remain within the organization in order for the process of improvement to progress and develop. The consultant should be perceived by the organization as an asset to assist with implementation and not as an initiator of TQM. It may be that the consultant is also learning on the job and any ideas, proposals and decisions should always be scrutinized carefully by the TQM steering committee for their applicability to the company's operations.

Management consultancies bring their expertise to the company and provide the resources, experience, disciplines, objectivity and catalyst for getting the process started. The consultants are usually involved in a wide range of activities, from planning through to training and project work and implementation of specific improvement initiatives. There is a myriad of consultancies, offering a variety of TQM products and packages, and not all of them will suit every organization. It is likely that organizations, in particular large ones, will use more than one consultancy as they make progress on the TQM journey.

A company intending to use a consultancy must consider its selection carefully so as to ensure that the one chosen is suited to its needs; this also applies to the individual consultant(s) who will actually carry out the work. There are a number of factors to be taken into consideration in the selection process, including:

- Presentation of the TQM approach used by the consultancy to senior management and other interested parties,

- Personality of the consultants and the perceived interaction with the people with whom they will work,

- Proposal details,

- Previously published material,

- Availability of educational material and supporting systems, programmes and tools,

- Reputation and track record of the consultancy and individual consultants, with existing clients,

- Knowledge of TQM and its application in practice in similar or related companies – not just in consulting, research and/or teaching,

- Rapport and ability to communicate with staff at all levels in the organization,

- Training skills and ability,

- Grasp of the client organization's culture and management style, and

- The extent to which the consultancy is prepared to assist in carrying out a quality management diagnosis and tailor the package to suit the needs of the client.

The decision to use a consultant organization is usually made by the CEO with support from the quality director. It is dangerous for the consultant to assume that other board members will contribute more than vocal support to the process of improvement.

The company needs to understand clearly what it is buying from a consultancy. It is often difficult to define in precise detail what is required in a TQM assignment, with the consequence that the terms of reference are vague. This sometimes results in a difference between what was ordered and what was delivered; wrangling over the deliverables from a TQM contract is a major detractor in a continuous improvement process. The company should also take care that a TQM assignment is not used to open the door for other consultancy work in problem areas such as manufacturing management, accountancy and business management. The easiest way of selling consultancy is on the back of a short-term successful assignment; this might have a negative influence on the long-term success of TQM.

A major complaint that organizations make about consultancies is the use of 'off-the-shelf' packages and prescriptive solutions that fail to maximize client involvement and do not reflect the client's business processes and business constraints, and the use of prescriptive words and terms that do not suit the culture of the organization.

For those considering the utilization of an external consultant, the main issues to be addressed and agreed on can be summarized as follows:

1 Clear terms of reference specifying the expected benefits to the organization of the consultancy project, with tangible objectives, milestones and timescales.
2 The precise nature of the relationship between the client management team and the consultancy. The management team will need to consider the precise form of consultancy input required, and identify success criteria for the project.

3   The mechanism for implementing the improvement strategy and managing the change process, together with the resources required. The issues involved include the role of the senior management team, the amount of time and energy individual senior managers are able or prepared to commit, and who might assume the day-to-day role of project coordination.

Frameworks and Models

A framework or model is usually introduced to present a picture of what is required in introducing TQM. They are the means of presenting ideas, concepts, pointers and plans in a non-prescriptive manner and are usually not considered to be a 'how-to' guide to TQM introduction and subsequent development. They are guides to action and not things to be followed in a slavish manner. Step-by-step approaches have a set starting point, usually follow one route and are rigid in general. They are more concerned with the destination than with the route to get there. A framework allows users to choose their own starting point and course of action, and to build gradually on the individual features and parts at a pace which suits their business situation and available resource. Aalbregtse et al. (1991) provide an excellent description of what a framework should consist of and its objectives. A number of writers (e.g. Burt, 1993; Chu, 1988; Dale and Boaden, 1993; Flero, 1992; Johnson. 1992) have proposed a range of TQM/improvement frameworks.

A typical framework for managing quality improvement is the UMIST generic improvement framework, which is described by Dale and Boaden (1993) and Boaden and Dale (1994). The framework is divided into four main sections, all of which need to be addressed once the motivation for starting a process of continuous improvement has been identified and the overall strategic direction set. The foundation of the framework is 'organizing' and the two pillars that form its structure are the use of 'systems and techniques' and 'measurement and feedback;'. 'Changing the culture' is the fourth section of the framework and is something which must be considered at all stages. Central to the whole process of improvement are people, both as individuals and working in teams without whose skills and commitment improvement will not occur. A diagrammatic

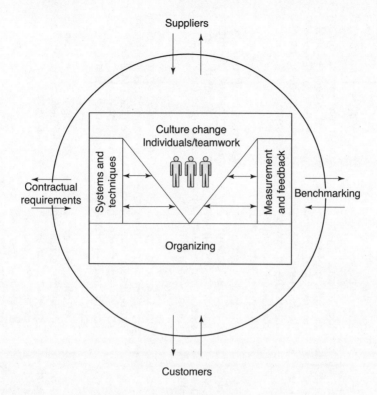

Figure 2.1 The UMIST quality improvement framework

representation of the framework is given in figure 2.1 and a summary of its features in table 2.1.

The framework provides an indication of how the various aspects of TQM fit together and is particularly useful for those organizations that:

- Are taking their first steps on the improvement journey.

- Have got ISO 9000 quality management system series registration and require some guidance and advice on what to do next.

- Are attempting to develop improvement plans and controls across a number of sites.

- Have less than three years' operating experience of continuous improvement principles and practices.

Table 2.1 UMIST quality improvement framework: a summary

Organizing	Systems and techniques	Measurement and feedback	Changing the culture
Formulation of a clear long-term strategy for the process of continuous improvement, integrated with other key business strategies, departmental policies and objectives	Identification of the tools and techniques applicable at different stages of the process of continuous improvement	Identification and definition of key internal and external performance measures to assess the progress being made and to ensure customer satisfaction	Assessment of the current status of organizational culture, before developing and implementing plans for change
Definition and communication of a common organizational definition of quality, TQM and continuous improvement	Development of the appropriate type of training in the use of tools and techniques, targeted at the right people	Discussion with customers, about expected performance, needs and expectations, using a variety of techniques	Recognition of the ongoing nature of culture change, rather than a prerequisite for TQM
Selection of an approach to TQM	Consideration of the use of a formal quality system, if one is not in place	Consideration of benchmarking, once the organization has taken some steps down the continuous improvement journey	The development of plans for change that enable it to take place in a consistent and incremental manner
Identification of the organizations and people (internal and external) who can be sources of advice on aspects of TQM	Identification and implementation of other systems and standards that may be required by customers, legislation or in order to compete	Consideration of various means for celebration and communication of success, and the development of methods for recognizing the efforts of teams and individuals	The recognition of the role of people within the organization

Table 2.1 Continued

Identification of stages of improvement activity, taking into account the starting point of the organization, the motivation for continuous improvement and the tools that may be applicable	Adoption of process analysis and improvement as a continual part of the organization's continuous improvement process	Identification of the interrelationships of all activities, and the way in which they contribute to quality within the organization in order to minimize conflict
Recognition of executive leadership, tangible commitment and support as being crucial at all stages	Consideration of linking rewards to quality improvement activities and results	Identification of factors that indicate that TQM has started to change culture
Development and communication of vision and mission statements that are concise and understandable to all employees	Utilization of some means of assessing the progress toward world-class performance	Consideration of the culture of a country and its people in planning for change
Establishment of a formal programme of education and training		
Establishment of an organizational infrastructure that will ultimately facilitate local ownership of the continuous improvement process		
Establishment of teamwork that is designed to become part of the organization's method of working		

Developing A Tailor-Made Organizational Route Map

A variation on these approaches is to absorb the 'received wisdom' and the experiences of other companies and extract the ideas, methods, systems and tactics that are appropriate to the particular circumstances, business situation and environment of the organization. Organizations starting with any of the popular approaches to TQM will eventually use this method.

In this approach management have to think through the issues and develop for themselves a vision, values, objectives, a policy, an approach, a route map for continuous improvement and the means of deploying the philosophy to all levels of the organization. A feature of organizations following this approach is that senior management will have visited other companies with a reputation for being 'centres of excellence' to see at first hand the lessons learned from TQM, and will have become involved in meetings relating to TQM with executives of like minds from different companies. They are also frequent attendees at conferences and are generally well read on the subject.

When getting started on the improvement process it is always beneficial for organizations to establish contacts with others that have a reputation for excellence in systems and products. There is much to be said for learning by association and sharing information through networks. In our experience, companies working with or competing directly against companies with advanced management processes develop their knowledge of TQM at a fast rate. A case in point is the influence that the resident Japanese automotive and electronic companies have had on the development of improvement practices of the UK supply base.

From the outset, organizations must accept that continuous improvement is a long and arduous journey, which has no end. Unfortunately, there are no short cuts and no one has a monopoly on the best ideas. Furthermore, once started, the momentum needs to be maintained, otherwise even the gains may be lost. Even the most successful organization has periods when little headway is made.

The method of getting started on improvement is less important than management commitment to its ideals and the leadership they are prepared to demonstrate; this is the key determinant of long-term success.

Self-Assessment and Quality Awards

If a process of continuous improvement is to be sustained and its pace increased, it is essential that organizations monitor on a regular basis which activities are going well, which have stagnated, what needs to be improved and what is missing. Self-assessment provides such a framework. There are many definitions of self-assessment provided by writers such as Conti (1993) and Hillman (1994) but an all-embracing definition is provided by the European Foundation for Quality Management (EFQM) (1977):

> Self-assessment is a comprehensive, systematic and regular review of an organization's activities and results referenced against a model of business excellence.
>
> The self-assessment process allows the organisation to discern clearly its strengths and areas in which improvements can be made and culminates in planned improvement actions which are monitored for progress.

Self-assessment implies the use of a model on which to base the valuation and diagnostics. There are a number of internally recognized models, the main ones being the Deming Application Prize in Japan, the MBNQA in American and the EFQM Model for Business Excellence in Europe. In addition, there are many national quality awards (e.g. the British Quality Award and the Australian Quality Award) and regional quality awards (e.g. the North West Quality Award). Most of the national and regional awards are more or less duplicates of the international models, with some modifications to suit issues of national or local interest. The models on which these awards are based comprise definitions of TQM in a broad sense; they are comprehensive, considering the whole organization and its various activities, practices and processes.

Since the establishment of these awards there has been an explosion in published material describing them (e.g. Brown, 1996; Cole, 1991; Conti, 1993; Hakes, 1996; Lascelles and Peacock, 1996; Nakhai and Neves, 1994; Steeples, 1993). In the view of the authors, the primary objective of self-assessment against one of these models should not be to win an award but to use the results to learn, improve and increase the velocity of the improvement process.

The award models and the application guidelines are helpful in defining TQM in a way that management can more easily understand. They also help organizations to develop and manage their improvement activities in a number of ways. For example:

● They provide a definition and description of TQM which gives a better understanding of the concept, improves awareness and generates ownership for TQM among senior managers.

● They enable measurement of the progress with TQM to be made, along with its benefits and outcomes.

● They force management to think about the basic elements of the organization and how it operates.

● The scoring criteria provide an objective measurement, gain consensus on strengths and weaknesses of the current approach and help to pinpoint improvement opportunities.

● Benchmarking and organizational learning is facilitated.

● Training in TQM is encouraged.

There is little doubt that the MBNQA and the European Quality Award (EQA) have helped to raise the profile of TQM in America and Europe, respectively.

To use any self-assessment method effectively, various elements and practices must be in place and management needs to have had some TQM experience to understand the questions underpinning the concept. What has not been implemented cannot be assessed. In our experience, the use of self-assessment methods based on a quality award model are best suited to those organizations that have had a formal improvement process in place for at least three years, although there is a clear need to assess progress before this time has elapsed. For example, Sherer (1995) (managing director of Rank Xerox, Germany), explaining how Xerox won the EQA in 1992, makes the point, 'Do not use the award programme, your application for the European Quality Award, as an entry point into your quality journey. It is something you should do after you have been on the road for a long time'. He also goes on to say, 'Do not try to run for the award too early'. A similar point is made in the Deming Prize

Guide for overseas companies (Deming Prize Committee, 1996): 'It is advisable to apply for the Prize after two to three years of company-wide TQM implementation effort or after top management has become fully committed and has begun to assume a leadership role'.

Having made this point, the TQM and Business Excellence models underpinning the quality awards are most helpful in demonstrating to those organizations experienced in TQM what is involved. However, such organizations must understand the potential gap that can exist between where they currently stand in relation to TQM and the model of the award being used to make the comparison.

DEMING APPLICATION PRIZE

The Deming Application Prize was set up in honour of Dr W. E. Deming, back in 1951, in recognition of his friendship and his achievements in the cause of industrial quality.

The original intention of the Deming Application Prize was to assess a company's use and application of statistical methods; later, in 1964 it was broadened to assess how TQM activities were being practised. The award is managed by the Deming Application Prize Committee and administered by the Japanese Union of Scientists and Engineers (JUSE). It recognizes outstanding achievements in quality strategy management and execution. There are three separate divisions for the award: the Deming Application Prize, the Deming Prize for individuals and the Quality Control Award for Factories. The Deming Application Prize is open to individual sites, a division of a company, small companies and overseas companies. It is awarded each year and there is no limit to the number of winners. It is made to those 'companies or division of companies that have achieved distinct performance improvement through the application of company-wide quality control' (Deming Prize Committee, 1996).

The Deming Application Prize is comprised of ten primary categories (see table 2.2) which in turn are divided into sixty-six sub-categories. Each primary category has six sub-categories except 'quality assurance activities' which has twelve categories. There are no pre-designated points allocated to the individual sub-categories. It is claimed that the reason for this is to maintain flexibility. However, discussions with JUSE indicated that each sub-category is scored out of ten. This checklist is prescriptive in that it identifies factors,

Table 2.2 Quality award criteria

Award	Category	Points (maximum)
Deming Application Prize	Policies	
	Organization	
	Information	
	Standardization	
	Human resources development and utilization	
	Quality assurance activities	
	Maintenance/control activities	
	Improvement	
	Effects	
	Future plans	
Malcolm Baldrige National Quality Award	Leadership	110
	Strategic planning	80
	Customer and market focus	80
	Information and analysis	80
	Human resource development and management	100
	Process management	100
	Business results	450
	Total	1000
European Quality Award	Leadership	100
	People management	90
	Policy and strategy	80
	Resources	90
	Processes	140
	People satisfaction	90
	Customer satisfaction	200
	Impact on society	60
	Business results	150
	Total	1000

procedures, techniques and approaches that underpin TQM. The examiners for the Deming Application Prize are selected by JUSE from quality management experts from not-for-profit organizations. The applicants are required to submit a detailed document on each of the Prize's criteria and this is followed by an on-site visit.

Considerable emphasis is placed on the on-site examination of the applicant organization's practices.

THE MALCOLM BALDRIGE NATIONAL QUALITY AWARD

The Malcolm Baldrige National Quality Improvement Act of 1987, signed by President Reagan on 20 August 1987, established this annual US quality award, some thirty-seven years after the introduction of the Deming Prize. The award is named after a former American Secretary of Commerce in the Reagan administration. The MBNQA programme is the result of the cooperative efforts of government leaders and American business. Its purpose is to promote quality awareness, recognize the quality achievements of American companies, and publicize successful management and improvement strategies. The US Department of Commerce and the National Institute of Standards and Technology are responsible for administering the award scheme.

Up to two awards can be given each year, out of the average number of one hundred applications, in each of these categories: manufacturing companies or subsidiaries, service companies or subsidiaries, and small business (defined as independently owned, and with not more than five hundred employees). Since its inception, in a single year there have never been fewer than two or more than five awards. The award is made by the President of the United States, with the recipients receiving a specially designed crystal trophy mounted with a gold-plated medallion. They may publicize and advertise their awards provided they agree to share information about their successful quality management and improvement strategies with other American organizations.

Every Baldrige Award application is evaluated in seven major categories with a maximum total score of 100 (US Department of Congress, 1997). These are: leadership (110 points), strategic planning (80 points), customer and market focus (80 points), information and analysis (80 points), human resource development and management (100 points), process management (100 points) and business results (450 points) (table 2.2, figure 2.2). Each of the seven categories is subdivided into twenty items, and the items are further defined by thirty areas to address. The framework (figure 2.2) has three basic elements: strategy and action plans, system, and information and analysis. Strategy and action plans are the set of

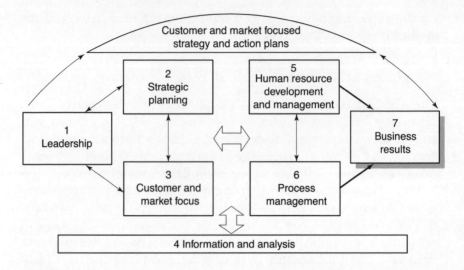

Figure 2.2 Baldrige Award criteria framework: a systems perspective
Source: US Department of Commerce (1997).

company-level requirements, derived from short- and long-term strategic planning, that must be done well for the company's strategy to succeed. They guide overall resource decisions and drive the alignment of measures for all work units to ensure customer satisfaction and market success. The system is comprised of the six Baldrige categories in the centre of figure 2.2 that define the organization, its operations and its results. Information and analysis (category 4) are critical to the effective management of the company and to a fact-based system for improving company performance and competitiveness.

The evaluation by the Baldrige examiners is based on a written application and looks for three major indications of success:

- Approach: the strategy, processes, practices, and methodology used by the organization in attempting to achieve world-class quality.

- Deployment: the resources being applied and how widespread (i.e. broad or narrow) is the quality effort throughout the organization.

- Results: evidence of sustained improvement over the last five years.

Following a first-stage review of the application by quality management experts, a decision is made about which organizations should receive a site visit. A panel of judges reviews all of the data, from both the written applications and the site visits, and recommends the award recipients to NIST. Quantitative results weigh heavily in the judging process, so applicants must be able to prove that their quality efforts have resulted in sustained improvements. The thoroughness of the judging process means that even applicants not selected as finalists get valuable feedback on their strengths and areas for improvement.

THE EUROPEAN QUALITY AWARD

The European Quality Award was launched in October 1991 and first awarded in 1992. According to the EFQM, it was intended to 'focus attention on business excellence, provide a stimulus to companies and individuals to develop improvement initiatives and demonstrate results achievable in all aspects of organizational activity'. Although only one European Quality Award is made each year, a number of European Quality prizes are awarded to those companies that demonstrate excellence in the management of quality through a process of continuous improvement. The EQA is awarded to the best of the prize winners in the categories of companies, public service organizations (i.e. healthcare, education, and local and central government) and small and medium sized enterprises. The winner of each of the three awards retains the EQA trophy for a year; all prize winners receive a framed holographic image of the trophy. The winners are expected to share their experiences of TQM at conferences and seminars organized by the EFQM.

The EFQM Model of Business Excellence is intended to help the management of European organizations to improve their understanding of best practices and to support them in their leadership role. The model provides a generic framework of criteria that can be applied to any organization or its component parts. The EQA is administered by the EFQM with the support of the European Organization for Quality (EOQ) and the European Commission. The EQFM, in developing the model, drew upon the experience in use and application of the MBNQA.

Applications for the EQA are assessed on nine criteria: leadership, people management, policy and strategy, resources, processes, people

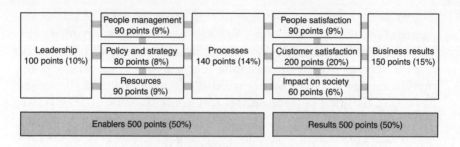

Figure 2.3 The EFQM Model for Business Excellence
Source: European Foundation for Quality Management (1997).

satisfaction, customer satisfaction, impact on society and business results (European Foundation for Quality Management, 1997). The criteria, which are shown in table 2.2, are split into two groups: 'enablers' and 'results', illustrated in figure 2.3. Nine elements of the model are further divided into thirty-two criteria parts. The EFQM model of business excellence is based on the principle that processes are the means by which the organization harnesses and releases the talents of its people to produce results. In other words, the processes and the people are the enablers that provide the results. The results aspects of the EFQM model are connected with what the organization has achieved and is achieving, and the enablers with how the results are being achieved. The rationale for this is that customer satisfaction, people satisfaction, impact on society and business results are achieved through leadership, driving policy and strategy, people management, and the management of resources and processes, leading to excellence in business results. Each of these nine criteria can be used to assess an organization's progress towards business excellence.

The enablers are scored in terms of approach and deployment. The approach is concerned with how the requirements of a particular criterion are approached and met. The deployment is the extent to which the approach has been deployed and implemented vertically and horizontally within the organization. The results criteria are evaluated in terms of degree of excellence and the scope of the results presented. The scoring framework consists of 1000 points, with 500 points each being allocated to enablers and results.

The EFQM Model of Business Excellence does not stipulate any particular techniques, methods of procedures that should be in place.

The organizations that put themselves forward for the award are expected to have undertaken at least one self-assessment cycle. Once an application has been submitted to the EFQM headquarters, a team of fully trained independent assessors examines the applications and decides whether or not to conduct a site visit. A jury reviews the findings of the assessors to decide who will win the award.

The Difficulties in Sustaining TQM

Based on work carried out by the UMIST Quality Management Centre over a period of three years on an Engineering and Physical Sciences Research Council (EPSRC) funded project, a number of issues have been identified that impact on the sustainment of TQM. They have been grouped into the five broad categories of (a) internal/external environment, (b) management style, (c) policies, (d) organizational structure and (e) process of change (table 2.3) Drawing on Dale et al. (1997), these five categories are described in the following subsections.

INTERNAL/EXTERNAL ENVIRONMENT

A common method to distinguish between internal and external environments and their influencing factors has been described using the Strength, Weaknesses, Opportunities and Threats (SWOT) framework.

Opportunities and threats are viewed as external variables:

> The *external environment* consists of variables (Opportunities and Threats) that exist outside the organization and are not typically within the short-term control of top management. (Wheelan and Hunger, 1988)

Strengths and weaknesses are part of the internal environment:

> The *internal environment* of a corporation consists of variables (Strengths and Weaknesses) within the organization itself that are also not usually within the short-term control of top management. (Wheelan and Hunger, 1988)

Table 2.3 TQM sustaining categories and issues

Internal/external environment	Management style	Policies	Organizational structure	Process of change
External: Competitors Employee resourcing, development and retention	Industrial relations Management/worker relationship	Policies that may conflict with TQM: Human Resource Management Financial Maintenance Manufacturing	Positioning of the quality function Departmental, functional and shift boundaries Communication	Improvement infrastructure Education and training Teams and teamwork Procedures
Internal: Customer focus Investment The 'fear' factor			Job flexibility and cover Supervisory structure	Quality Management system Quality management tools and techniques Confidence in management

Source: Dale et al. (1997).

The point of making these distinctions is that there are several environmental variables that are often outside the direct control of managers, although they can affect a business through the perceived negative and destabilizing effect that they have on both employees and the improvement process. Therefore, managers need a knowledge of these variables, so that they can, where possible, plan around them.

MANAGEMENT STYLE

This category distinguishes between macro and micro levels and implications of management style, using the sub-categories of industrial relations and management/worker relationships, respectively. The former defines the way in which a business manages employee relations, as outlined typically by Fox (1974) and Marchington and Parker (1990). The latter concerns the attitudes, values and interpersonal skills of managers and supervisors, and their interactions with their subordinates.

POLICIES

It is not unusual to find policies within the organization that conflict, are inconsistent, with or overlap with TQM. Typical of such policies are:

- Human resource management (HRM), where the policy is to pursue individualistic practices, supported by the reward system, which undermine the teamwork methods of TQM. Other aspects of HRM policies, that may conflict with TQM include the level of salaries in relation to the type of work done, lack of transparency of salaries across the organization, perceived discrimination in relation to regard and effort, a complex salary grading structure, and levels of salaries relative to those within the geographical area. Other examples of conflicting HRM policies include lack of consistency in applying appraisal systems, and discrimination between shop-floor workers and staff on issues of sickness and leave of absence.

- Financial policies that encourage short-term decision making and business results in order to maintain stock market credibility and benefits to shareholders. These prevent managers pursuing the longer term objectives of TQM.

- Maintenance policies that, because of a need to reduce costs, limit the amount of work carried out on planned maintenance. This in turn impacts on the performance of the machinery and its ability to produce conforming product.

- Manufacturing policies that focus on output rather than quality performance and customer satisfaction. This focus also has a detrimental effect on training, which, as a consequence, may be perceived as unnecessary or time wasting, and the holding of improvement team meetings.

ORGANIZATIONAL STRUCTURE

This category is concerned with the issues that arise from the way in which a business is structured, and includes functions, roles, responsibilities, hierarchies, boundaries, flexibility and innovation. Structure has been defined by Wilson and Rosenfield (1990) as:

> the established pattern of relationships between the component parts of an organization, outlining both communication, control and authority patterns. Structure distinguishes the parts of an organization and delineates the relationship between them.

PROCESS OF CHANGE

The issues underpinning this category relate to the improvement process itself and/or are a direct result of some form of improvement activity and action. They refer to the training, coaching and development of employees as well as changes in organizational structure and management style, and the adoption of new working practices that are required as part of the TQM initiative. Many of the issues in this category relate to the ability of management to complement change and integrate TQM into the working practices of the organization. The process of change involved in integrating the philosophy of TQM into an organization is complex and wide ranging. If the process is to be effective, it requires the creation of an environment where employees are motivated to want to improve on a continuous basis. If the managers cannot create this environment then any system, tools, techniques or training employed will be ineffective.

Summary

There are a number of approaches to TQM, and these have been examined in the chapter. It is senior management's responsibility to select that which best suits its business and operating environment and any constraints that may exist. The approach should always be tailored to the organization, and 'off-the-shelf' packages should be avoided. Senior managers have much to gain by networking with their counterparts in different businesses, and this exchange of ideas and concerns and discussion of common issues can help to fine-tune the approach that is being used to advance the improvement process.

The chapter also examined the role of self-assessment and the main award models for measuring progress, but pointed out the dangers of using them without adequate knowledge and understanding of continuous improvement principles and mechanisms.

References

Aguayo, R. 1990: *Dr. Deming: The American who Taught the Japanese about Quality*. New York: Simon and Schuster.

Aalbregtse, R. J., Heck, J. A. and McNeley, P. K. 1991: TQM: how do you do it? *Automation*, 38(8), 30–2.

Boaden, R. J. and Dale, B. G. 1994: A generic framework for managing quality improvement: theory and practice., *Quality Management Journal*, 1(4), 11–29.

Brown, G. 1996: How to determine your quality quotient: measuring your company against the Baldrige criteria. *Journal for Quality and Participation*, June, 82–8.

Burt, J. T. 1993: A new name for a not-so-new concept. *Quality Progress*, 26(3), 87–8.

Chu, C. H. 1988: The pervasive elements of total quality control. *Industrial Management*, 30(5), 30–2.

Cole, R. E. 1991: Comparing the Baldrige and Deming awards. *Journal for Quality and Participation*, July/August, 94–104.

Conti, T. 1993: *Building Total Quality: A Guide to Management*. London: Chapman & Hall.

Crosby, P. B. 19979: *Quality is Free*. New York, McGraw-Hill.

Dale, B. G. 1991: Starting on the road to success. *The TQM Magazine*, 2(6), 321–4.

Dale, B. G. and Boaden, R. J. 1993: Improvement framework. *The TQM Magazine*, 5(1), 23–6.

Dale, B. G., Wilcox, M., Boaden, R. J. and McQuarter, R. E. 1997: Total quality management audit tool: description and use. *Total Quality Management*, in press.

Deming, W. E. 1986: *Out of the Crisis*. Cambridge, Mass.: MIT Press.

Deming Prize Committee 1996: *The Deming Prize Guide for Overseas Companies*. Tokyo: Japanese Union of Scientists and Engineers.

European Foundation for Quality Management 1997: *Self Assessment 1997: Guidelines for Companies*. Brussels: EFQM.

Feigenbaum, A. V. 1983: *Total Quality Control*, 3rd edn. New York, McGraw-Hill.

Feigenbaum, A. V. 1991:*Total Quality Control*, 4th edn. McGraw-Hill.

Flero, J. 1992: The Crawford Slip method. *Quality Progress*, 25(5), 40–3.

Fox, A. C. 1974: *Beyond Contract: work, trust and power relations*. London: Faber and Faber.

Hakes, C. 1996: *Total Quality Management: the key to business improvement*, 3rd edn. London: Chapman & Hall.

Hillman, P. G. 1994: Making self-assessment successful. *The TQM Magazine*, 6(3), 29–31.

Johnson, J. W. 1992: A point of view: life in a fishbowl: a senior manager's perspective on TQM. *National Productivity Review*, 11(2), 143–6.

Juran. J. M. (ed.) 1988: *Quality Control handbook*, 4th edn. New York: McGraw-Hill.

Kilian, C. S. 1992: *The World of W. Edwards Deming*. New York, SPC Press.

Lascelles, D. M. and Peacock, R. 1996: *Self-Assessment for Business Excellence*. Maidenhead: McGraw-Hill.

Marchington, M. and Parker, P. 1990: *Changing Patterns of Employee Relations*. Brighton: Harvester Wheatsheaf.

Nakhai, B. and Neves, J. 1994: The Deming, Baldrige and European Quality Awards. *Quality Progress*, April, 33–7.

Scherkenbach, W. W. 1991: *The Deming Route to Quality and Productivity: Roadmaps and Road Blocks*, 2nd edn. Milwaukee, Wis.: ASQC Quality Press.

Sherer, F. 1995: Winning the European Quality Award – a Xerox perspective. *Managing Service Quality*, 5(2), 28–32.

Steeples, M. M. 1993: *The Corporate Guide to the Malcolm Baldrige National Quality Award*. Milwaukee, Wis.: ASQC Quality Press.

US Department of Commerce 1997: *1997 Award Criteria Malcolm Baldrige National Quality Award*. Gaithersburg, Md.: National Institute of Standards and Technology.

Wheelan, H. and Hunger, G. 1988: *Strategic Management and Business Policy*, 3rd edn. Menlo Park, Calif.: Addison-Wesley.

Wilson, D. C. and Rosenfield, R. H. 1990: *Managing Organizations*. Maidenhead: McGraw-Hill.

Yoshida, K. 1995: Revisiting Deming's 14 points in light of Japanese business practice. *Quality Management Journal*, 3(1), 14–30.

3 Managing Human Resources for TQM

Introduction

This subject is important for one simple reason: in practice, the success or failure of TQM depends on the way it is made to work by employees at all levels, from the front line through all levels of management (Hill and Wilkinson, 1995). According to Evans and Lindsay (1995), the TQM focus is 'changing the role of human resource management by changing the perspectives of employees, HRM professionals and line staff managers from an adversarial control oriented relationship to a co-operative position based on mutual organisational and individual goals, trust and respect'. Oakland (1989) has stated that:

> TQM is concerned with moving the focus of control from outside the individual to within; the objective being to make everyone accountable for their own performance, and to get them committed to attaining quality in a highly motivated fashion. The assumptions a director or manager must make in order to move in this direction are simply that people do not need to be coerced to perform well, and that people want to achieve, accomplish, influence activity and challenge their abilities.

In fact, each of the internationally respected quality experts (Juran, Crosby, Deming and Feigenbaum) places a rather different emphasis on the people-management aspects of the system (Dale and Plunkett, 1990; Oakland, 1989). For Crosby and Juran the role of employees in continuous improvement is minimal. While Crosby (1979) recognizes a need for quality awareness to be raised among employees to generate more personal concern, his approach suggests that employees should simply be encouraged to communicate to management the obstacles they face in achieving their improvement goals. Moreover, he rejects outright the redesign of work, regarding work itself as a secondary motivator to how employees are treated (Crosby, 1986). Juran (1988) sees little role for shop-floor employees, with the primary responsibility resting with professionals and to a lesser extent middle management, although he warns against exhortation. His emphasis is on training and top management.

A central problem in this area is that the prescriptive TQM literature says more about what organizations are attempting to achieve in terms of employee commitment and involvement than about HOW they are to reach these ideals (Hill, 1991; Wilkinson et al., 1991). Traditional working practices and management styles may be inconsistent with TQM, and attempts to change the culture of organizations may be problematic (Snape et al., 1995) because they are likely to affect not just shop-floor employees but also professional, supervisory and managerial staff. Managers, for example, may feel that they need to worry about TQM, given the emphasis on empowering their subordinates (Marchington et al., 1992, p. 38), and the evidence indicates that TQM may make managers' jobs more demanding (Wilkinson et al., 1993). Many of the problems identified from research conducted on TQM appear to have been those relating to human resource (HR) issues (defined broadly) such as management style, commitment and understanding, attitudes and culture. One possible explanation for this is that TQM has developed from a quality assurance perspective and consequently focuses on the 'hard' technical aspects such as production/operation performance to the relative neglect of the so-called 'soft' aspects. Indeed, these hard aspects received much of the focus of the original work carried out by the experts and the early research carried out by academics such as Dale and Oakland.

From this viewpoint, the limitations of TQM in practice can be at least partially attributed to the neglect of HR policies in the organization, and a failure to align the HR policies with TQM to ensure integration (Dawson, 1994). As Schuler and Harris (1991) put it, 'HR practices must be brought in line with the mission. Treating human capital inconsistently with a quality philosophy will sabotage all other efforts; people make the process work'. However, while these critical 'soft' issues are commonly raised by reports, they remain relatively unexplored in comparison with the use of quality management tools and techniques and quality systems (Wilkinson, 1992). Furthermore, change is a constant today, and workforce diversity and mobility are creating new employee needs and expectations (Petrick and Furr, 1995). There is some acknowledgement of the importance of HR issues in the major quality award bodies. For example, the Malcolm Baldrige National Quality Award provides for 100 out of 1000 points to be based on HR utilization. Other categories are leadership, information and analysis, strategic planning, customer and market focus, process management and business results. The European Quality Award has allocated 90 points for people management and 90 points for people satisfaction out of a total of 1000 points. The assessment model is one where customer satisfaction, people satisfaction and impact on society are achieved through leadership drive, policy and strategy, people management, resources and processes leading ultimately to excellence in business results. However, van de Wiele (1996), reporting on a study of 117 European organizations with considerable experience of self-assessment, pointed out that in these organizations 'self-assessment is perceived to be more related to the hard issues of TQM rather than the soft issues'.

Hard and Soft Aspects of TQM

Much of the traditional TQM literature concentrates on what might be termed the hard side. This emphasizes systems data collection ('management by fact') and measurement, and involves a range of techniques, including statistical process control, design processes and basic quality control tools used to interpret data and make improvements to the process. As mentioned earlier, this emphasis reflects the background orientation of many of the TQM gurus. However, as quality is no longer considered simply a manufacturing issue or something affecting only part of the organization, this brings in wider issues concerned with managing staff.

The so-called 'soft' side of TQM received a good deal less attention in traditional texts, although it was not completely ignored. Deming, for example, included a number of HR concerns within his fourteen points remedy (Bowen and Lawler, 1992):

1   Institute training on the job.

2   Break down barriers between departments to build teamwork.

3   Drive out fear from the workplace.

4   Eliminate quotas on the shop floor.

5   Advocate conditions that allow workers to have pride in their workmanship, including abolishing annual reviews and merit ratings.

6   Institute a programme of education and self-improvement.

Clearly there are implications for the entire workforce in the TQM philosophy, with the message that 'quality is everyone's business', and as organizations are urged to move away from old-fashioned supervisory approaches to quality control towards a situation where employees themselves take responsibility. The soft side thus puts the emphasis on the management of human resources in the organization: a well-trained and motivated workforce is more likely to contribute to organizational success.

TQM is said to minimize the cost of poor and uncertain quality because it is a way of getting everybody to improve what they do and to build on best practice. Every employee has a common focus based on the customer, so that people with different jobs, abilities and priorities are able to communicate in the pursuit of a common organizational purpose (Wilkinson and Witcher, 1991). Thus, improved communication is an essential requirement of TQM. Team-working, both as a mechanism of continuous improvement and as a form of work organization, is advocated by most quality management experts and features particularly prominently in the work of Juran (1988). It is also assumed that continuous improvement increases employee involvement in decision making, although the scope and magnitude of this – whether it is simply task-centred involvement or a more empowering form of participation and shared decision making – is not addressed (Hill and Wilkinson, 1995).

The TQM literature has little to say on the HRM issues of selection, performance appraisal and reward, and has a distinctly negative view of performance appraisal and performance-based remuneration. One explanation for these omissions and differences is that they reflect a fundamental disagreement about the relative importance of systemic and individual contributions to performance (Waldman, 1994). For the quality gains, performance and employee effectiveness depend less on individual factors and more on the system itself. Since most employees cannot affect this directly, HRM policies that focus on individual performance are less relevant and, indeed, are seen as something of a blind alley. However, from a people management perspective, this is oversimplistic and employers are likely to be reluctant to discard what they regard as key management tools.

In recent years there has been both a shift in emphasis towards HR issues within the TQM field and growing interest and involvement of personnel and HR specialists. This reflects two factors. Firstly, there has been a move away from quality assurance to a broader TQM-based approach, with a consequently greater emphasis being placed on people management issues. Secondly, growing evidence suggests that TQM has major problems in the so-called 'soft' areas (A. T. Kearney, 1992; Cruise O'Brien and Voss, 1992; Plowman, 1990). According to Cruise O'Brien and Voss (1992, p. 11):

> Quality depends on broad based employee involvement and commitment. New and innovative human resource policies were reported by managers in a number of organizations, but these were not often related to quality . . . divorce of human resources from quality, except in name, could seriously retard the spread of quality through the firm.

Similarly, Guest (1992) has argued that TQM is inextricably linked to HRM through the vehicle of training, because of the need for a quality and committed workforce; because the credibility of the initiative is partly governed by management's treatment of the workforce; and, finally, because quality, with its emphasis on involvement and flexibility, implies a high-trust organization. He suggests that 'the need for total quality management linked to and integrated with HRM is increasingly recognised' (1992, p. 111). As with HRM, TQM can be seen as demanding a more strategic approach to the management of human resources. However, it is all too common to point to the failure of many organizations to adopt such a strategic approach (Wilkinson et al., 1991). Moreover, it is argued that TQM writers have understated the difficulties of winning employee commitment and have focused on an overly limited range of change levers (Hill, 1991; Snape, et al., 1995).

Human Resource Policies and Practices

The question of 'fit' between the 'hard' and 'soft' sides of TQM necessitates a re-examination of existing HR policies and practices. Clearly, the HR policies must be consistent with and reflect the quality policy values, vision and mission of the organization, so that different and contradictory messages are not being disseminated by management, and so that HR policies and practices actually facilitate and support the implementation of TQM.

There are a number of critical HR issues, which are discussed in the following subsections.

EDUCATION AND COMMUNICATION

Companies place great emphasis on this, through a variety of vehicles – videos, briefing, magazines, newsletters, notice-boards, story boards and so on – so as to promulgate and reinforce the quality message. However, it is inadequate for senior management to express their commitment solely through communicating vision and mission statements. The 'levers' at the disposal of the HR department (see below) may be more powerful in providing clear messages of change and taking this message beyond the talking stage. However, there has been criticism of some communication programmes that exhort workers to higher effort. Deming (1986), for example, is against such motivational approaches:

> Eliminate slogans, exhortations and targets for the workforce asking for zero defects and new levels of productivity. Such exhortations only create adversarial relationships as the bulk of the causes of low productivity belong to the system and thus lie beyond the power of the workforce.

RECRUITMENT AND SELECTION

There is some evidence in the UK that TQM has had an effect on selection procedures (IRRR, 1991). Some companies use sophisticated recruitment and selection techniques, including psychometric and aptitude tests and assessment centres, to identify teamworkers or problem solvers appropriate to a quality culture. 'Realistic job previews' help produce a stable workforce that fits the organizational

culture. The careful recruitment and selection of workers also charac-
terizes many Japanese companies that have established plants in the
UK and want to facilitate the appropriate 'culture', as well as firms
like Jaguar. Aptitude tests are also being used by companies considering which of the current staff might be moved into 'new' plants
(that is, those with new and more sophisticated technology).

APPRAISAL

Performance appraisal is seen as playing an important role as a tool
to communicate to managers whether quality standards are being
met although in practice it often ends up as an empty ritual (Snape et
al., 1994). Given the importance of the 'customer' in ideas of TQM, it
may be appropriate to include customer evaluation of managerial
performance in the overall appraisal. More organizations appear to
be doing this, with a growing use of 'mystery shoppers', whereby
individuals, either company employees or contracted in, pose as
customers, and monitor and report in their experience to senior
managers. At BP and Rank Xerox managers' subordinates were used
to evaluate their managers' commitment to TQM. Furthermore, there
are cases where managers used their own survey data of customer
satisfaction with their unit's performance to verify and, indeed, challenge the ratings of senior managers (Snape et al., 1994). Certainly,
there is evidence that companies are re-assessing their appraisal
systems to incorporate quality criteria so as to reinforce the critical
importance of the 'quality' message. This is a prime area in which the
gap between the broad organizational philosophy (e.g. 'quality
is king') and managerial practices/systems (e.g. people are not
appraised on the basis of quality) can be most easily observed. Any
contradiction between espoused policies and operational reality can
easily lead to employee cynicism and frustration. Upward or peer
appraisal can also be used as one way of attempting to develop a
more open management style.

Some of the quality gurus, in particular Deming, have argued that
performance appraisal is inconsistent with TQM, and have characterized appraisal and management by results as one of the 'deadly
diseases' of Western management. Under these approaches, dubbed
'management by fear' by Deming, people look for short-term individual achievements to meet their immediate appraisal objectives and

instead of seeking out problems are more likely to cover them up. The emphasis is one of avoiding risk. According to Deming (1986):

> Merit rating rewards people that do well in the system, it does not reward attempts to improve the system. Don't rock the boat.

> Evaluation of performance, merit rating or annual review . . . it nourishes short-term performance, annihilates long-term planning, builds fear, demolishes teamwork, nourishes rivalry and politics.

Moreover, the performance of most low-level employees is dependent on systems controlled by others. However, Western management appears to be implementing TQM with existing structures of appraisal (Snape et al., 1996). It might be that the key is to incorporate quality indicators into the appraisal system (Bowen and Lawler, 1992). For example, in Hill's (1991) account of a US office automation company, managers were appraised on the basis of their adherence to TQM procedures, which included targets for their employees' involvement in quality management activities.

Thus, in practice, companies that have introduced TQM have found that they have had to use appraisal and incentives in order to align managerial behaviour with the principles of quality management, even when initially they followed the prescriptive advice to make TQM voluntary (Hill, 1991). Daniel and Reitsberger (1991) provide evidence that the Japanese have modified control systems to encourage continuous quality improvement, with goal setting and feedback information about specific quality items. However, how is this done? If Kohn (1993) is right in his view that performance-related pay only 'motivates people to get rewards', then there are clearly dangers in simply measuring people's participation in processes (e.g. how many suggestions have been made, how many improvement teams established, how many control charts are in use). Are people to be appraised and rewarded for their individual achievements or for their ability to work in teams? Are quality indicators (e.g. customer satisfaction, internal rejection rate, cost of quality, process capability index, EFQM Model of Business Excellence score, the amount of quality enhancement activity) to replace older measures of performance? All of these matters need to be carefully thought through (Hill and Wilkinson, 1995).

TRAINING AND DEVELOPMENT

Pfeffer (1992, p. 45) argues that worker autonomy, self-managed teams and even a high wage strategy depend on having people who are not only empowered to make changes and improvements but who also have the necessary skills to do so. Consequently, he argues that an integral part of most new work systems is a greater commitment to training and skill development. He argues that training can reduce employees turnover and absenteeism, and lead to higher performance ratings. Technical training (tools and techniques) predominates in TQM texts but there is less emphasis on the necessary soft skills (e.g. teamwork), which may also be required. An increased emphasis on both types of training was apparent in one organization that was studied in research undertaken by UMIST for the IPM. The case of CarCom illustrates that training can be seen as a key litmus test of management commitment to developing employees. Training had increased in volume despite the business losses incurred, and the appointment of a training officer was also seen as significant. Similarly, at another company, Photochem, the HR department had recently initiated training sessions that – a least in part – were geared up to improving interpersonal and teamworking skills (IPM, 1993). A Malcolm Baldrige Award winner, Federal Express, approached training from several angles: firstly, basic training to explain 'quality', secondly, training in quality tools, techniques, teamwork and problem solving; and thirdly, exploiting the technical skills of each employee (Herbig et al., 1994). An Institute of Management survey found a strong relationship between an individual manager's assessment of the adequacy of training and the degree of success of the quality management programme (Wilkinson et al., 1993). Indeed, training is a primary mechanism through which individuals are socialized to new organizational values (Walton, 1985).

TQM may also have implications for management development, especially in relation to management style. If there have been moves towards becoming a more flexible organization with fewer explicit guidelines, this may put a greater emphasis on the use of interpersonal skills to motivate staff. In the longer run, as flatter structures evolve, this may require cross-functional career moves and horizontal reassignments such as those that have characterized Japanese operations over some years (Bowden and Lawler, 1992).

The research findings from the Institute of Management study (Wilkinson et al., 1993) point to the greater emphasis on teamwork and demands on managers' time (table 3.1). Quality management (QM) appears to make managerial jobs more demanding, requiring more in terms of both people management and technical skills. A majority felt that QM made employees more questioning of managerial decisions, while just under half said that it placed managers under greater scrutiny from their superiors. Thus, managers appear to be pressurized from above and below.

While there was broad agreement about the impact of QM on jobs among managers at board, senior, middle and junior management levels, there were some differences between these groups. The research shows a significant relationship between job status and the perceived effect of QM on the amount of discretion afforded to the manager in the job. Thus, the further down the management hierarchy we go, the less likely were managers to see the QM programme as increasing their level of discretion. Many junior managers in particular saw QM as actually reducing their level of discretion.

Senior managers appear to be more aware of the skills implications of QM. Thus, while managers at all levels felt that QM placed greater emphasis on both people management skills and technical skills and knowledge, this feeling was more pronounced among more senior managers. Interestingly, while the majority of managers felt that QM made greater demands in their time, this feeling was particularly pronounced for those in the middle of the management hierarchy (Wilkinson et al., 1993).

REWARD AND RECOGNITION

Pfeffer (1992) argues that 'fairness and justice virtually dictate that if people are responsible for enhanced levels of performance and profitability, they will want to share in the benefits'. Lack of perceived fairness will lead to a demotivated workforce and reduced productivity. In attempts to reinforce the quality message, it seems sensible that companies should abandon pay policies that simply reward output.

The TQM literature assumes that employees are keen to participate in the pursuit of quality improvements with little concern for extrinsic reward. Moreover, some managements take the line that

Table 3.1 Research findings from the Institute of Management study

Thinking about managers' jobs at your level in the organization, what effect has the Quality Management programme had on the following aspects of managers' jobs?
(Percentage of respondents, answering on a five-point scale)

	1	2	3	4	5	
To make them more demanding Mean score = 1.11	16	60	21	3	0	To make them less demanding
To increase the level of discretion Mean score = 1.91	4	30	42	21	4	To reduce the level of discretion
To place managers' decisions under more scrutiny from superiors Mean score = 1.59	9	39	38	12	2	To place managers' decisions under less scrutiny from superiors
To make employees more questioning of managerial decisions Mean score = 1.37	10	51	33	6	1	To make employees less questioning of managerial decisions
To place more emphasis on people-management skills Mean score = 1.12	19	57	19	4	2	To place less emphasis on people-management skills
To make more demands on managers' technical skills and knowledge Mean score = 1.35	13	49	29	8	1	To make fewer demands on managers' technical skills and knowledge
To put more emphasis on teamwork Mean score = 0.86	34	49	15	2	1	To put less emphasis on teamwork
To make more demand on managers' time Mean score = 0.96	32	44	19	4	1	To make less demands on managers' time
To improve the prospects for career development Mean score = 1.77	6	27	56	9	3	To limit the prospects for career development

Base: Respondents reporting that they have or have had a formal quality management campaign.
Source: Wilkinson et al. (1993).

continuous improvement is a part of employees' routine work, and hence should not be directly rewarded.

Crosby and Deming, two of the major quality gurus, have argued against the use of financial incentives (Drummond and Chell, 1992). For example, Crosby (1979) argues that to reward an individual's commitment to quality with financial incentives is to risk demeaning them by attaching a price tag to their efforts. For Crosby, recognition should be central, with the awarding of prizes and trinkets of more symbolic value. Deming also has been very critical of such attempts to use pay as a tool to change attitudes, seeing the emphasis on individual contribution as working against the ideas of cooperation and teamwork espoused by TQM. However, writers in the remuneration and the organizational behaviour fields have argued that pay is a critical lever for change, and signals the way for new directions in organizational strategy. For example, Brewster and Richbell (1983) point out that too often employees see the gap between espoused strategy (what management say) and operational strategy (how managers act or expect employees to act). Payment is a good case. Managers may say that 'quality' is the top priority but if they continue to emphasize output and getting goods out of the factory gate to meet deadlines and pay workers by piece rates, the gap between rhetoric and reality is all too clear. Piddington et al. (1995) outline an approach to recognition and reward called the 'Improvement Opportunity Scheme', which has been successfully used by Betz Dearborn to encourage employees to become more fully involved in the improvement process. In the scheme points are awarded for ideas, and once the points total has reached 1000 there is a payout of £25 000 divided equally between all of the company's employees. The case for rewarding quality has been put by Bowen and Lawler (1992), who point out that 'the value orientation in many countries says individuals and groups should be paid more when they perform better. When they are not paid more they tend to feel inequitably treated'.

For many writers the key issue is not *whether* to use payment systems but *how* to develop them in line with TQM principles. Thus, Bowen and Lawler (1992) suggest that incentives need to focus on skills acquisition, and on team and unit performance. Skills-based pay, profit sharing and gain sharing linked to quality improvements and efficiency savings are seen as the appropriate forms of incentives to underpin continuous improvement.

JOB DESIGN

This has been emphasized by James (1991), who links TQM with the Quality of Working Life debates, suggesting that employees are more likely to show commitment when jobs are meaningful and involve significant responsibility, and where employees are able to get direct feedback on their performance (see chapter 7). TQM's emphasis on flexibility and teamwork may also require a move away from detailed fixed job descriptions (Bowen and Lawler, 1992).

SINGLE STATUS

This may also be important in providing some underpinning of the sense of shared responsibility or continuous improvement, and may help to break down 'them' and 'us' attitudes. This would certainly be consistent with the ideas of Deming. Clearly, visible senior management commitment is crucial. Thus, at one organization, Electron, the interviewing of all staff on a one-to-one basis by the MD, together with addressing employee unhappiness at certain aspects of the work environment, clearly marked off the quality initiative from past fads (Wilkinson, 1996). Pfeffer (1992) argues that the symbols that separate people from each other are an important barrier to decentralizing decision making and eliciting employee commitment and cooperation. He argues that 'symbolic egalitarianism' is a way of signalling to both insiders and outsiders that there is comparative equality, and it is not the case that some think and some do. Such policies are often associated with Japanese implants in the UK. Initiatives that fall under this banner are single-status canteens, identical workwear, unreserved parking places, all staff being salaried (rather than the shop-floor workers being on hourly rates), open access to management and offices, and the location and size of those offices. However, managers can resist these changes because they object to losing their status symbols. In research undertaken at UMIST by Godfrey et al. (1996), it was argued that single-status is also displayed in more psychological ways, for example, how people are treated during everyday contact, how they are spoken and listened to, and the use of first names, etc. In short, ensuring that everyone is treated as a human being deserving equal respect involves both structural and attitudinal changes.

EMPLOYEE INVOLVEMENT

This can take a number of forms, ranging from direct downward communication from managers to other employees or the seeking of employee opinions via problem solving groups through to high-level meetings between directors and trade union representatives on works councils or company boards. Equally, the subject matter can vary from the mundane to the strategic, focusing on social and sports items through to high-level financial and commercial information. Wilkinson et al. (1992) differentiate between employee involvement defined as:

1 Education, communications, customer care.

2 Amended job responsibilities, hierarchically and at the same skill level.

3 Problem solving and the tapping of employee opinion.

Even though these may not be radical in orientation, their successful operation depends to a large extent on the climate within which they are introduced, the motives and abilities of managers to make them work, and their primacy in relation to other organizational goals and objectives (see chapter 7). Pfeffer (1992), for example, argues for broader employee empowerment and participation in controlling their own work processes – employees should be encouraged to analyse their own jobs and search for improvements, coming up with their own ideas. The desire is for self-management, with 'every employee a manager'. He argues that the evidence is that participation increases both employee satisfaction and productivity, although there have been major criticisms of these links and any positive correlation between involvement and employee satisfaction and/or performance (Marchington et al., 1992).

EMPLOYEE RELATIONS

TQM, if done properly, requires significant organizational change and a re-examination of operating methods and working practices. The traditional TQM literature suggests that persuading workers to take responsibility for quality assurance/improvement and adjusting traditional job roles requires little more than a dose of motivation and training. However, these are issues that (certainly in the manufacturing sector) involve questions of job control and working practices and possibly compensation as well. At Photochem, for example, as decision was made to 'work with' the stewards in introducing change rather than ignoring or bypassing them (IPM, 1993). Employee relations considerations may also be important where TQM is associated with a programme of job losses and work intensification. Furthermore, trade unions may also be concerned that TQM can marginalize the union as a communications channel, at the same time strengthening the sense of commitment to what might be seen as 'managerial' objectives. However, trade unions are not necessarily opposed to TQM. The TUC report on HRM in 1994 suggested that management and unions could come together in a cooperative partnership in implementing organizational change (Marchington, 1995). Much depends on management motives and the precise nature of organizational change. Thus Thurley and Wirdenius (1989) point out that 'managers need to be reminded that the commitment of employees to production system objectives will depend on the acceptability of objectives as legitimate and the perceived justice of the arrangements governing employee work'. These are issues beyond the usual 'teething problems' of the management of change because of fear of the unknown.

In one study, TQM in its early stages was regarded as essentially management policy and outside the union sphere of influence. However, while TQM at business strategy level was not seen as a union concern, TQM as implemented throughout the organization was. Thus, as it worked down the organization, industrial relations issues were increasingly involved. For example, workers in a machine tool company wanted additional payments because of their enhanced role in quality assurance. Such issues may be more limited in the service sector, where a high degree of managerial prerogative extends over issues concerning the management of staff (Wilkinson et al., 1992).

Management may see its approach as a set of 'neutral' techniques and tools but, as Deming (1986) points out, the system is often seen as repressive by workers. While workers and unions may find it difficult to challenge the 'logic' of management action in principle, the workforce almost invariably interprets, evaluates and reacts towards managerial initiative and, in its own way, 'audits' their introduction and operation.

Thus, while TQM presents a positive message offering opportunities to employees, it is important to appreciate that these are defined by management. Consequently, employee involvement may be seen as beneficial but it can also be seen, depending on the context of its introduction, as intensifying work and increasing responsibility without tangible reward. In other words, TQM contains an implicit unitarianism, assuming that everyone in the organization shares common interests and values and that management prerogative is seen as legitimate and, indeed, legitimized by customer-defined goals, even if management actually interprets customer demands. The adversarial, low-trust dynamic of UK industrial relations has been much written about (Guest, 1987), and if TQM is implemented within this context it is unlikely that anything more than employee compliance will be the result. Thus, Pfeffer (1992) argues that security of employment signals a long-standing commitment by the employer to its workforce. An employer that signals through 'word and deed' that its employees are dispensable is not likely to generate loyalty, commitment or willingness to expend extra effort for the organization's benefit. Employees who feel relatively secure in their employment are, he argues, more likely to become involved in and contribute to improvements in the work process because they no longer fear loss of their own or their colleagues' jobs. Employment security also has implications for recruitment (which is likely to be more selective) and for training, where both employer and employees will have a greater incentive to invest in training (see Godfrey et al., 1996).

The emphasis we have given to HR issues raises the question of the role of the personnel department. Recognition of the significance of HR issues *in principle* is by itself inadequate. In a classic analysis of personnel work, Legge (1978) points out that:

> Non-specialists, while formally recognising the importance of effectively utilising human resources, lacking as they did the expertise to develop a systematic view of what this entailed in terms of personnel strategies and actions, in practice tended to underestimate the importance of the human resource variable in decision making issues that were not explicitly personnel management.

Consequently, a specialist personnel contribution is likely to be crucial to a full consideration of HR issues (Herbig et al., 1994). Thus, Giles and Williams (1991) suggest that TQM could either be an opportunity for the personnel function (because of the HR implications of TQM), or, alternatively, could actually lead to a declining role since the issues are seen to be too important to be left to personnel! Yet they argue that personnel professionals have much to offer quality management, acting as 'guardians' of such key processes as selection, appraisal, training and reward systems. These are key levers in any attempt to achieve and maintain strategic change. Quality can be the business issue that brings senior managers and HR specialists together, moving HR to strategic HRM (Bowen and Lawler, 1992).

The type of personnel work that is carried out can be related to the dimensions of level and profile. In relation to the notion of *level*, and in particular, *strategic* versus *operational* level, it is clear that there are different roles for personnel, perhaps exemplified most clearly by the distinction between the 'clerk of the works' and the 'architect' (Tyson, 1987). The existence of a personnel presence on the board would be one indicator of this, but it may also be illustrated by the most senior personnel member reporting directly to the managing director, or by the implicit promotion of HRM ideas by the senior management team. Personnel work can also be related to some notion of *power* or *profile*, which is apparent in the distinction between terms such as intervention, innovation or visibility, and responsiveness, support or low profile. This provides some measure of the degree to which personnel merely supports the activities of line managers and operates behind the scene, or, in contrast, attempts to make its activities known across the organization by a more proactive style. By combining these two dimensions, a cell diagram can be constructed which categorizes the personnel role into four categories; strategic/high profile, strategic/low profile, operational/high profile and operational/low profile (figure 3.1).

This model enables us to examine the broad range of personnel roles in terms of *how* the function is organized. In research conducted for the IPM, personnel departments were involved in a wide variety of activities to do with TQM (Marchington et al., 1993; Wilkinson and Marchington, 1994). While all personnel departments played a basic *facilitating* role (in many respects little different from that normally expected of personnel), in most cases they played a

Figure 3.1 The role of personnel in TQM

more significant additional role specific to TQM. These were defined as the *change agent* role, the *hidden persuader* role and the *internal contractor* role.

The change agent role (strategic/high profile) can be characterized by a high-level contribution that is also highly visible to others in the organization. At one end, this would include a situation in which personnel is responsible for driving through the quality initiative or plays a central role in evaluating the structure or culture to enable TQM to be introduced. In one manufacturing company, the function played a change agent role, both through the influence of the HR director at board level and in the Quality Improvement Steering Committee. The managing director referred to HR as 'helping to create an organization culture and structure in which TQM is possible', the quality manager regarded HR as providing 'the engine of change', and the union convenor saw the recent HR package as 'the extension of TQM to people management'.

The second role, that of hidden persuader (strategic/low profile), was rather less common in the IPM research. With this role, the personnel operated at strategic level, working closely with the chief executive of the organization or site in question, although the presence of personnel as a function was much less visible to others in the organization. However, the managing director decided that 'personnel' could help the quality manager to develop QM because it was seen as 'neutral' and could take an overview of the change process. The personnel manager was used as a 'sounding board' for new ideas before they were discussed with the wider management team. Thus, while the influence of personnel can be quite high, and it operates at a strategic level regarding TQM, its role is not particularly visible to other managers (or employees).

The third role is that of internal contractor (operational level/high profile), and this was apparent in several of the IPD cases. Organizations had attempted to draw up and publicize targets or standards for the delivery of personnel and HR practices to internal customers. At a software consultancy that had achieved ISO 9000 system series registration several years ago, the personnel department produced its own 'simply quality targets of Personnel Products and Services' after discussions with a 'selection of customers'. The overall objective of the personnel function was to 'provide services for obtaining and maintaining a productive workforce for the group, through the provision of employment policies, services and information for Directors, managers and staff; and by liaising, on employment matters, with outside training, recruitment and statutory bodies'. Such products and services include offers and contracts, administration of induction, and advice on dismissal and disciplinary procedures, and are related to a specific 'customer'. The level of service (e.g. the response times) was also specified.

At all organizations, the personnel function performed a *facilitator* role. Personnel played some role in the training of employees in quality management awareness and principles; in some cases, most of the training was provided by personnel, whereas in others it was a joint activity between the quality and personnel functions. Training initiatives ranged from awareness training or the training of staff on the use of tools and techniques to teamwork courses and new management development programmes. Communications is also an area where personnel plays a role, including publicizing mission statements and preparing booklets and leaflets. In addition, some functions also played a role in the design and administration of attitude surveys, which provided insight into the effectiveness of TQM in changing the views of employees.

In practice, HR departments have taken on more than one of these roles in addition to acting as a facilitator. This can happen because a single-site personnel function may intervene at different levels on separate occasions or over time; or, in multi-establishment organizations, members of the personnel function may themselves be located at different levels, e.g. corporate/division/site.

It is important to appreciate that the four roles discussed do not simply represent a 'menu' of choices from which personnel departments can select. There are three critical factors influencing which role is adopted. The first is the existing approach and status of the function; clearly, a function that performs basic operational work is unlikely suddenly to become transformed by the onset of TQM into a strategic role. Thus, departments that have carried out 'nuts and bolts' work tend to continue in a similar vein under a TQM regime. The second is the origins of the TQM initiative: the instigators will already have their own perspective on what TQM is about; schemes driven by a marketing director are likely to be different from those designed by operations specialists. Thirdly, the nature of the initiative itself provides a context for the involvement of personnel professionals. The launch of TQM was in some cases partly a reflection of the need to develop from a quality assurance based initiative. This can provide an opportunity for personnel practitioners to offer/claim a more strategic foothold on organizational change by pointing to past failures, and putting themselves forward as the appropriate people to overcome these problems (Wilkinson and Marchington, 1994).

Personnel is often regarded by some managers as free from the typical conflicts that take place between production, marketing and design, and thus more likely to be 'objective' in its approach to managing change. It may well be up to personnel to point to the contradictory nature of the organizational cures embarked upon; for example, the differing emphasis on the group and the individual. The following list indicates how Bowen and Lawler (1992) see the HR function being redefined by applying quality principles:

1   Quality Work for the First Time. The HR department which has to redesign a pay system or orientation programme because employees don't understand it, can be seen as a form of rework. Cause and effect analysis can be utilised within the department.

2   Focus on the Customer. The HR department can be more service oriented, that is it aims to satisfy clients (e.g. other managers) rather than being driven simply by their own pet programmes. 'Customers' can be involved here in decisions that affect them.

3   Strategic Holistic Approach to Improvement. Quality improvement may involve changes in mission, structure, job design and management practices.

4   Continuous Improvement. HR can try to build values and practices to support the idea of continuous improvement.

5   Mutual Respect and Teamwork. HR has to lead by 'driving out fear'. As the hierarchical structure of the organization is

redesigned, employee involvement and collaborative working must be championed.

It is also important to appreciate the dynamics of the role. It could be argued that the very nature of the approach (that is, a continuous process rather than a programme) gives the personnel function a number of windows of opportunity to contribute.

In research carried out for the Institute of Personnel Management, it was reported that there were five possible phases of intervention (Marchington et al., 1993). Personnel professionals could play a role in shaping TQM initiatives at the formulation stage. Personnel people may be able to play a creative role here in terms of the philosophy behind TQM and its degree of interaction with current organizational practice and ethos. However, much depends upon the existing influence of the function, and its ability to gain access to senior levels of decision making within the organization. Assuming this to be the case, the following are examples of areas in which interventions may be made:

- preparing and synthesizing reports from other organizations that have experience of TQM,

- assisting with choices about the TQM approach to be adopted,

- influencing the type of TQM infrastructure and culture appropriate to the introduction of TQM, and

- shaping the type of organizational structure and cultural appropriate to the introduction of TQM, and

- designing and delivering senior management development courses that create the right climate for TQM.

At the implementation stage, personnel professionals can play a rather facilitating role in ensuring that TQM is introduced in the most appropriate way. The following types of activity may be undertaken:

- training of middle managers and supervisors in how to develop the TQM process with their staff,

- training facilitators, mentors and team members in interpersonal skills and how to manage the TQM process,

- coaching managers on the behaviour that is necessary with the TQM approach,

- designing communication events to publicize the launch of TQM,

- consulting with employees and trade union representatives about the introduction and development of TQM,

- assisting the board to adapt mission statements and prepare quality objectives for dissemination to staff and customers, and

- deciding how to deal with those managers and employees who resist improvement initiatives.

Having shaped and implemented a new TQM initiative, the personnel function can play an effective part in attempting to maintain and reinforce its position within the organization. Interventions in the third area are designed to ensure that TQM continues to attract a high profile and does not lose impetus. The contribution can be in the following sorts of areas:

- introducing or upgrading the TQM component within induction courses,

- ensuring that training in tools, techniques, systems and processes continues to be provided within the organization,

- redesigning appraisal procedures so that they contain criteria relating to specific TQM objectives,

- preparing/overseeing special newsletters of team briefs on TQM,

- assisting quality improvement teams or suggestions schemes to work effectively and produce ideas, and

- ensuring that the methods of rewarding success are established.

Personnel may also be able to make a contribution to TQM at the fourth, review, stage, either on a regular basis or as part of an ongoing procedure for evaluating progress. Such intervention could include:

- contributing to leading the preparation of an annual TQM report,

- assessing the effectiveness of the TQM infrastructure; steering committees, quality service teams, improvement groups etc.,

- preparing and administering employee attitude surveys on TQM,

- facilitating and assisting with benchmarking the effectiveness of the organization's TQM with that of competitors or employers in other sectors/countries, and

- facilitating and assisting with self-assessment using criteria such as the EFQM Model of Business Excellence or the Malcolm Baldrige National Quality Award.

Finally, and to some extent in conjunction with each of the above contributions, personnel functions can apply TQM processes to a review of their own activities, along the lines of that undertaken by the internal contractors, as analysed earlier. The precise list of practices obviously depends on the organization and function involved, but some of the more typical might be those described below:

- preparing offer and contract letters within a specified time,

- advising staff on their terms and conditions of employment,

- evaluating training provision on an annual basis,

- preparing and disseminating absence and labour turnover data to line managers on a monthly basis,

- providing advice on disciplinary matters within a specified and agreed time period, and

- continual review of its activities using the people-related criteria in the EFQM model and MBNQA.

However, it should not be assumed that the more of these that are undertaken the better. Indeed, this may lead to resources being spread too thinly and the function getting the reputation of being faddish and pushing initiative regardless of their organizational relevance.

Summary

In this chapter we have examined the implications that TQM has for the management of human resources and the centrality of HR issues to implementation. We have suggested that the difficulties on changing attitudes are often underestimated and that management needs a wholesale review of existing HR policies and practices. The role of the HR function in contributing to the introduction and development of TQM has been outlined. It is our view that organizations that fail to utilize fully the skill and abilities of their HR professionals are less likely to achieve success with TQM.

References

Kearney, A. T. 1992: Total quality: time to take off the rose tinted spectacles, IFS Report.

Bowen D. and Lawler, E. 1992: Total quality-oriented human resources management. *Organizational Dynamics*, 20(4), 29–41.

Brewster, C. and Richbell, S. 1983: Industrial relations policy and managerial custom and practice. *Industrial Relations Journal*, 14(1), 22–31.

Crosby, P. B. 1979: *Quality is Free*, New York: McGraw-Hill.

Cruise O'Brien, R. and Voss, C. 1992 In search of quality, London Business School Working Paper.

Dale, B. G. and Plunkett, J. J. (eds) 1990: *Managing Quality* 1st edn. London: Philip Allan.

Daniel, S. and Reitsberger, W. 1991: Linking quality strategy with management control systems: empirical evidence from Japanese Industry. *Accounting, Organizations and Society*, 6(7), 601–15.

Dawson, P. 1994: Total quality management. In J. Storey (ed.), *New Wave Manufacturing Strategies*. London: Paul Chapman, pp. 103–21.

Deming, W. E. 1986: *Out of the Crisis: Quality, Productivity and Competitive Position*. Cambridge, Mass.: MIT Press.

Drummond, H. and Chell, E. 1992: Should organizations pay for quality? *Personnel Review*, 21(4), 3–11.

Evans, J. and Lindsay, W. 1995: *The Management and Control of Quality*, 3rd edn. St Paul, Minn.: West.

Giles, E. and Williams, R. 1991: Can the personnel department survive quality management? *Personnel Management*, April, 28–33.

Godfrey, G, Wilkinson, A. and Marchington, M. 1997: Competitive advantage through people? UMIST Working Paper.

Guest, D. 1987: HRM and industrial relations. *Journal of Management Studies*, 24(5), 503–22.

—— 1992: Human resource management in the UK. In B. Towers (ed.), *The Handbook of Human Resource Management*. Oxford: Blackwell.

Herbig, P., Palumbo, F. and O'Hara, B. S. 1994: Total quality and the human resource professional. *The TQM Magazine*, 6(2), 33–6.

Hill, S. 1991: Why quality circles failed but total quality might succeed. *British Journal of Industrial Relations*, 29(4), 541–68.

Hill, S. and Wilkinson, A. 1995: In search of TQM. *Employee Relations*, 17(3), 8–25.

IPM 1993: *Quality, People Management Matters*. London: Institute of Personnel Management.

IRRR 1991: The start of selection, 24 May.

James, G. 1991: Quality of working life and total quality management, occasional paper no. 50, Work Research Unit, ACAS.

Juran J. 1988: *Quality Control Handbook*. New York: McGraw-Hill.

Kohn, A. 1993: *Punished by Rewards*. Boston, Mass.: Houghton Miflin.

Legge, K. 1978: *Power, Innovation and Problem Solving in Personnel Management*. Maidenhead: McGraw-Hill.

Marchington, M. 1995: Fairy tales and magic wands: new employment practices in perspective. *Employee Relations*, 17(1), 51–66.

Marchington, M., Goodman, J., Wilkinson, A. and Ackers, P. 1992: New developments in employee involvement, Department of Employment Working Paper, London.

Marchington, M., Wilkinson, A. and Dale, B. 1993: Quality and the human resource dimension: the case study section. *Quality, People Management Matters*. London: Institute of Personnel Management.

Oakland, J. 1989: *Total Quality Management*. London: Heinemann.

Petrick, J. and Furr, D. 1995: *Total Quality in Managing Human Resources*. Delray Beach, Fla.: St Lucie Press.

Pfeffer, J. 1992: *Competitive Advantage through People*. New York: Free Press.

Piddington, H., Bunney, H. S. and Dale, B. G. 1995: Rewards and recognition in quality improvement: what are they key issues? *Quality World*, March (technical supplement), 12–18.

Plowman, B. 1990: Management behavior. *The TQM Magazine*, 2(4), 217–9.

Schuler, R. and Harris, D. 1991: Deming quality improvement: implications for human resource management as illustrated in a small company. *Human Resource Planning*, 14, 191–207.

Snape, E., Redman, T. and Bamber, G. 1994: *Managing Managers*. Oxford: Blackwell.

Snape, E., Redman, T., Wilkinson, A. and Marchington, M. 1995: Managing human resources for total quality management. *Employee Relations,* 15(3), 42–51.

Snape, E., Wilkinson, A. and Redman, T. 1996: Cashing in on quality? pay incentives and the quality culture. *Human Resource Management Journal,* 6(4), 5–17.

Thurley, K. and Wirdenius, H. 1989: *Towards European Management.* London: Pitman.

Tyson, S. 1987: The management of the personnel function. *Journal of Management Studies,* 24(5), 523–32.

van de Wiele, T., Williams, A. R. T., Dale, B. G., Carter, G., Kolb, F., Luzon, D. M., Schmidt, A. and Wallace, M. 1996: Self assessment: a study of progressive Europe's leading organisations in quality management practices. *International Journal of Quality and Reliability Management,* 13(1), 84–104.

Waldman, D. 1994: The contribution of total quality management to a theory of work performance. *Academy of Management Review,* 19(3), 510–36.

Walton, R. 19985: From control to commitment. *Harvard Business Review,* March/April, 72–9.

Wilkinson, A. 1992: The other side of quality: soft issues and the human resource dimension. *Total Quality Management,* 3(3), 323–9.

—— 1994: Managing human resources for quality in B. G. Dale (ed.), *Managing Quality,* 2dn edn. London: Prentice Hall, pp. 273–91.

—— 1996: Variations in total quality management. In J. Storey (ed.), *Blackwell Cases in Human Resource and Change Management.* Oxford: Blackwell, pp. 173–89.

Wilkinson, A. and Marchington, M. 1994: TQM – instant pudding for the personnel function? *Human Resource Management Journal,* 5(1), 33–49.

Wilkinson, A. and Witcher, B. 1991: Fitness for use: barriers to full TQM in the UK. *Management Decision,* 29(8), 44–9.

Wilkinson, A., Allen, P. and Snape,. E. 1991: TQM and the management of labour. *Employee Relations,* 13(1), 24–31.

Wilkinson, A., Marchington, M., Goodman, J. and Ackers, P. 1992: Total quality management and employee involvement. *Human Resource Management Journal,* 2(4), 1–20.

Wilkinson, A., Redman, T. and Snape, E. 1993: Quality and the manager: An IM Report, Corby Institute of Management.

4 What Senior Management Need to Know about Quality Costing

Introduction

The collection and use of quality-related costs is a crucial factor in a process of continuous improvement. The task is not an easy one. There may be internal opposition and obscuration of the data, but these organizations that have persevered and succeeded have found the exercise to be beneficial. Many executives are surprised when they learn of the scale of their quality costs and soon want to develop their quality-related costing systems to gain greater benefits and cost control and to realize the potential savings. It has also been found helpful to ensure that the CEO and senior management teams persevere with their TQM and improvement initiatives.

The purpose of this chapter is to provide senior managers with an overview of the subject of quality costing and the wherewithal to understand what is involved in a quality costing exercise, and how the data may be used to assist with the development of an improvement process.

The Role of Quality Costing in Total Quality Management

Most senior managers want tangible evidence of the benefits of TQM in order to gain their interest. One of the means of providing this evidence and a factor in promoting a process of continuous improvement is the collection, reporting and use of quality-related cost information.

As already mentioned in this book, continuous improvement requires patience, tolerance, tenacity, and considerable commitment from people at every level in the organization, in particular from the senior management team. It requires some considerable effort to sustain this process and, more often than not, the management of an organization, in particular those based in the West, will need to justify to its parent company, board and shareholders that the investment in the improvement process is cost effective and that definable outputs and deliverables are being made.

Some people may argue that there should be no need to justify investment in a formal improvement process, taking the line that the benefits will always outweigh the costs. The environment in the West is such that organizations and their managements are judged over relatively short time periods. Indeed, one of the criticisms made of executives is that they place too much emphasis on short-term objectives. This short-termism is often engendered by the financial institutions. Committing huge expenditure on improvement activities as a blanket approach without some measure of cost effectiveness and whether or not the money being expended is concentrated on the right activities can be considered an act of faith and is contrary to the way in which many Western businesses operate. Executives, after twelve months or so of TQM activities in terms of training, operation of improvement teams and tackling of projects, tend to become nervous if tangible benefits are not starting to surface. A number of writers (e.g. Schaffer and Thomson, 1992) have criticized some of those TQM approaches that are heavily oriented towards cascade training and action-centred activities and which fail to produce early results and savings (i.e. high on input but short on output).

In Japanese organizations the situation is quite different. Investment in improvement initiatives over a long period of time without thought of immediate benefits, appears to be accepted without question by executives, senior managers, shareholders and financial institutions. There are a number of well-publicized examples where Japanese companies have established a manufacturing plant outside of Japan and planned for it not to reach a breakeven situation for at least five years from start-up. The Japanese have considerable tangible evidence, over the past thirty years or so, of the wisdom of pursuing this long-range management view (see chapter 9).

In addition to quality, organizations need to be competitive on cost and delivery (QCD). In today's climate of 'more for less and more for less' (that is, improved performance for less money) a considerable number of organizations need to achieve substantial cost reductions if they are to survive as business entities. Consequently, intense effort is being expended by management in deciding what their core businesses are and identifying waste and non-value-adding activity. In the automotive and electronic industries, suppliers are often assisted by their customers in this activity by a joint analysis of all costs using an 'open book' and target cost approach. Many organizations, particularly in complex and high technology industries, are vulnerable to any breakthrough by their competitors in relation to improvement and technology. In many instances, quality-related costs are a major potential source of the necessary savings that help to maintain a competitive age. Quality costing is one of several quality management techniques that can assist organizations with improving the processes of identifying and eliminating excessive costs, waste and non-value-adding activities.

Quality costing may be considered by some to be more useful for organizations taking the first steps along the TQM journey than it is for those that have considerably more operating experience of TQM. However, a number of world class organizations do employ quality costing measures as an indication of internal performance. Quality costing is about knowing what non-quality is costing the organization, tracking the causes and effects of the problem, working out solutions using improvement teams and monitoring progress.

A knowledge of quality costs helps executives to justify the investment in an improvement process and assists them in monitoring the effectiveness of the efforts made and assessing the impact of various improvement activities. It is used to reduce the number of errors and mistakes, along with the associated costs. In this way it frees-up employees' time and helps utilize them in a more effective way. Quality costing expresses an organization's quality performance in the language of the CEO, board, senior management team, shareholders and financial institutions – money. It is often found that the board and the senior management team are unmoved by quality assurance data but are spurred into action when the same data are expressed and presented in monetary terms. The majority of management consultants when contracted to assist a company with its introduction of TQM will carry out an assessment of quality costs.

This analysis, no matter how broad-brush, is used to indicate the potential for TQM. It is not unusual to find that the representatives of financial institutions and venture capitalists on company boards start to take a particular interest in quality issues when they see the potential loss of profit caused by waste and failure to meet customer requirements. Operators and line supervision are also found to react positively when failure data, in addition to the normally expressed measures of numbers and percentages, are presented in this way.

Many organizations are surprised when they learn of the potential savings, and soon want to develop their quality-related costing systems to gain greater benefits and improve cost control. However, the fact that improvements in quality performance do not necessarily produce pro rata changes in quality-related costs should not be overlooked by senior management. It is not enough to have the necessary mechanisms in place for collecting quality-related costs; it is also necessary for the CEO and the senior management team to have the will to carry out the analysis and use the results.

The following are some comments made by executives in the Department of Trade and Industry Booklet, *The Case for Costing Quality* (Dale and Plunkett, 1990).

> It is important that we invest more at the front end of our programmes in design and development, if we are to reduce the high failure costs. The need for programmes designed for ease of manufacturing at the earliest possible stage is essential if profitable trouble-free production is to be achieved. This does not require an increase in project cost overall, but a re-allocation of costs. (Norman Wallwork, Quality Director, British Aerospace (Dynamics) Ltd)

> Quality costs allow us to identify the soft targets to which we can apply our improvement efforts. (John Asher, Managing Director, Crown Industrial Products).

> Four years ago we could still use quality as a selling feature for our products, now that's all changed. If you are still a supplier to the automotive industry today you will have achieved a high level of quality that is the accepted norm in the industry. Those companies who have failed to improve their quality are no longer suppliers. Customers expect to share in the benefits of our continuous quality improvement efforts through agreed cost reduction programmes and extended warranty agreements. Without tracking quality costs we could seriously impair our bottom line profitability and not know the reason why. (Tony Harman, Managing Director, Garret Automotive).

With the prospect of increased competition as a result of activities surrounding 1992, it is important for us to continually improve our operational methods. The formal measurement of quality costs is central to that process, and has the added benefit of showing us how we can tackle certain areas of costs. (John Barbour, Managing Director, John Russell (Grangemouth) Ltd)

Quality must be one of the cornerstones for a growing company, otherwise spectacular growth can be followed by an equally spectacular rapid descent and quality costs are one of the measures by which this can be monitored. (Ian Elliot, Managing Director, Pirelli Focom)

While there is clearly a good case for quality costing it is not a panacea for solving quality problems and must not be treated as an end in itself. The bottom line objective, as with any other tool, technique or system, is to improve performance.

What Are Quality Costs?

When considering the nitty-gritty of quality costs, there can be considerable controversy about which activities and costs are quality related. There is by no means a uniform view of what is meant by a quality cost and what should be included under the quality cost umbrella. Definitions are a key feature in quality costing. Without clear definitions, there can be no common understanding or meaningful communication on quality costs. The definition of what constitutes quality costs is by no means straightforward and there are many grey areas where good production/operations procedures and practices overlap with quality-related activities. The comparability of sets of data is also dependent on the definitions of the categories and elements used in compiling them. If definitions were not established and accepted, the only alterative would be to qualify every item of data so that at least it might be understood, even though it may not be comparable with other data. The value of much of the published data on quality-related costs is questionable because of the absence of precise definition and lack of qualification. Senior management always resist the temptation to compare the quality costs of their organization with those of other organizations without being aware of these issues.

Many definitions of quality-related costs are in fairly specious terms. Admittedly, there are difficulties in preparing unambiguous acceptable definitions and in finding generic terms to describe tasks having the same broad objectives in different cases. It should also be appreciated that problems of rigorous definition arise only because of the desire to carry out costing exercises. Consideration of quality in other contexts (such as training, supplier development, design and engineering changes and statistical process control) does not require such a sharp distinction to be made between what is quality-related and what is not.

Overambition or overzealousness may prompt people, including management consultancies, to try to maximize the impact of quality costs on the CEO and members of the senior management team. Consequently, they tend to stretch their definitions to include those costs that have only the most tenuous relationship with quality. This attempt to amplify quality costs can backfire. Once costs have been accepted as being quality-related there may be some difficulty in exerting an influence over the reduction of costs that are independent of quality management considerations. It is not always easy to disown costs after one has claimed them, especially if ownership is in a 'grey area' or 'white space', and no one else wants them.

Definitions of the categories and their constituent elements are to be found in most standard quality management texts. Detailed guidance is given in specialized publications on the topic (BS 6143: Part 2, 1990; Campanella, 1990; Dale and Plunkett, 1995; Hagan, 1986).

Ideas of what constitutes quality have been changing rapidly in recent years. Whereas only a few years ago the costs of quality were perceived as the cost of running the quality assurance department and the laboratory, plus scrap and warranty costs, it is now widely accepted that they are the costs incurred in the design, implementation, operation and maintenance of a quality management system, the cost of organizational resources committed to introducing and sustaining a process of continuous improvement, and the costs of system, product and service failures and inefficiencies which, over the years, have been built into the business.

Quality systems may range from simple inspection to those surpassing the requirements of the ISO 9000 series or any other recognized Quality System Standard (e.g. QS 9000). System failures can result in obsolescent stocks, lost items, production or operational delays, additional work, scrap, rectification work, late deliveries, additional transportation costs, poor service and non-conforming products. Product and/or service failures result in warranty, guarantee and product liability claims, product replacement, complaint administration and investigation, product recall, additional customer service costs and loss of customer goodwill.

So quality-related costs are not, as is sometimes thought, just the cost of quality assurance, inspection, monitoring, testing and scrap materials, components, products and services that do not conform to requirements. Quality-related costs arise from a range of activities and involve a number of departments in an organization, all of which impinge on the quality of the product or service, for example:

- Sales and marketing
- Design, research and development
- Purchasing, storage handling
- Production and operations planning and control
- Manufacturing/operations
- Delivery
- Installation
- Service

Nor are costs wholly determined or controlled from within the manufacturing or service organization. Suppliers, subcontractors, tradespeople, stockist, agents, dealers, customers and consumers can all influence the incidence and level of quality-related costs.

Why are Quality Costs Important?

The answer firstly, is because they are very large – very large. In 1978 they were estimated by the UK government to be £10 000 millions, equal to 10 per cent of the UK's Gross National Product. There is no reason to suppose that they are any less now. The findings of a National Economic Development Council (NEDC) task force on Quality and Standards (1985) claim that some 10–20 per cent of an organization's total sales value is accounted for by quality-related costs and, using the figure of 10 per cent, it is estimated that UK manufacturing industry could save up to £6 billion each year by reducing such costs. The information available from a variety of

UMIST research projects on the topic indicates that quality-related costs commonly range from 5 to 25 per cent of a company's annual sales turnover. The costs depend on the type of industry, business situation or service, the view taken by the organization of what is or is not a quality-related cost, the approach to TQM and the extent to which continuous and company-wide improvement is practised. Crosby (1985) claims that manufacturing companies incur costs amounting to 25–30 per cent of their sales by doing things over again, while in service organizations he estimates that 40–50 per cent of operating costs are wasted, although he produces no evidence to support this view.

The following are examples of quality costs taken from the Department of Trade and Industry Publication, *The Case for Costing Quality* (Dale and Plunkett, 1990). (Unless stated, all current quality costs are based on 1988 figures).

- In 1980 the quality costs of Bridgeport Machines were 4 per cent of annual sales turnover (£1 million); by 1988 they had fallen to 2 per cent of annual sales turnover.

- British Aerospace Dynamics quality costs are 11 per cent of the total cost of production.

- In British Aerospace Technical Workshops, staff time on quality-related activities are: failure (22.9 per cent), prevention (19.4 per cent) and appraisal (6.8 per cent).

- The quality costs in Courtaulds Jersey have been reduced from 12.1 to 7.6 per cent of annual sales turnover over a period of four years.

- The quality costs of Standfast Dyers and Printers have been reduced from 20 to 7 percent of annual sales turnover over a period of four years.

- In 1986, the quality costs at Crown Industrial Products were 13 per cent of raw material usage cost; by late 1988 they were down to 8 per cent.

- In 1986 the quality costs of Garrett Automotive (Turbocharger Division) were 6.5 per cent of annual sales turnover; by 1988 they had fallen to 4 per cent of annual sales turnover.

- At Grace Dearborn the quality costs are 20 per cent of annual sales turnover.

- In 1987 the quality costs at ICL (Manufacturing and Logistics) were £60 million.

- In 1988 the quality costs at John McGavigan were 22 per cent of annual sales turnover.

- At National Westminster Bank, 25 per cent of operating costs is absorbed in the difference between the cost actually incurred in accomplishing a task and the cost that should be incurred if a 'right first time' approach is successfully adopted.

- Philip Components Blackburn have reduced their plant-wide quality costs by 60 per cent over a period of six years.

Secondly, 95 per cent of the quality cost is usually expended on appraisal and failure type activities. These expenditures add little to the value of the product or service, and the failure costs, at least, may be regarded as avoidable. Reducing failure cost by eliminating causes of non-conformance can also lead to substantial reductions in appraisal costs. The research evidence of Dale and Plunkett (1995) suggests that quality-related costs may be reduced by one-third of their present level, within a period of three to five years, by the commitment of the organization to a formal process of continuous and company-wide improvement.

Thirdly, unnecessary and avoidable costs make goods and services more expensive. This in turn affects organizational competitiveness and, ultimately, wages, salaries and standards of living.

Fourthly, despite the fact that the costs are large, and that a substantial proportion of them is avoidable, it is apparent from the UMIST research (Eldridge and Dale, 1989; Hesford and Dale, 1991; Machowski and Dale, 1995; Plunkett and Dale, 1988; Pursglove and Dale, 1995) that the costs and economics of many quality-related activities, including investment in prevention and appraisal activities, are not known by many companies.

Why Measure Quality Costs?

The measurement of costs allows quality-related activities to be expressed in monetary terms. This, in turn, allows quality to be treated as a business parameter like, for example, marketing, research and development, and production/operations. Drawing

quality costs into the business arena helps to emphasize the importance of quality to corporate health. The emphasis should be on
identifying improvement opportunities and not just costing areas of
failure, nor should quality costs be considered as just another financial measure. They will help to influence employee behaviour, attitudes and values at all levels in the organization towards TQM and
continuous improvement. In many organizations there will be
employees who will need to be convinced that their senior management are serious about TQM. Typical of the comments are 'we have
heard all this before', 'TQM is the latest management fad and it will
not last'. Quality costing is a way of highlighting to all employees the
importance of quality to business profitability (see chapter 1).

Quality cost measurement focuses attention on areas of high
expenditure and identifies potential problem areas and cost-
reduction opportunities. It allows measurement of performance and
provides a basis for comparison between products, services, processes and departments. Measurement of quality-related costs also
reveal quirks and anomalies in cost allocation, standards and disposal of products that may remain undetected by the more commonly used production/operation and labour-based analyses. It can
uncover non-conformances that conventional accounting procedures
do not pick up. The questioning of the norm helps to identify
situations that have been overlooked or ignored by traditional practices. Measurement can also obviate the dumping of embarrassing
after-sales costs under quality-related headings.

Finally, and perhaps most importantly, measurement is the first
step towards control.

Uses of Quality Costs

There is no point in collecting quality costs if the data are not to be
used. The usefulness of the data is the only justification for their
collection and clearly this is one of the most important criteria in
setting up a cost collection system. Most executives are looking to
quality costs data to show things that their own quality-related
information and reports do not reveal. The use of quality costs are
numerous and diverse; what follows are the main uses.

Quality costs display the importance of quality-related activities to
the CEO and senior management in meaningful terms, and help to

shock people into action. They can also be used to educate staff in the concept and principles of TQM and why the organization is embarking on the TQM journey.

Knowledge of quality-related costs enables business decisions about quality to be made in an objective manner. It permits the use of sensitivity analyses, discounted cash flow and other accounting techniques that are used for the evaluation of expenditure as in any other area of the business. In this way, it helps companies to decide how, when and where to invest in preventative activities and/or equipment.

Costs may be used to monitor performance, to identify products, processes and departments for investigation, to set cost-reduction targets and to measure progress towards targets. They may be used to evaluate the cost benefit of individual quality activities and initiatives, such as quality management system certification, SPC and supplier development, or to compare performances between departments, works or divisions. Quality costs are the means of initiating improvement projects, and levers for uncovering quality problems and areas of chronic waste.

Costs are the bases for budgeting and eventual cost control. They also enable valid comparisons to be made with other costs via the usual measurement bases (such as sales turnover, units of saleable product or standard hours).

Quality costs help to provide information for quotations for products or contracts having onerous quality conditions.

Lastly, costs keep quality aspects of the business under the spotlight – but only if they are featured in the regular management accounts and reporting systems.

Pointers for Setting up a Quality Costing System

A number of pointers are now offered to executives on how their organization might approach the collection, analysis and reporting of quality costs:

(1) It is unlikely that an organization's management accounts will contain the necessary information in the right form. Hence it is essential to involve accountants in the cost collection exercise right from the outset.

(2)   There is no point in collecting quality-related costs just to see what they may reveal. Many executives and managers have success-fully resisted pressure to cooperate in the collection of quality costs on the grounds that they would not reveal any problems of which they were not already aware from the organization's existing quality management information system.

The purpose of quality costing should be clarified at the start of the project because this may influence the strategy of the exercise and will help to avoid difficulties later. If, for example, the main objective of the exercise is to identify high-cost problem areas, approximate costs will suffice. If the CEO and members of the senior management team already accept that the organization's cost of quality is within the normally quoted range and are prepared to commit resources to the improvement process then there is no point in refining the data. If, on the other hand, the purpose is to set a percentage cost-reduction target on the organization's total quality-related costs, it will be necessary to identify and measure all of the contributing cost elements in order to be sure that costs are reduced and not simply transferred elsewhere. If the intention is only to get a snapshot from time to time as a reminder of their magnitude, the strategy will be to identify and measure large and ongoing costs.

Another aspect that needs to be considered is whether to collect and allocate costs on a departmental or business unit basis or across the whole company. In some cases analysis at company level would be inadequate because it would result in the problems being set out in terms too global to generate ownership at departmental or process level. On the other hand, analysis at too detailed a level would lead to a trivialization of problems. These types of issues will also have a bearing on the definition and identification of cost elements. The incidence of such diverse objectives with their differing requirements serves to reinforce the case of a rational approach, in which the purpose of the exercise is clearly established at the outset. Thus, the matter is important, not only from a philosophical point of view but from purely practical considerations as well.

(3)   It will also be necessary to decide how to deal with overheads, since many quality-related costs are normally included as part of the overheads, while others are treated as direct costs and attract a proportion of overheads. Failure to clarify this can lead to a gross dis-tortion of the picture derived from the quality-related cost analysis. It

is also easy to fall into the trap of double counting. For these and other reasons, quality-related costs should be made the subject of a memorandum account. However, the costs should not include recovery of overheads on calculating costs of personnel. Another issue to be decided is how costs are allocated to components that are scrapped. For example, a common practice encountered is to value scrap at 100 per cent material costs plus 50 per cent of the finished part total labour/burden costs, irrespective of the actual state of manufacture of the scrapped component. These are areas where the accountant's advice and assistance can prove invaluable.

(4) Another area of difficultly is deciding whether some activities, usually of a setting-up, testing or running-in type, are quality activities or an integral and essential part of the production/operations activity. These costs are often substantial and can alter quite markedly the relative proportions of quality-related costs categories. There are also factors that serve to ensure the basic utility of the product and/or service, guard against errors, and protect and preserve quality. Examples are the use of design codes, preparation of engineering, technical and administrative systems and procedures, capital premiums on machinery and equipment, document and drawing controls, and handling and storage practices. Whether such factors give rise to costs that may be regarded as being quality-related is a matter for judgement in individual cases. These problems need to be discussed with purchasing, engineering, production/operations and accountancy personnel, as appropriate, in order to resolve them. There is little doubt that deciding which activities should be included under the quality-related umbrella is by no means straightforward, and there are many grey areas. Some quality assurance managers have a tendency to include costs that are difficult to justify as being quality-related and over which they have no control or influence. As mentioned earlier, this can backfire if the costs later prove not to be influenced by quality management initiatives.

(5) One of the maxims of quality costs collection seems to be that, in general, costs need to be large to hold the attention of people, in particular, that of senior executives. Magnitude is often regarded as being synonymous with importance, although it is magnitude coupled with relevance and potential for reduction that determines the real importance of costs. Clearly it may be much more advantageous to pursue a small percentage reduction in a large cost than a

large reduction in a small costs, depending on the ease of achievement. This creates something of a dilemma for the cost collector because large costs are often insensitive to changes. But the collector cannot omit large costs and concentrate only on smaller costs, which may be seen to change readily. Hence, cost groupings need to be chosen carefully so that the cost reductions that are achieved are displayed in such as way that both the relative achievement and the absolute position are clearly shown Another dilemma facing the cost collector arises from the fact that one-off estimates of quality costs tend not to change and some people take the view that there is no point in costs that do not change. The only way out of this dilemma is to measure, directly, or though surrogates, those costs that it is thought worth collecting.

Prior to the collection of costs an assessment should be made of the type of data that is available from the quality management information system. This assessment should include accuracy and realiability.

(6)   A checklist of quality costs elements can provide a useful starting point for the cost collection exercise. BS 6143: Part 2 (1990) provides such as a list of elements under the cost categories of prevention, appraisal, internal failure, and external failure. However, there is no substitute for a thorough analysis of all of an organiza-tion's activities, and some key elements may be missed if only this method is used. In some organizations cost elements have been identified by scanning the quality costing literature, and other organ-izations, from analysis of their processes, have identified the costs of non-conformance incurred from not getting operations right first time. In non-manufacturing situations the process cost model out-lined in BS 6143: Part 1 (1992) can prove a useful aid and stimulus in identifying quality costs.

(7)   In the absence of an established quality-related cost reporting system, the exercise should commence by investigating failure costs, namely:

- Failure costs attributable to supplier and/or subcontractors.

- In-house mistakes, scrap, rework and rectification costs.

- Downgraded products or 'seconds'.

- Free repairs or replacements for products or services that are defective as delivered and/or fitted.

- Warranty and guarantee costs and field failures.

- Litigation costs.

This should be followed by inquiring into the costs of inspection, checks, false starts, disruption to routine production and operations activities, wastage, non-value-adding activities and quality-related inefficiencies (e.g. excess material allowances, and deliberate over makes) built into standard costs. The way in which quality-related costs are completed should be recorded so that the validity of comparisons made across departments, products, processes or time may be checked.

(8) When cost information is available it should be analysed and costs attributed to department, defect type, product, cause, supplier, etc. The responsibility for costs should be identified with functions and people. Problems and cost-reduction projects need to be ranked by size and importance. The collection, analysis and reporting of quality-related costs should be integrated into the organization's accounting system with the aim of keeping paperwork to a minimum and the whole process as automatic as possible.

(9) The reporting of quality costs should be such that costs make an impact and the data are used to their full potential. In most organizations the standard of quality costs reporting is poor. In developing a reporting mechanisms consideration needs to be given to issues such as:

- A standardized reporting format.

- Clarity and simplicity of reporting with minimum use of words.

- Presentation of the quality cost data.

- The completeness of the data.

- Clarity of the decisions to be taken by the CEO and members of the senior management team on the basis of the reported data.

- The needs of the people receiving the data, if quality costs are to be reported to different levels of the organizational hierarchy. Typical questions to be kept in mind are: 'What are we trying to communicate?' and 'What will they understand from the data?'.

The summarized data should be supported by detailed information – especially the failure costs. Attention should also be given to the use of histograms and pie charts with standard range and scales. This ensures that the relative magnitude of cost elements plotted on separate charts is kept in perspective, thus making comparisons and judgements easy. The quality costs should always be separated from other aspects of product and service quality and presented in the context of other costs. The actions required of executives in relation to quality costs data should not be to disentangle and analyse data in order to pursue and ensure provision of necessary resources.

(10) Successful quality costing systems, as an everyday feature of an organization's management activities, take a long time to establish. It can take up to five years to reach the status of credibility and usefulness that should be expected of data featured in a management information system.

Summary

The value of cost data should not be underestimated. Costs are a most effective way of drawing attention to and illuminating situations in ways that other data cannot. It has been found that even the most rudimentary attempts at quality costing have been beneficial in identifying areas of waste and trends in performance. It should also not be forgotten that quality costs are already being incurred by an organization; the primary purpose of the quality costing exercise is to identify these 'hidden costs' from various budgets and overheads, the objective being to allocate these indirect costs to a specific cost activity.

Senior management must make up their own minds on the value of the quality costing concept and assess whether or not it is worth the effort. There is clearly a good case for it but senior management need to decide when, how and whether to use the technique.

All the signs are that interest from organizations in the concept of quality focusing is growing. A number are now seeking and getting practical evidence on quality-related costs and others are developing formalized quality costing systems. They are keen to develop their knowledge of the technique to help them better understand the effectiveness of their decisions on wastage, and to save money.

Acknowledgement

Barrie Dale is indebted to his friend and colleague the late Ian Plunkett for allowing some of his research findings to be used in this chapter.

References

BS 6143, Part 1: *Guide to the Economics of Quality*, Part 1: *Process Cost Model.* London: British Standards Institution.

BS 6143 Part 2: 1990: *Guide to the Economics of Quality*, Part 2: *Prevention, Appraisal and Failure Model.* British Standards Institution.

Campanella, J. 1990: *Principles of Quality Costs; Principles, Implementation and Use.* Milwaukee, Wis.: ASQC Quality Press.

Crosby, P. B. 1985: *The Quality Man.* London: BBC Education and Training.

Dale, B. G. and Plunkett, J. J. 1990: *The Case for Costing Quality.* London: Department of Trade and Industry.

—— 1995: *Quality Costing*, 2nd edn. London: Chapman & Hall. London.

Eldridge, S. E. and Dale, B. G. 1989: Quality costing: the lessons learnt from a study in two parts. *Engineering Costs and Production Economics*, 18(1), 33–44.

Hagan, J. T. (ed.) 1986: *Principles of Quality Costs.* Milwaukee, Wis.: ASQC Press.

Hesford, M. and Dale, B. G. 1991: Quality costing at British Aerospace Dynamics: a case study. *Proceedings of the Institution of Mechanical Engineers*, 205(G5), 53–7.

Machowski, F. and Dale, B. G. 1995: The application of quality costing to engineering changes. *International Journal of Materials and Product Technology*, 19(3–6), 378–88.

National Economic Development Council 1985: *Quality and Value for Money.* London: NEDO.

Plunkett, J. J. and Dale, B. G. 1988: Quality-related findings from an industry-based study. *Engineering Management International*, 4(4), 247–57.

Pursglove, A. B. and Dale, B. G. 1995: Developing a quality costing system: key features and outcomes. *Omega*, 23(5), 567–75.

Schaffer, R. H. and Thomson, H. A. 1992: Successful change programs begin with results. *Harvard Business Review*, January/February, 80–9.

5 The Role of Senior Management in Total Quality Management

Introduction

In opening this chapter on the role of management in TQM it must be mentioned that more than one director has commented to the authors that the word 'quality' should be removed from the term Total Quality Management. The reasoning for this argument is that TQM is all about good management behaviour and practice, and is an integral and natural part of the management of an organization, its structure and its business processes. Therefore, taking this line, can any current or would-be executive who wishes to improve his or her management skills and abilities afford not to understand more about the subject of TQM and get involved with its introduction and development?

As examined in chapter 1, quality is an influencing factor on the competitive performance and success of any organization. Today it is a qualifying criterion in the global market-place and in some situations it can provide the competitive edge. Therefore executives need to understand how TQM can help to address business problems and increase the value-added activities of their organization's key processes.

This chapter outlines the main reasons why it is important that senior managers should become personally involved in TQM. It examines what they need to know about TQM and what they should do in terms of positive actions. Middle management and first-line management also have a key role to play in putting the principles of TQM in place at the sharp end of the business, and the activities that they need to get involved in are outlined here; this listing of activities can serve as a checklist of what they should be doing.

The Need for Senior Executives to Get Involved in TQM

The decision to introduce TQM can only be taken by the CEO in conjunction with the senior management team. Developing and employing organization vision, mission, philosophy, values, strategies, objectives and plans, and communicating the reasons behind them along with the underlying logic is the province of senior management. This is why senior managers have to become personally involved in the introduction and development of TQM and demonstrate visible commitment and confidence in it by leading this way of thinking and managing the business. They have to encourage a total corporate commitment to continually improve every aspect of the business. This not only requires their personal commitment but also a significant investment of time.

The responsibility for quality rests with the CEO and the senior management team. TQM requires the commitment, confidence and conviction of the CEO; if this is achieved, it avoids false starts and helps to ensure longevity. Everyone in the organization has a role to play in continuous improvement but this effort is likely to be disjointed and spasmodic if the senior management team have not made the organizational requirements clear. If they fail to get involved, it is likely that the improvement process will stagnate and disillusionment will set in amongst employees. Quality is an integral part of the management of an organization and its business processes and is too important to delegate to technical and quality specialists.

There is a very strong relationship between the business achievements of an organization and the CEO's understanding of and commitment to TQM. If TQM is to become a way of organizational and business life, it is only the CEO who can ensure that this becomes a reality. As chapter 4 demonstrated, the cost of non-conformance or mismanaging quality is likely to be between 5 and 25 per cent of an organization's annual sales turnover or operating costs in not-for-profit organizations. If these figures are compared to profit as a percentage of sales turnover or expenditure in not-for-profit organizations, the key questions are: Can the CEO afford not to get involved in TQM? How much will it cost the organization not to put in place a process of continuous improvement? Is investment in TQM and continuous improvement worthwhile?

McKinsey and Company (1989), reporting on a survey of the CEOs of the top 500 European corporations (see chapter 1 for details) in relation to the key requirements for success in TQM, found the following:

- Top management attention: 95 per cent agreement

- People development: 85 per cent agreement

- Corporate team spirit: 82 per cent agreement

- Quality performance information: 73 per cent agreement

- Top management capability building: 70 per cent agreement

- Sense of urgency: 60 per cent agreement

It is clear from this that the role of senior management is critical to success. Lascelles and Dale (1990a), reporting on their research, also make the point that 'the CEO is the primary internal change agent for quality improvement'. They go on to say that in this capacity the CEO has two key roles: 'shaping organizational values, and establishing a managerial infrastructure to actually bring about change'.

The CEO must have faith in the long-term plans for TQM and should not expect immediate financial benefits. However, there will be achievable benefits in the short-term, providing that the introduction of TQM is soundly based. Ultimately, the CEO is responsible for the organizational environment, behaviour, values, climate and style of management in which TQM will either flourish or wither. The CEO and his or her senior managers need to create and promote an environment in which, for example:

- People can work together as a team, and teamwork becomes an integral part of business activities.

- People cooperate with their peers and teams work with teams.

- Mistakes are freely admitted without recriminations and these mistakes are perceived as an opportunity for improvement (i.e. a 'blame-free' culture).

- People are involved in the business through decision making.

- People improve on a continuous basis the processes under their control (i.e. the continuous improvement mindset).

- People, direct their attention to identifying, satisfying, delighting and winning over customers, whether they be internal or external.

- Ideas are actively sought from everyone.

- Development of people is a priority.

- Employee involvement in the business is worked at continually.

- Permanent solutions are found to problems.

- Departmental boundaries between functions are non-existent.

- Effective two-way communication is in place.

- Recognition is given for improvement activities.

- Status symbols are removed.

Change is not something that any department and individual takes to easily, and administering changes in organizational practices has to be considered with care (this is discussed in chapter 7). In the majority of Western organizations, people have witnessed the latest fads and 'flavours of the month' that have come and gone. They have become accustomed to senior managers talking a lot about a topic or issues, but failing to demonstrate visible commitment to what they are saying. Typical, of the comments made by employees are, 'They're at it again, let's humour them', 'TQM will go the way of all other fads and fancies' and 'Let's keep our heads down and things will revert to normal'. It is only senior executives who can break this cynicism, influence the indifference and persuade people that the organization is serious about TQM. It is they who have to communicate in person to their people why the organization needs continuous improvement and demonstrating that they really care about quality. This can be done by getting involved in activities such as:

- Setting up and chairing a TQM Steering Committee or Quality Council.

- Identifying the major quality issues facing the organization and becoming personally involved in investigating the issues, ideally as a leader, member, sponsor or foster parent to an improvement team, problem elimination team or the like.

- Getting involved in quality planning, audit, improvement meetings and organizational housekeeping.

- Chairing individual sessions with operatives about the importance of following procedures and working instructions.

- Organizing and chairing defect review and customer return committees.

- Instigating and carrying out regular audits and diagnosis of the state-of-the-art of TQM and continuous improvement (i.e. self-assessment against a model of business excellence such as the EFQM Model).

- Dealing with customer complaints, and visiting customers and suppliers.

- Leading customer workshops, panels and focus groups.

- Visiting, on a regular basis, all areas and functions of the business, and discussing improvement issues.

- Developing, communicating and then following a personal improvement action plan.

- Communicating as never before on TQM; for example, carrying out team briefs, preparing personal thank you notes to both team and individuals and writing articles for the company newsletter.

- Practising the internal customer–supplier concept (figure 5.1). (With this approach, a supplier identifies his or her customers and determines their requirements. In some cases the supplying process may have to be developed to meet the stated requirements. The supplier then undertakes the task and carries our self-inspection and control before the work is passed to the internal customer. Taking responsibility for following processes is part of this approach).

In ways such as these, senior executives lead and teach by example and employees can develop a sense of purpose to continuous

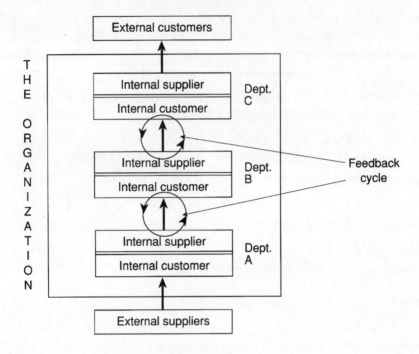

Figure 5.1 The customer-supplier network

improvement. It is only by getting personally involved that a full understanding of the philosophy underlying continuous improvement can be developed. Once commitment and leadership have been demonstrated, ideas, innovations and improvements can start to feed through from the lower levels of the organizational hierarchy. At this stage in the development of TQM the CEO must also be aware that some employees will be complying through fear and will have no real commitment or belief in the concept. It takes time to change attitudes and culture (see chapter 7).

The improvement process is a roller-coaster of troughs and peaks (see figure 5.2). At certain points in the process, the situation will arise that while a considerable amount of organizational resources is being devoted to improvement activities, little progress appears to be being made. In the first three or so years of launching a process of continuous improvement, and when the process is at one of these low points, it is not uncommon for some middle and first-line managers and functional specialists to claim that TQM is not working and start to ask questions such as: Why are we doing this? Are we

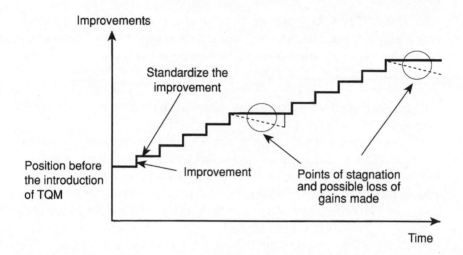

Figure 5.2   The quality improvement process

seeking real improvements? What are the benefits? Have we the time to spend on the 'outside our function' activities? They may say that 'improvement teams are a waste of time' and 'such and such a concept would be a better bet'. Consequently, they will perhaps wish to switch their attention to what they claim are other more pressing matters, such as Business Process Re-engineering (BPR). If the CEO is personally involved in TQM and visibly perceived to be so, people are much less likely to express this type of view. The CEO and senior managers have a key role to play in helping to get their people through this crisis of confidence in TQM. There are a number of mechanisms that can assist with this. For example, the managing director of a speciality chemicals company introduced the concept of 'Quality Action Days' to give all employees the opportunity to meet him and express their views and concerns on the company's progress with TQM and what could be done to speed up the process of involvement.

In most Western organizations, a few key people are vital to the advancement of the improvement process, and if one of these people leaves, it can result in a major gap in the management team. In the case of leadership and organizational changes, the CEO plays a major role in developing understanding and diffusing beliefs with respect to TQM to new managers and technical and business specialists. In this way, the effects of any organizational changes are minimized. When key people leave and the improvement process continues without interruption, and improvement teams continue to meet and make a contribution, this is an indication that an environment that is conducive to TQM is firmly in place. These type of issues are explored in detail by Bunney and Dale (1996) as part of a longitudinal study in a speciality chemical manufacturing organization.

Organizations are not usually experienced in holding the gains made in TQM. In addition to leadership and organizational changes, factors such as takeovers, human resources and industrial relations problems, short-time working, redundancies, cost cutting, downsizing, streamlining, no salary increases, growth of the business, and pursuit of policies that conflict with TQM in terms of resources etc. can all have an adverse effect on the gains made and damage the perception of TQM. People will be looking to senior management to provide continuity and leadership in such circumstances. For example, whenever there is a shortfall in the order book, Western organizations tend to either lay people off and operate a policy of short-time working or make people redundant. This can perhaps be considered as a short-sighted action driven, by and large, by traditional accounting practices; in most companies labour costs are less than one-quarter of the material costs. When there is such a downturn, a CEO who is totally committed to TQM could have people engaged in housekeeping, improvement activities, advanced quality planning, additional training, visiting customers and suppliers etc. Many business managers would consider it slightly naïve to suggest that avoiding labour cost is possible as a short-term measure to offset falling sales. However, these suggested actions, in addition to the practical benefits arising from the types of activities, would help to build loyalty among the workforce and provide clear signals to them of what the senior managers of the organization consider to be important.

What Executives Need to Know about TQM

The first thing executives must realize from the outset is that TQM is a long-term and not a short-term intervention. It is an arduous process. They must also realize that TQM is not the responsibility of the quality function. There are no:

- quick fixes
- easy solutions
- universal panaceas
- tools, techniques and/or systems that will provide all the answers
- ready-made packages that can be plugged in and that will guarantee success.

What we are talking about here is a long-term culture change. The planning horizon to put the basic TQM principles into place is between eight and ten years. The Japanese manufacturing companies typically work on sixteen years made up of four four-year cycles – introduction, promotion into non-manufacturing areas, development/expansion, and fostering advancement and maintenance (see chapter 9 for details). Consequently, executives have to practise and communicate the message of patience, tolerance and tenacity. It is highly likely that there will be some middle management resistance to TQM, in particular from those managers with long service who are concerned about the new style of managing – more so than from staff and operatives.

Despite the claims made by some writers, consultants and 'experts', senior management must recognize that there is no single or best way of introducing and developing TQM. There are, however, common standards and principles that apply in all organizations. Organizations are different in terms of their:

- people
- culture
- history
- customs
- prejudices
- structure
- products
- technology
- processes
- operating environment

What works successfully in one organization and/or situation will not necessarily work in another. A good example of this is TQM awareness training. There are two main approaches: (a) cascade ('sheep dipping'), in which training is given to everyone over a relatively short time frame, and (b) infusion, where people are trained on a 'need to know' basis. In some organizations 'sheep dipping' has been successful and in others it has been a dismal failure. The same two-way argument is true for the infusion approach.

In the long run what really matters is that senior managers demonstrate long-term, commitment to and leadership of the process of continuous improvement. Senior management must be prepared to think out the issues for themselves and test out ideas and thoughts, modify them and adapt them, as appropriate to the operating environment of the business. The key point is to learn from experience. Employees may be more forgiving of management, if mistakes are openly admitted, rather than covered up, and explanations given.

It must also be recognized that while quality systems and procedures and tools and techniques are important features of TQM, the concept is very much dependent upon people (see chapter 8).

Senior managers need to commit time in order to develop their own personal understanding of the subject. They need to read books, attend conferences and courses, visit the best practices in terms of TQM and talk to as many people as possible. The self-assessment criteria of quality awards schemes such as the MBNQA and the EFQM Model for Business Excellence (as outlined in chapter 2), can assist in developing this overall understanding. It is also important that improvement ideas are forever circulating in the minds of senior managers along the lines of the PDCA (Plan–Do–Check–Act) cycle. In this way they will avoid the false trails laid down by their own staff, consultants and 'experts'.

This understanding of TQM will also assist the CEO in deciding, together with other senior managers and key staff, how the organization is going to introduce TQM. For example:

- What method and format of training is required?

- How many and what type of teams will be introduced?

- How many teams can be effectively supported?

- What form should a TQM Steering Committee take? Should it be the management committee, should it meet separately or should TQM be the top item on the management agenda? What should its meeting frequency be? What is its role?

- Which tools and techniques should be used?

- What is the role of a quality management system?

- How will TQM contribute to reducing warranty claims?

The issue of getting started is not an easy one. Prior to embarking on TQM, most organizations will already have undertaken a number of improvement initiatives, and a key issue is how to bring together those initiatives and build on them. A number of elements of TQM, such as empowerment, are nebulous and senior managers sometimes have difficulty in seeing how they might operate in their organization. It is important that the more nebulous elements are combined with the readily understood aspects, such as quality systems, procedures and practices, teamwork, and tools and techniques. As part of the getting started process the CEO and senior managers must also be involved in diagnosing the organization's strengths and areas of improvement in relation to the management of quality. This typically takes the form of an internal assessment of employees' views and perceptions (internal and group assessments, and questionnaire surveys), a systems audit, a cost of quality analysis, and obtaining the views of customers (including those accounts that have been lost) and suppliers about the organization's performance in terms of product, service, people, administration, innovation, strengths and weaknesses etc. This type of internal and external assessment of perspectives should be carried out on a regular basis to gauge the progress being made towards TQM and help decide the next steps. This is the benefit of self-assessment against a recognized model of business excellence (see chapter 2).

Once senior management have realized the need for TQM they need to translate this awareness into effective action. At this stage they need to ask questions such as:

- What should we do?

- What are the priorities?

- What advice do we need?

- From whom should we be taking advice?

- Can we get unbiased advice?

- Should the approach be top-down or bottom-up?

- Do we have to use the term TQM? What are the alternatives? Quality improvement, continuous improvement, business improvement? Customer care? Customer focus? Customer first?

- How quickly should we proceed?

- Which tools, techniques and systems should we apply?

- How do we apply these tools and techniques?

- What courses and conferences should we attend?

- Can we make use of the EFQM Model for Business Excellence?

- Which companies should we visit?

- Which network of companies should we attempt to join?

- What training do we need?

- What packages and programmes should we buy?

- Should we call in a management consultant and, if so, which one?

- Should we develop the quality management system to meet the requirements of the ISO 9000 series?

- How important is quality management system registration?

- How do we embrace our current improvement initiatives under the TQM umbrella?

Their dilemma is often compounded not just by a lack of knowledge of TQM and the process of continuous improvement but also by a lack of experience in managing organizational change. The overwhelming quantity and variety of advice, which is often conflicting, sometimes biased and sometimes incorrect, simply adds to the confusion and chaos. In this deliberation senior managers should be aware that: (a) meeting the requirements of the ISO 9000 series should be considered as the minimum and (b) tools and techniques should be chosen carefully.

THE REQUIREMENTS OF THE ISO 9000 SERIES

to he better than

The organization should be encouraged to surpass the requirements of the appropriate standard (i.e. ISO 9001, ISO 9002 and ISO 9003). These requirements tend to be a static representative of an organization's quality system at one point in time, and do not adequately encourage year to year improvements. The 'management review', 'internal audit', 'corrective action' and 'preventative action' procedures can be used to develop this continuous improvement spirit, but only if the action is focused on long-term improvements. It is unfortunate that a number of organizations and their managements view ISO 9000 system series registration as the pinnacle of their achievements and go to amazing lengths to publicize this.

There is much more to TQM than achieving the twenty set requirements in the ISO 9001 standard. Indeed, possession of certification can result in a sense of complacency and it should not be forgotten that there are almost certain to be lapses in the system. The only signals being given from such certification are that an organization's quality system has procedures, controls and disciplines in place and that the organization has got its feet on the first rung of the TQM ladder. Registration to the ISO 9000 system series should be treated as a matter of course and not a highlight or hype.

TOOLS AND TECHNIQUES

Whatever the TQM approach chosen by an organization, it will need to use a selection of tools and techniques to assist with the improvement process, from introduction and promotion to fostering its development and advancement. However, it is important that organizations do not rush headlong into the use of plethora of tools and techniques. Senior management should understand how these tools and techniques work and their various uses and be in a position to ask sensible questions of the people responsible for their day-to-day application.

From the UMIST research of tools and techniques (e.g Dale, 1994; Dale and Shaw, 1990; Lascelles and Dale, 1990b) the following points need to be considered carefully by executives.

The application of any tool and technique in isolation will only provide short-term benefits of tools and techniques to be effective over the long-term. Major organizational changes in behaviour, attitudes, values and culture are required. The key factor is not the tools and techniques themselves, but how they are used within a process of continuous and company-wide improvement. Lascelles and Dale (1990) make the point that it is important for managers to address questions such as those outlined below, when considering the use of a particular tool or technique.

- What are the purposes of the technique?

- How will it help us to improve the way we manage quality?

- Is it right for our product, processes, people and culture?

- Are we being given the right advice concerning which technique and how to use the technique itself?

- What organization changes are necessary to make the best use of the technique?

- What resources, skills, information, education, training, etc. do we need in order to introduce the technique successfully?

- Have we the staff, financial resources and commitments to make the technique work over the longer-term?

- How will the technique fit into, complement, or support other techniques, and quality assurance methods and systems that are already in place, and any that might be introduced in the future?'

No single tool or technique should be regarded as more important than another; they all have a role to play in a process of continuous improvement. It is a mistake to single out for special attention one tool or technique. Executives need to view with some considerable suspicion those organizations, consultants and internal personnel peddling one technique or tool.

Tools and techniques fulfil a number of roles; for example, planning for quality, improving the design of the product and process, listening to the voice of the process, improving the process, controlling the process, capturing and documenting quality system data, modelling the quality system, solving problems, involving people, motivating and promoting quality awareness. It is important that organizations are fully aware of the main purpose and use of the tools and techniques that they are considering applying.

Every person in the organization should be taught and encouraged to use the seven basic quality control tools (that is, Pareto diagrams, cause and effect diagrams, control charts, histograms, check sheets, scatter diagrams and graphs); simple tools and techniques can be just as effective as the more complex ones (Ishikawa, 1976). Senior managers must be sure that their people are not dismissive of the more simple tools.

When a major customer insists upon the use of a particular tool or technique by its supplier community, there are two observable phases in its use (Dale and Shaw, 1990). In the first place, the tool or technique is applied just to satisfy the demands of the major customer in order to maintain the business. During this phase, the supplier resorts to a number of camouflage measures, fakes and ruses in a bid to convince the customer that it is serious about application of the technique. The theme of this phase is satisfying the paperwork requirements. The second phase is when the supplier starts to question how it might use the technique to its own best advantage in order to advance the process of continuous improvement. Senior managers must ensure that the organization gets into the phase-two mode as quickly as possible.

McQuater et al. (1995) make the point that organizations run into a number of difficulties with the use and application of tools and techniques. They have identified the common ones as:

- Poorly designed training and support.
- Being unable to apply what has been learnt.
- Inappropriate use of tools and techniques.
- Resistance to the use the tools and techniques.
- Failure to lead by example.
- Poor measurement and data handling.
- Not sharing and communicating the benefits achieved.

The CEO and the senior management team may need to develop a company vision and mission statement; this should include developing an organizational definition of quality. However, the vision and mission have to be supported by organized changes rather than simply being stand-alone statements of objectives (see chapter 9 for more details).

As a final point, senior managers should be sufficiently knowledgeable about TQM to know what type of questions to ask their people in relation to the improvement mechanisms. They should also be able to query results and the process by which they were obtained, and have some indication of what non-conforming products and/or service is costing their organization.

What Executives Need to Do about TQM

This section opens with a review of the leadership criteria of the EFQM Model for Business Excellence (European Foundation for Quality Management, 1997; see chapter 2). The criteria detail the behaviour of all managers in driving the company towards business excellence. They concern how the executives and all other managers inspire and drive excellence as an organization's fundamental process for continuous improvement. The leadership criteria cover the following four parts:

- How leaders visibly demonstrate their commitment to a culture of Total Quality Management.

- How leaders support improvement and involvement by providing appropriate resources and assistance.

- How leaders are involved with customers, suppliers and other external organizations.

- How leaders recognise and appreciate people's efforts and achievements.

Senior management need to decide the actions they are going to take to ensure that quality becomes the number one priority for the organization. They need to allocate time and commitment to:

- Communicate their views on TQM. Executives should take every opportunity to talk and act in a manner consistent with the principles of TQM.

- Decide how the company will approach the introduction and advancement of TQM.

- Lead education and training sessions including the review of courses.

- Assess the improvements made.

- Get personally involved in improvement activities.

- Understand how key competitors are using TQM.

- Become involved in benchmarking because this will enable them to see, for example, what the superior performing organizations have achieved and the discrepancies or gap with their organization's performance.

- Lead and encourage the use of self-assessment methods and principles.

Executives should consider how they are going to demonstrate to people from all levels of the organizational hierarchy their commitments to TQM. They need to visit every area to see what is happening in relation to TQM, ask about results and problems, give advice and create good practice through leadership. In relation to this latter point, executive should take the lead in organizational housekeeping with the objectives of seeing that the plant is a model of cleanliness and tidiness.

There are considerable demands on senior managers' time and a vast number of projects and matters seeking their attention. A CEO of a small but complex high-technology printed circuit board manufacturer uses the term 'spinning like a top' to describe this situation. However, if TQM is to be introduced successfully it has to take precedence over all other activities. The CEO should plan his or her diary to ensure that some time each week is devoted to TQM activities. The experience from the superior performing companies is that once the process is bedded in, the time devoted by the CEO to TQM can be reduced and he or she can focus on maintenance issues and the promotion of new themes and concepts.

It is the responsibility of the CEO and other senior managers to ensure that everyone in the organization knows why it is adopting TQM and that people are aware of the potential of TQM in the area, department, function and/or process. The commitment of the CEO and the senior management team must filter down through all levels of the organizational hierarchy. It is important that all employees feel they can demonstrate initiative and have the responsibility to put into place changes in their own area of work. This involves the establishment of owners for each business process. Consideration needs to be given to how this should be addressed.

The senior management team needs to commit resourses to TQM; for example, releasing people for improvement activities and ensuring that key decision makers are made available to spend time on TQM issues. The CEO needs to delegate responsibility for continuous improvement to people within the organization. Some organizations appoint a total quality facilitator/manager/coordinator to act as a catalyst or change agent. However, if this is to be effective the CEO must have a good understanding of TQM and the continuous improvement process. The CEO needs to develop an infrastructure to support the improvement activities in terms of:

- Monitoring and reporting the results (there is nothing like success to convert cynics and counter indifference).

- Providing a focus and the people to make it happen.

- Developing and deploying improvement objectives and targets.

- Involving people from non-manufacturing areas.

It is helpful to establish a TQM Steering Committee Quality Control Council to oversee and manage the improvement process. The typical role of such a group is to:

- Agree plans and goals, provide and manage resources.

- Monitor progress.

- Determine actions.

- Create an environment that is conductive to continuous improvement.

- Concur on issues of continuous improvement.

- Facilitate team work.

- Ensure that firm foundations are laid down.

- Identify impediments to progress.

From the vision and mission statements a long-term plan needs to be drawn up that sets out the direction of the company in terms of its development and management targets. This plan should be based on the corporate philosophy, sales forecast, current status, previous achievements against plan and improvement objectives. From this long-term plan an annual policy should be compiled, and plans, policies, actions and improvement objectives established for each factory, division, cost, delivery, safety and the environment. Middle managers and first-line supervisors should, at the appropriate point, participate in the formulation of these plans, targets and improvement objectives. This ensures that the policies and objectives initiated by the CEO and the senior management team are cascaded down through the organizational hierarchy so that all employees in each function of the business can carry out their activities within their own area of influence with the aim of achieving common goals and improvement targets. A typical framework for policy deployment is shown in figure 5.3; details of policy deployment are given by Dale (1990) and Akao (1991) and also in chapter 9.

The process of policy deployment ensures that the quality policies, targets and improvement objectives are aligned with the organization's business goals. The ideal situation in policy deployment is for the senior person at each level of the organizational hierarchy to make a presentation to his or her staff on the plan, targets and improvements. This ensures the penetration and communication of policies, objectives and continuous improvements throughout the organisation, with general objectives being converted into specific objectives and improvement targets. In some organizations, as part of this policy deployment, a plan is formulated every year which focuses on a different improvement theme. One of the key aspects of policy deployment is its high visibility, with company and departmental policies, targets, themes and projects being displayed in each section of the organization.

There must also be some form of audit at each level to check whether or not targets and improvement objectives are being achieved, and to assess the progress being made with specific improvement projects. This commitment to quality and the targets and improvements made should be communicated to customers and suppliers. Some organizations use seminars to explain these policies and strategies. The respective reporting and control systems must be designed and operated in a manner that will ensure that all managers cooperate in continuous improvement activities.

The CEO must ensure that the organization really listens to what customers are saying and understands what they truly need and their concerns. This is more easily said than done; none of us likes

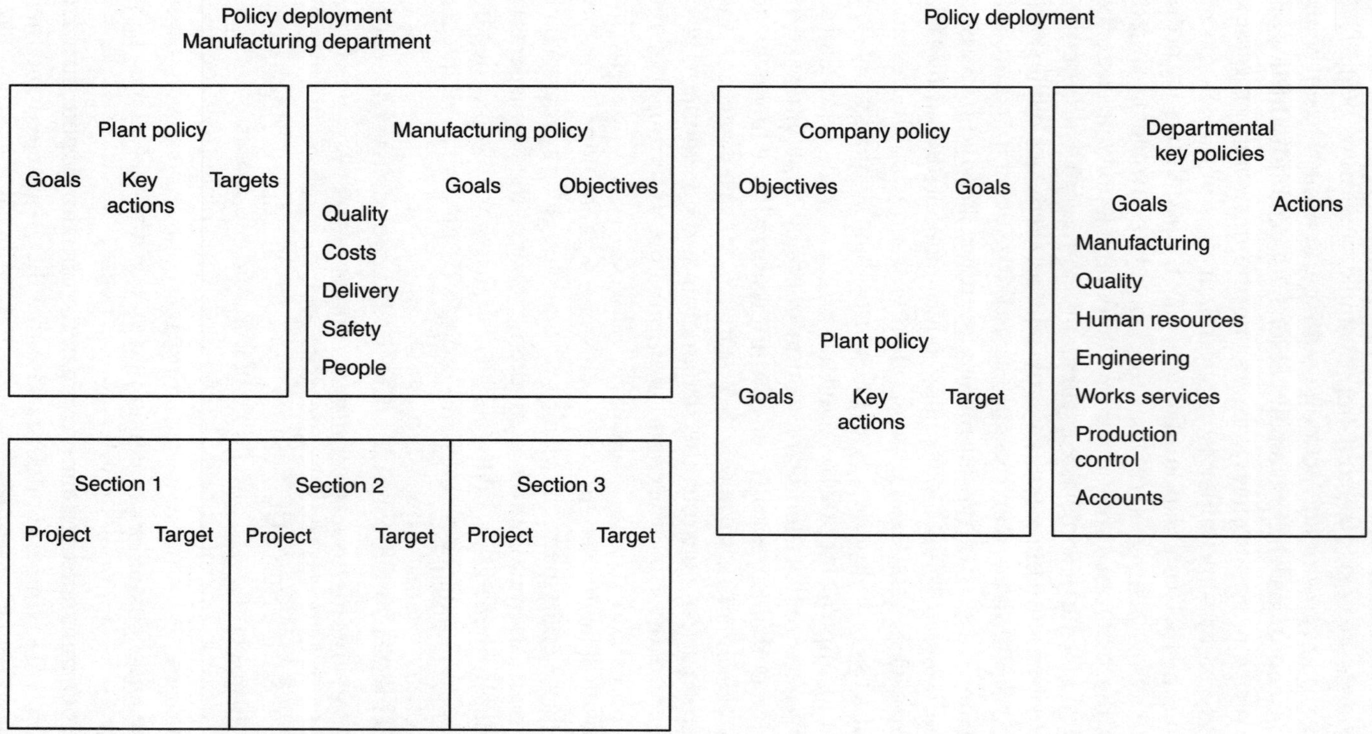

Policy deployment

Policy deployment
Manufacturing department

Company policy

Objectives   Goals

Plant policy

Goals   Key   Target
         actions

**Departmental
key policies**

         Goals   Actions

Manufacturing
Quality
Human resources
Engineering
Works services
Production
control
Accounts

Manufacturing policy

Goals   Objectives

Quality
Costs
Delivery
Safety
People

Plant policy

Goals   Key   Targets
         actions

Section 1

Project   Target

Section 2

Project   Target

Section 3

Project   Target

Figure 5.3 A typical framework for policy deployment

criticism and we have a tendency to think we know best. This customer information is the starting point of the improvement planning process. In many organizations this type of information is collected directly by computer links to and from customer processes, particularly in process industries.

Executives must ensure that they do not disguise things from the customer; honesty is the byword in TQM. Senior managers should ensure that their organization takes every opportunity to join the customers' and suppliers' improvement processes; mutual improvement activities can strengthen existing partnerships and build good working relationships. For example, a major blue chip packaging manufacturer works with its customers to ensure that the packaging produced is suited to the packaging equipment of the customers. Senior managers must ensure that corrective action procedures and defect analysis are pursued vigorously and a closed-loop system operated to prevent repetition of mistakes.

It is important that the CEO ensures that the organization has positive quantifiable measures of quality as seen by its customers. This enables the organization to keep an outward focus on the market in terms of customer needs and future expectations. These typical performance measures include:

- field failure statistics
- reliability performance statistics
- customer returns
- customer complaints
- 'things gone wrong' data
- adverse customer quality communications
- customer surveys
- lost business
- non-accepted tenders
- prospect to customer conversion rate

Internal performance measures also need to be developed such as:

- non-conformance levels

- quality audit results
- yield results
- quality costs
- employee satisfaction
- employee involvement

It is usually necessary to evaluate the current internal and external performance measures to assess their value to the business.

A measurement system to monitor the progress of the continuous improvement process is a key necessity; without it improvement will be more difficult. In the words of Scharp, President and CEO of A B Electrolux (1989), 'What gets measured gets done'; consequently, people will focus on those actions necessary to achieve the targeted improvements. All of the evidence from the Japanese companies (Dale, 1993) indicates that improvement targets and objectives act as key motivators. However, these need to be carefully set and monitored. It is possible to improve indicators without improving real performance, especially if targets are unrealistic or not seen as controlled by the individuals responsible for them, who fear that they will be blamed, and consequently focus on indicators not performance.

Senior managers should never overlook the fact that people will want to be informed about how the improvement process is progressing. They need to put into place a two-way process of communication for ongoing feedback and dialogue; this helps to close the loop. Communications up and down the organizational hierarchy are one of the most important features of the relationships between directors, managers and staff. Regular feedback needs to be made about any concerns raised by employees, which will help to stimulate further involvement and improve communication.

Continuous improvement can be facilitated by the rapid diffusion of information to all parts of the organization. A visible management system and a story-board style presentation in which a variety of information is collected and displayed is a very useful means of aiding this diffusion. The CEO needs to consider seriously this form of transparent system.

As already touched upon in this chapter, senior managers need to understand that TQM is not a campaign, nor a programme – it is a process that is company-wide and continuous. The CEO and the senior management team must never become satisfied and complacent with the process the organization has made in TQM; they must strive continually to achieve improvements in the product, service and associated processes. They need to adopt the philosophy and mindset that there is no ideal situation and the current state can always be improved upon. Areas of organizational waste and uselessness need to be identified and attacked in a ruthless manner.

The Role of Middle Managers

Middle managers have a vital part to play in the introduction and development of TQM. They will only be effective, however, if they are committed to it as a concept. Their role typically involves:

- Developing specific improvement plans for the departments and processes for which they are responsible.

- Ensuring that the objectives, values, policies and improvement initiatives of their departments are aligned with the company's business goals, TQM strategy and quality management system.

- Communicating the company's approach to TQM in common-sense and jargon-free language to first-line and other employees.

- Acting as TQM coach and counsellor to the employees for whom they are responsible.

- Ensuring that first-line managers are individually trained in the use of techniques and tools and that these are used effectively.

- Acting as a guardian, sponsor or mentor to improvement teams and securing the means to reward employees.

- Providing top management with considered views on how to manage the continuing implementation and development of TQM, taking into account feedback from first-line managers and employees on potential difficulties or obstacles.

The Role of First-Line Managers

First-line managers and supervisors are at the forefront of TQM. They have the key role of encouraging its implementation in the workplace, and are especially important because of the number of people they influence and lead. If first-line managers lack commitment, training, appropriate resources and a supportive management system and culture then the TQM cascade will fail at its most critical level. They are directly responsible for:

- Analyzing the individual procedures and processes for which they are responsible in order to identify areas where improvements might be annotated and made.

- Encouraging individual employees and operators to contribute improvement ideas, and ensuring that good ideas and efforts are acknowledged and rewarded by middle and top management.

- Ensuring that any quality concerns reported by employees are analyzed and resolved through permanent long-term corrective action.

- Participating in improvement teams in their own and related work areas.

- Providing workplace training in the use of specific techniques and tools to capture improvement data.

- Communicating the results of improvement activities and initiatives effectively to middle managers.

- Providing the data and responses required by the company's formal quality management system, including, where applicable, the requirements of the appropriate part of the ISO 9000 series.

- Providing the data for the self-assessment process.

- Representing the people and processes they supervise in management discussions about TQM resources and strategies.

Summary

This chapter has examined the role that senior managers need to take and the leadership they need to display if TQM is to be successful. Senior management will often ask what they need to do to demonstrate their commitment to TQM. The chapter has outlined some of the things they need to get involved with, including chairing the TQM Steering Committee, organizing and chairing Defect Review Boards, leading self-assessment of progress against a model of business excellence, developing and then following a personal improvement action plan and sponsoring improvement teams. The chapter has summarized in brief what senior management need to know about TQM and what they need to do to ensure that TQM is successful and is treated as part of normal business activities.

It has also pointed out that middle managers and first-line managers have a vital role in putting the principles of TQM in place and that they must have unified thinking with senior management. Typical activities they should get involved with have been outlined.

References

Akao, Y. (ed.) 1991: *Hoshin Kanri: policy deployment for successful TQM.* Cambridge, Mass.: Productivity Press.

Bunney, H. S. and Dale, B. G. 1996: The effect of organisational change in sustaining a process of continuous improvement. *Quality Engineering,* 8(4), 649–57.

Dale, B. G. 1990: Policy deployment. *The TQM Magazine,* 2(6), 125–8.

—— 1993: The key features of Japanese total quality control. *Quality and Reliability Engineering International,* 9(3), 169–78.

—— 1994: *Managing Quality,* 2nd edn. London: Prentice Hall.

Dale, B. G. and Shaw, P. 1990: Failure mode and effects analysis in the motor industry: a state-of-the-art study. *Quality and Reliability Engineering International,* 6(3), 179–88.

European Foundation for Quality Management 1997: *Self-Assessment 1997 Guidelines for Companies.* Brussels: EFQM.

Ishikawa, K. 1976: *Guide to Quality Control.* Tokyo: Asian Productivity Organisation.

Lascelles, D. M. and Dale, B. G. 1990a: Quality management: the chief executive's perception and role. *European Management Journal,* 8(1), 67–75.

—— 1990b: The use of quality management techniques. Quality Forum, 16(4), 188–92.

McKinsey, and Company 1989: Management of quality: the single major important challenge for Europe, European Quality Management Forum, 19 October, Montreux, Switzerland.

McQuater, R. E., Scurr, C. H., Dale, B. G. and Hillman, P. G. 1995: Using quality tools and techniques successfully. *The TQM Magazine*, 7(6), 37–42.

McQuater, R. E., Dale, B. G., Boaden, R. J. and Wilcox, M. 1996: The effectiveness of quality management tools and techniques: an examination of the key influences in five plants. *Proceedings of the Institution of Mechanical Engineers*, 210(B4), 329–39.

Scharp, A. 1989: What gets measured gets done: the Electrolux way to improve quality, European Quality Management Forum, 19 October, Montreux, Switzerland.

6 Total Quality Management: Some Common Failings of Senior Management

Introduction

As discussed in chapter 5, it is the responsibility of the CEO and the senior management team to create the right organizational environment, atmosphere, values and behaviour in which TQM can achieve its potential. This requires changing, through a deliberate, structured and systematic process, the behaviour and attitudes of people at all levels in the organizational hierarchy. Because of a number of factors – including the respective cultures of the organizations in which people have worked, lack of TQM education and training, lack of opportunity, neglect, mistreatment, and so on – people in manufacturing industry have regarded quality as a means of sorting the conforming from non-conforming product and reworking product to prevent non-conforming goods being passed to customers, while those in service situations have sometimes adopted a 'take it or leave it' attitude to the consumer.

It is not an easy task to create an organizational culture in which each person in every department is fully committed to improving his or her own performance and is dedicated to satisfying internal customers' needs and future expectations. Implementing quality management techniques, such as SPC, is much easier. A change in culture takes many years and requires executives to take a long-term view. Along the TQM journey it is easy for people, especially when under pressure, to slip back into the old traditional fire-fighting way of doing things. There is also the tendency for employees to question why the organization is going on the TQM journey. It should be expected that a number of employees will tend to be cynical and expect TQM to go the way of all new 'programmes' and initiatives, and eventually fizzle out. So it is not surprising that organizations do encounter a wide range of obstacles in pursuing a process of continuous and company-wide improvement. In our experience the road blocks often emanate from senior and middle management.

This chapter explores some of the common mistakes that executive management make in relation to TQM, and examines the reasons for the apparent lack of TQM commitment, awareness and vision that still exists in some organizations and among their employees. It should be mentioned that if executives did all of the things that were outlined in chapter 5, they would not fall as easily into the traps that are now discussed.

Time

Executives and other key organizational decision makers are not prepared to devote the time to learn about TQM and take personal leadership for continuous improvement. The impression given is that TQM is not such a pressing priority as financial, marketing, production and technical, and research and development issues. Frequent comments of subordinates are: 'there is plenty of rhetoric, but tangible and visible commitment is much more scarce', 'strong on words but short on deeds' and 'all talk and no action'. There is little doubt that a majority of executives devote too little time to improvement activities. They would find it revealing to undertake a time analysis of their weekly activities using the broad categories of:

1 housekeeping (e.g. regarding reports and attending meetings)

2 travel

3 fire-fighting

4 control (e.g. dealing with programme changes, organizational restructuring and the introduction of new products, services and technology)

5 improvement

TQM is the prime responsibility of senior management and they need to become immersed in it: without this commitment nothing of any significance will happen. They often claim that they simply do not have the time. The attitude of those CEOs who have emerged as true leaders of continuous improvement is that you create time simply by doing every task in a quality manner. For example, the CEO and chief operating officer at Milliken devote more than half their time to the company's 'Pursuit of excellence' process (Anonymous, 1989). To ensure that senior managers focus their attention on issues of continuous improvement there is emerging evidence that a proportion of the remuneration (e.g. bonus or performance-related pay) is related to metrics such as customer satisfaction and employee satisfaction figures and to scores achieved against the EFQM model.

Some CEOs brief their senior staff that the organization is setting out on the TQM journey. These staff are then given delegated responsibilities in relation to TQM and told to get on with the tasks they have been allocated, and not to involve them because they are going to be busy dealing with some financial, marketing, new technology, product substitution, organizational restructuring, etc., project. They are, however, told that from time to time they are to report back on the progress made.

The CEO tends to assume that these delegated tasks are being carried out in the manner ascribed. This may not be the case. The people to whom the tasks have been delegated will have their own day-to-day job responsibilities and consequently insufficient attention may be given to the task. They may misinterpret what the CEO expects of them, or the given tasks may conflict with their own beliefs and/or self interest. On either count, the tasks are sometimes not accomplished as envisaged by the CEO, and the most unfortunate thing is that some CEOs are not aware of the true situation. CEOs operating in this passive way are verbally supporting TQM, but neatly sidestepping the issue; continuous improvement is seen as something for others. They have fallen into the trap of: 'do as I say, not as I do' and 'you change your ways before I change mine'.

On the other hand, there is a tendency for the senior management team who have spent some considerable time assimilating and distilling the received TQM wisdom, developing their own personal knowledge of the subject and planning the organization's route map for TQM failing to allow sufficient time for other people in the organization to develop the same level of understanding and be involved in the process. These senior managers then become frustrated with this state of affairs, and cannot understand why staff are not acting in the manner expected of them. This often surfaces in the form of mixed jargon, incorrect application of tools and techniques, poor deployment of objectives, inadequate operation of improvement teams and a lack of action. Out of the sheer frustration that emanates from this patchy understanding of TQM, an executive during management meetings may be tempted to point the finger at managers and departments who are perceived not to be making sufficient progress. This should be avoided at all costs because it tends to isolate individuals and functions.

It is a common complaint among middle management that the CEO and members of the senior management team often opt out of TQM training courses and elect a substitute to attend in their place or else they only attend the course for a short duration of time. Any executive who has done this should be aware that the signal being given to his or her people is that continuous improvement is not such a demanding priority. The Ford Motor Company has established, in the UK, three external centres, which it has accredited for training suppliers in SPC. The standard three-day SPC course, offered by each of the centres, was designed for members of senior management teams. However, all three centres have consistently reported to the Ford Motor Company that an insufficient number of senior executives is attending this course. Consequently, a one-day SPC appreciation course has been developed to ensure that the members of the senior management team are aware of the 'what and how' of SPC and the need for a strategic plan of implementation.

During the past decade a vast number of conferences have been held on the subject of TQM. However, the conference delegates are more likely to be from the ranks of middle managers than the CEO and board members. It is only when a conference or course on TQM is specifically aimed at senior management that they are likely to attend – an environment in which they can share concerns and problems, without threat, with peers. A case in point is the annual Forum conference of the EFQM. This is unfortunate because senior management have so much to learn by mingling with quality management specialists and hearing, at first hand, some of their frustrations in trying to facilitate a process of continuous improvement without sufficient support from executives.

Resources

In some cases there is a failure to commit the right level of managerial resources to TQM. To start and then develop a process of continuous improvement, an infrastructure is required to support the associated tasks and departments, and people need to be able to devote time to quality planning, prevention and improvement activities. Cook and Dale (1995) point out that management do not give sufficient care to reviewing the effectiveness of their organizational improvement infrastructure to ensure that the momentum of the improvement process is being maintained. Their research evidence indicates that the initial infrastructure is sometimes removed too quickly, before the process has become embedded.

In terms of the quality management structure it should be understood that day-to-day control and assurance of quality should be separated from improvement and TQM promotion activities. If this is not done, quality assurance staff quite naturally will focus their efforts on the daily short-term type activities and those related to the quality management system and commit little time to long-term planning and improvements. It is a fact of business life that people will give more priority to the day-to-day activities for which they are responsible. These tasks are more easily recognized, assessed and regarded than are those related to improvement, especially those involving some form of teamwork. In particular, this applies when assessment and appraisal of individual performance takes no account of improvement achievements. People must be encouraged to take part in improvement activities, and to do this they need to be released from their day-to-day work routines. The employment of a full-time quality coordinator and/or facilitator(s) relieved of day-to-day work pressures can help to integrate individual improvement activities under a common umbrella in addition to providing advice and guidance on matters of improvement to the senior management team.

The CEO should also be prepared to invest in people through a continuous process of education and training in quality. Too many executives view this as a cost rather than as an investment. In a number of cases senior management have authorized the purchase of some particular TQM training package, often as a result of customer pressure, but then the package fails to be used to its full potential because of a lack of resources given to its application. In other instances a programme of TQM education and training has been put into place, only to be cut back or put on hold when production volumes have to be increased.

The ultimate aim is to have people taking ownership for the quality assurance of their processes and having a mindset of continuous improvement. This state of affairs is not a natural phenomenon and does not happen overnight, and executives must be prepared to spend time coaching their people along this path. Once people have seen the CEO leading the TQM initiative, and respect has been earned, then this will start to happen and will encourage the emergence of quality leaders and champions.

'Getting things done' is a frequent cause of complaint among people who are committed to pursuing improvement activities. This complaint appears to be more the case with established products and services to which improvements are sought than with products, processes and services that are being planned and are high profile.

A frequent sticking point in the improvement activity is gaining the involvement of manufacturing engineers, production preparation staff, technical specialists, designers, and sales and marketing personnel. For example, even when simple mistake-proofing devices are pointed out to engineers and technical specialists, they often claim that they do not have the time to construct the device and put it into place. Technical specialists and staff from non-manufacturing departments often fail to recognize and employ some of the simple quality control techniques. The use of quality planning techniques such as Failure Mode and Effects Analysis (FMEA) and Quality Function Deployment (QFD) and the development of control plans are other areas where many people are not prepared to commit resources, because they encroach on the time available for carrying out day-to-day activities. Surprisingly enough, it is not that people remain unconvinced of the value of such tools and techniques, but rather it is the perceived time taken to use them. Considerable selling activity is required to gain progress on these fronts. The CEO is often not aware of such road blocks and this can act as a serious impediment to the process of continuous improvement. The protagonists of these types of improvement have to resort to making presentations to the CEO and senior management team to convince them of the value of advanced quality planning techniques. This should not have to be the case.

In administration and sales and marketing functions, staff are frequently slow at picking up the improvement theme. This is often because they are unsure of how the various ideas and techniques apply to their area of responsibility and what to do. A good way of getting started in these areas is the use of the 'twenty-four hour improvement' concept developed by the precision bearings operation of RHP Bearings Ltd at Newark. The scheme, which is part of a strategy to demonstrate RHP Precision's commitment to people involvement, enables employees to be involved in direct improvements to their own workplace. The aim of the scheme is to demonstrate to people that their day-to-day concerns will be met and that senior management are committed to putting things right. A group, typically comprising engineering, site services, quality and production operatives, meets at a nominated workstation at a set time each day to listen to improvement ideas from a selection of people responsible for a process. The maximum time allowed for these meetings is fifteen minutes. The focus is on those ideas that can be actioned or sanctioned within a period of twenty-four hours. However, this does not mean that longer-term improvements are ignored; quite the opposite – they are logged and dealt with using one of the other improvement initiatives operating on the site. When the team meets at a designated workstation they also check to see that the previous day's improvements have been implemented, generate the present day's improvement idea and record its details, with a copy to the managing director. The type of improvement submitted usually falls within one of three categories: efficiency, housekeeping and safety. The scheme is monitored on a daily basis and this tends to make the generation and implementation of improvement ideas normal practice.

Another common problem caused by a lack of resources committed to improvement is insufficient attention given to removing basic causes of errors. People put in quick fixes to prevent nonconforming products and services reaching the customer, but then there is a lack of subsequent follow-up effort devoted to long-term corrective action and developing systematic recurrence prevention measures. Consequently, the chronic problems persist and increase. A related difficulty caused by a failure of managing the improvement activities is that the solving of one problem tends to generate several others which are outside the scope of the original project. These types of problems would be less likely to occur if executives understood the resources required in TQM, and if they did get involved in improvement and diagnosis activities and the auditing and assessment of the progress made.

It should also be pointed out that organizations, from time to time, have to introduce a number of cost-cutting or streamlining measures. Senior managers need to be careful about how these measures are communicated and implemented, otherwise they are likely to have a negative impact on the process of continuous improvement.

Teamwork is Not Practised

Senior managers should work as a team to develop improvement objectives and plans, and identify the means by which they can measure organizational improvement (i.e. self-assessment). They are responsible for pinpointing opportunities, prioritizing projects and steering the improvement efforts. In some organizations, there is managerial obsession for preferential dealing with 'events of the moment' and 'today's problems' such as reorganization, and technical or marketing innovation. This is at the expense of the systematic improvement process and teamwork. While a CEO and senior managers meet from time to time, rarely do they function as a team to identify and consider strategies that will lead to organizational improvement. In more than one case a CEO has remarked that he is 'banging his head against the wall', a comment made in frustration at some of his management team for failing to take the actions they have promised to respond to the quality concerns of the customer. In certain cases we have observed the CEO playing senior managers off one against the other, with each senior manager, in turn, attempting to get the attention of the CEO for his or her particular plan, policy and/or project. In such cases the members of the senior management team appear to have different objectives and agendas.

Teamwork is an essential element of TQM, providing an opportunity for cooperative action in pursuit of continuous improvement. The CEO and senior managers need to give more thought to the means by which teamwork may be facilitated and how the achievements of effective team members can be recognized. The use of teams is a way of involving everyone in a continuous improvement initiative. Teams:

- Aid the commitment of people to the principles of TQM

- Provide an additional means of communicating between individuals, management and their direct reports, across functions, and with customers and suppliers

- Provide the means and opportunities for people to participate in decision making about how the business operates

- Improve relationships, develop trust and facilitate cooperative activities

- Help to develop people and encourage leadership traits

- Build collective responsibility

- Aid personal development and build confidence

- Develop problem solving skills

- Facilitate awareness of improvement potential, leading to behaviour and attitude change

- Help to facilitate a change in management style

- Solve problems

- Improve morale

- Improve operating effectiveness as people work in a common direction

There are a variety of team work approaches to team building, some of which are discussed in chapter 8.

Senior managers should not lose sight of the fact that middle and first-line management have been victims of previous 'flavour of the month' management. There is also a fear from middle managers that they will be bypassed as a result of improvement activities. A number of middle managers shine as troubleshooters (this is how they have achieved promotion), and do not know anything else. They commonly express the concern that 'if there is no fire-fighting what else can they do?' and naturally fear for their jobs, especially in the current climate of developing flatter organizational structures.

Some CEOs are not good at selecting senior colleagues who will be good team players in TQM, and one of the 'old guard' as part of the team will have a considerable negative influence on the concept.

In a number of cases this has been recognized too late, and the middle or senior manager has had to be moved to a position/site where he or she can do least damage. In one such situation the person was moved to an offshore site but made no attempt to modify his management style to take into account the culture of the country, and this prevented the improvement process from developing. Some individuals, if not dealt with by the CEO, create doubts in employees' minds of the commitment of the organization to continuous and company-wide improvement. In a German automotive components manufacturer, middle managers, because of the very strong hierarchical structure of working with little cross-functional communications and interactions, put road blocks in front of those employees at a lower level in the organization who were taking the initiatives to make improvements. There was also little follow-up and completion of projects because of the absence of feedback by senior management to the people taking the initiatives. This situation perpetuated itself down through the organization, with foremen not being willing to allow some of their activities to be taken over by cell leaders. This is discussed in some detail by Dale and McQuater (1997).

Training

The ability of the Japanese to manage the process of continuous improvement more successfully and at a faster rate than appears possible in European organizations is a key factor in their success story. One of the major factors appears to be the depth of knowledge and training in quality skills, tools, techniques and problem solving possessed by the Japanese management and supervisory structure. The current response of Japanese manufacturing companies to the increase in value of the yen in terms, for example, of product substitution, globalization, seeking out new markets, developing joint ventures, cycle time reductions, higher improvement targets etc. is a good example of their commitment to continuous improvement. Further details of the Japanese approach to TQM are given in chapter 9. Western organizations often do not invest sufficient monies in TQM education and training, and in developing the problem analysis skills and expertise of their people.

It is important that organizations invest in technology, machinery and systems but also in their people's education and abilities; TQM requires a new set of skills. An increasing number of organizations now provide all of their employees with a basic understanding of business, finance and where they, as individuals, fit into the organization. In this way, they are aware of what they can do to improve matters within their own area of responsibility. Regular training is required to reinforce the message in such a way that the improvement concept become an integral part of people' day-to-day work and not an additional task. In a number of organizations, an indication of their depth of commitment to TQM is that quality-related training courses are mandatory for all employees. An alternative to this approach is to specify the number of hours of training each employee should receive on an annual basis and allow the employees to choose the training which they themselves need.

There is a tendency for senior managers to look for and expect massive benefits arising from the implementation of quality systems and procedures, and tools and techniques. Any such benefits will only be short lived unless there are major changes in people's behaviour and attitudes. A company-wide education and training programme needs to be planned and undertaken to facilitate the right type and degree of changes. The aims of this programme should be to promote a common TQM language, awareness and understanding of concepts and principles, to ensure that there are no knowledge gaps at any level in the organizational hierarchy and to provide the skills to assist people with improvement activities. This should include team leadership, counselling and coaching skills. A planned programme of training is required in order to provide employees with tools and techniques on a timely basis. In most organizations it is frequently found that there is a good deal of variation in relation to understanding what the process of continuous improvement actually involves. Executives also need to consider the best ways of making an input to leading some of the quality-related training.

In relation to TQM training, it is worth considering the points made by Payne and Dale (1990) in relation to the disadvantage of conventional training courses. The CEO and senior managers should be aware of the following:

- Chief executives, whose actions determine whether or not a company has a corporate culture where quality comes first, rarely attend such courses, in particular 'open' courses.

- The training department, in conjunction with departmental managers, identify individual training needs and delegates are directed to attend a course. This often produces a negative reaction from delegates when they return to work after attending a course with complaints such as 'a mountain of paperwork', 'the number of queries which require resolving', 'all these telephone calls to return and letters to answer', etc.

- When course are run in-plant they are often of a 'one-off' nature, with minimum follow-up instruction and advice.

- The typical approach adopted in courses is to first teach principles, techniques and systems, followed by their application through general examples and problems. The courses by their very nature and experiences of the lecturer(s) involved, cannot deal with specifics relating to the delegates' individual needs.

- Prior to taking the course, it is not easy for delegates to assess the expertise of the course leader.

- The people giving the course are sometimes limited in their knowledge of the application of these principles, techniques and systems to industrial problems, and are short of suitable material to use as training examples.

- The delegates are likely to experience a problem of transferring the new knowledge gained whilst on the course and effectively applying it in their own working environment. The course has only changed the behaviour and attitudes of individuals; delegates on their return to their company have to motivate and change the behaviour, attitudes and direction of both their peers and senior management, and it is not uncommon for them to experience resistance from their respective company cultures.

- There is little attempt to integrate the knowledge imparted on the course with controlled projects carried out in the trainees' organisation.

- The problems associated with influencing other people's behaviour and attitudes in conjunction with day-to-day work pressures, results in a lack of practice in applying the new knowledge. This causes a rapid decline in the individual's motivation and in the meantime the course notes have been filed and forgotten.

Training is often carried out in a vacuum, with little thought being given to how the training provided can assist the process of continuous improvement. There is little point in training without clearly specified improvement objectives. The training is often wasted, with no follow-up projects pursued by the trainees and/or people being trained too far in advance of the introduction of particular quality initiatives and techniques. To coin a term, the training should be carried out 'just-in-time'. It is the responsibility of managers to ensure that those who have been on training courses use the knowledge that has been imparted in their day-to-day work activities. Organizations not considering such issues fail to get value for money from their investment in training.

Understanding

The lack of time devoted to learning about TQM means that many executives have insufficient understanding of the philosophy and logic underlying TQM and the associated techniques, systems and procedures. The concept and philosophy of TQM and the continuous improvement methods are well known and have been for years, and are very clearly outlined by internationally recognized quality experts such as Crosby (1979), Deming (1982), Feigenbaum (1991) and Juran (1988). This is despite the concept being regurgitated in various disguises. The main problem is communication of the concepts and the understanding of them by executives, followed by action. It should not be forgotten that 'I do not understand' is usually an excuse for doing nothing, and it is all too easy for executives and middle managers to do nothing.

In Europe, at least, this knowledge gap at one time was exacerbated by the lack of TQM education at undergraduate and postgraduate level in universities, business schools and polytechnics (see van der Wiele et al. 1993). Among the original objectives of the EFQM (1989) were:

Business schools and universities are encouraged to develop, implement and upgrade quality management education programmes.

EFQM has an objective to intensify Western European research programmes directed at strengthening quality management capabilities, programmes and achievements.

Today, the subject of TQM is now being given more attention in the European higher educational system, with courses featuring TQM being on the increase in most European universities and business schools (van de Wiele and Dale, 1996).

The majority of executives have had little or no exposure in their formal education and professional training of the concept and philosophy underlying TQM and continuous improvement. Consequently, many senior managers do not have well-developed quality improvement instincts and beliefs. This lack of understanding manifests itself in a number of ways, including:

- A lack of TQM organizational vision, mission and guiding principles. This results in a lack of harmony among functions, people and improvement activities, and of clear focus, priorities and planning; it also results in a failure to develop an environment in which everyone is an active participant. People do not have a common understanding and values regarding quality; this results in people having different expectations and working to different standards and requirements. Problems often arise because quality is not sufficiently defined. In short, there is a lack of cohesion.

- Senior managers are not sure of what is required of them in terms of their responsibilities for TQM, what activities they need to get involved in and how they can help. They often spend time discussing quality-related problems; it is frequently the case that they themselves do not have the knowledge and skills to solve such problems on their own.

- Worries about giving employees more involvement in the business and greater powers of decision making. They frequently fail to recognize the detailed know-how and enthusiasm that exists at the operating level of the business. Trust in each other and mutual respect for abilities are contributing factors.

- Senior managers are sometimes worried about exchanging information and ideas with their people, and fail to communicate on a person-to-person basis. TQM demands that there are no secrets. A case in point is that the membership, activities and outcomes of the TQM Steering Committee should be freely communicated throughout the organization.

- There is a failure to understand the role that each function in the organization has to play in TQM. This frequently leads to a lack of cooperation and collaboration in identifying and solving problems and ensuring that prevention activities are practised. This also manifests itself in the attitude that it is always someone else's problem: 'let them get it right, then everything will be ok'. In such situations the improvement initiative is restricted to a small number of departments, it is not company-wide and a critical mass of people is missed out. This applies, in particular, to service departments of manufacturing companies

- No milestones, checkpoints, phases of activity, key results indicators, critical success factors, criteria and plans are established by the senior management team. So, people within the organization are unsure of what progress has been made and the next steps.

- TQM is just viewed as a paperwork requirement to satisfy the demands of major customers. It is not uncommon to find quality managers and technical specialists resorting to a number of camouflage measures, fakes and ruses to convince the customer that the organization is serious about TQM, and also portray to the CEO that they are doing an effective job in terms of the management of quality. Senior managers are often not aware of the measures being used and the state-of-the-art of TQM within the organization. The increasing use of self-assessment against a recognized business excellence model, if applied in the spirit in which it was first intended, will help to rectify this situation. However on a more negative note, organizations are being encouraged, in the aim for recognition of achievement by some quality bodies to publicize the scores they achieve against the EFQM model – commercial, public relations and marketing instincts are taking over from improvement ideals.

- The concept of TQM conflicts with the education and professional training that many executives have received and also with their fundamental experience, beliefs, management style and company culture. In their 'heart of hearts' and 'personal beliefs' they do not consider it is the right way.

- Some CEOs argue that their organization's particular sphere of operation, whether it be service, commerce, manufacturing or not-for-profit, is different and some particular aspect of the Total Quality approach – tool, technique, system, procedure etc. – is not suitable and will not work.

- Too many CEOs isolate themselves in their offices and fail to visit the areas producing the product and/or service, and have little empathy with what is going on in the plant. This is the case in large organizations, where there is always a certain degree of remoteness and anonymity of management. In the words of the vice president of a speciality chemical manufacturers, 'what are offices for? To keep managers from getting wet'.

- Some CEOs are forever looking for the next fad and next wave (e.g BPR and Business Process Management). This indicates that they are not aware or remain unconvinced of the competitive edge that TQM can give to the organization.

- Some CEOs think that the principles of TQM can be put into place very easily and become frustrated about the lack of progress. It is often the case that they do not realized the full implications of the concept. They are too easily convinced of the benefits and taken in by the hype surrounding the subject. The difficulties encountered in doing this simple thing well and consistently, the diagnostics required to get to the root cause of problems, the need to be a role model etc. are completely underestimated.

- Staff are not encouraged to identify factors that prevent them from turning in an error-free performance. Everyone in the organization should be encouraged to identify and correct problems that affect quality. Employees must be asked what they think and listened to carefully. Listening is a key aspect for broad participation in the continuous improvement process.

- Some CEOs encourage effective systems to manage the rework and scrap. However, it is not the management of scrap that is important but the management of continuous improvement.

- There is failure to recognize and reward the efforts of individuals and teams. A process of recognition and celebration acts as a key motivator and demonstrates to staff that the executives know what is going on within the business. This also applies to the communication of success. Reporting and communicating business results tends to boost employees' morale.

- In relation to communication it is often found that what is going on in the market-place in terms of customers is not fed back on a frequent basis to operating staff.

● Insufficient attention is given to the key role of line personnel in the process of continuous improvement.

Mistaken Beliefs

Some CEOs and senior managers have picked up the wrong signals and are failing to follow the fundamental principles involved in a process of continuous improvement. This problem is related to the difficulties caused by lack of understanding about the concept and principles of TQM. It is unfortunate that a number of the mistaken beliefs that are discussed here are created by people who should know better. For example, one of the authors was contacted by a 'consultant' who was enquiring about whether or not TQM had peaked, and if 'continuous improvement' was now the issue that companies were pursuing. Other typical examples include (a) consultants encouraging organizations to carry out self-assessment against the EFQM model before the basics of quality management are in place, so much so that there is more focus on the points scored than on continuous improvement activities, and (b) consultants and academics encouraging the belief that BPR has replaced TQM.

Continuous improvement is seen to be the responsibility and province of the quality manager and his or her department. In addition, TQM is just seen as a function of production and operations, and something that can only be used by operating personnel in a manufacturing environment.

Senior managers believe that the answer to all their quality problems lies in the implementation of a particular tool, technique or system, and that they do not need any formal training in the quality skills and techniques required to develop an effective improvement strategy.

There is a tendency to respond solely to meeting the requirements of customers in terms of quality management system standards, and the use of techniques such as SPC and FMEA, because they are a contractual requirement. Many organizations never achieve much more than this and consequently become stuck at first base. The approach to be recommended is that followed by the CEO of an electronics manufacturing organization, when addressing delegates to the three-day course on SPC; his usual words are along the lines

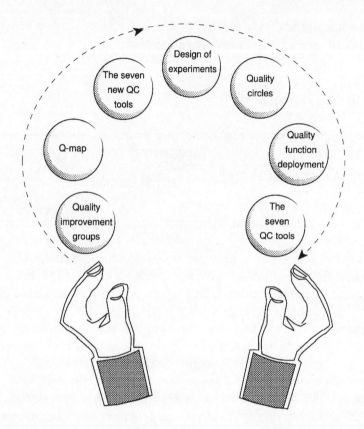

Figure 6.1 The use of quality management tools and techniques

'forget the Ford Motor Company and General Motors: we need SPC for our own corporate well-being'.

Senior managers frequently expect too much from the introduction and use of a single tool or technique, quality system, quality proced-ure etc. Consequently, following a short period of usage there is a tendency to believe that 'such and such a technique' is not working, and to look for the next technique or tool (see figure 6.1). The benefits from the use of tools, techniques systems and procedures is cumulative, and the temptation to isolate the effect of single tools and techniques should be resisted (see figure 6.2).

In other cases, some CEOs still hold the view that organizational quality ills can be cured by just changing the operators' behaviour and attitudes. There is a tendency for them to look for quality-improving

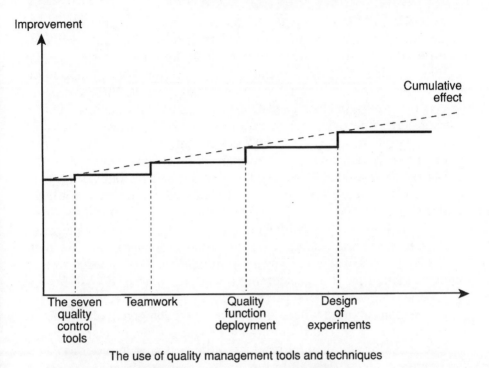

The use of quality management tools and techniques

Figure 6.2 Incremental improvement through the use of quality management tools and techniques

changes at the bottom of the organization rather than at middle and senior management level. Senior managers should be aware that the degrees of opportunity for change are considerably greater at the top of the organizational hierarchy. Along a similar line, there is a belief that quality problems are caused by people, and by employing different forms of automation, advanced technology and computing systems, the problems will be eradicated. There is a tendency to undervalue the simple things (e.g. housekeeping and doing the basics right) and the influence of people.

Production Output and Cost are the Main Priorities

The CEO and the senior management team are more often than not measured by their shareholders, financial institutions and main board on numbers – profit, cost, headcount, sales turnover, numbers of products produced in a period, stock turnover etc. Consequently, most senior managers tend to be very concerned about numbers, especially if they are from a financial background. This results in them placing considerable emphasis on meeting production, output and most targets, with quality taking a lower priority the focus is on accounts and systems. It is relatively easy to influence numbers in the short-term; improving quality requires a long-term view. In this type of situation today's events will always take priority. Also, if the company is performing well in financial terms many executives do not see the need for TQM. The fact that the benefits of TQM are not immediate and are sometimes of an intangible nature does not help this situation.

The traditional measurement system, such as monthly targets, encourages a concentration on numbers. It is often the case that quality considerations are given top priority for the first three weeks of a month, then if targets are not being met there is a drive to ship product to meet the targets. This approach is self-defeating.

Situations abound where, despite having been given advice that a shipment contains non-conforming product, a senior manager has instructed the shipment of product to the customer in order to meet monthly output targets and/or to achieve delivery promises. Concessions are also sometimes used to legalize this action. Some organizations go to elaborate lengths to disguise the situation in the hope that the customer will not find the non-conforming products or will not bother to complain. It may even be the case that the CEO expects to have moved to a new company by the time the non-conforming products are returned. The main reason for this type of situation arising is that the number achieved and/or delivered is a black and white figure, and is a direct measure of the plant's performance that requires a simple judgement. The resulting customer complaints, warranty claims, costs incurred and time spent putting the problem right are not as easy to measure and can be attributed to a wide variety of different events.

Statistical Inadequacies

The majority of senior managers do not understand 'process variation and capability'. They frequently have concerns about their lack of knowledge of statistical methods and, for fear of exposing their own inadequacies, tend to shy away from using statistical techniques in their own decision making. They should be sufficiently knowledgeable about the concepts of 'variability' and 'statistical thinking' to enable them to ask sensible questions about the key business processes to get answers to improve their own decision making. The use and limitations of statistical methods should be understood and executives need to be able to interpret statistical analysis and use effective reporting.

Consider, for example, the application of SPC. As part of the organization's total commitment to continuous improvement, members of the senior management team should be prepared to learn about statistical methods, use them in their decision making processes, and demonstrate an active interest and involvement in SPC. When passing through manufacturing and office areas, they should get into the habit of looking at the control charts on display and directing questions to the people responsible for charting and analyzing the data. They can also learn, from the data portrayed on the charts, of any problems that the operator is experiencing with the process. The control chart is a communication to senior management in the condition of a process, and ignoring the message will only cause frustration among those involved with SPC and hinder the improvement process. It should also not be forgotten that SPC teaches people to ask questions about the process.

Summary

Given the importance of TQM in distinguishing an organization from its competitors, the effects on business efficiency and survival of an organization, and the publicity given to organizations winning prestigious quality awards and the benefits of superior performing companies in relation to quality, the key issue should be how CEOs and senior managers show sufficient commitment and dedication to TQM.

References

Anonymous, 1989: Xerox and Milliken get Baldrige Award. *Business America*, 110(23), 2–11.

Cook, E. and Dale, B. G. 1995: Organising for continuous improvement: an examination. *The TQM Magazine*, 7(1), 7–13.

Crosby, P. B. 1979: *Quality is Free*. New York: McGraw-Hill.

Dale, B. G. and McQuater, R. E. 1997: *Tools and Techniques for Business Improvement*. Oxford: Blackwell.

Deming, W. E. 1982: *Quality, Productivity and Competitive Position*. Cambridge, Mass.: MIT Press.

European Foundation for Quality Management 1989: *Introduction to EFQM*. Brussels: EFQM.

Feigenbaum, A. V. 1991: *Total Quality Control*. New York: McGraw-Hill.

Juran, J. M. (ed.) '1988: *Quality Control Handbook*. New York: McGraw-Hill.

Payne, B. J. and Dale, B. G. 1990: Total quality management training: some observations. *Quality Assurance*, 16(1), 5–9.

van der Wiele, A. and Dale, B. G. 1996: *Total Quality Management Directory 1996: TQM at European Universities and Business Schools*. Rotterdam: University Press.

van der Wiele, T., Timmers, J., Bertsch, B., Williams, R. and Dale, B. G. 1993: Total quality management: a state-of-the-art survey of European industry. *Total Quality Management*, 4(1), 23–38

7 Motivation, Change and Culture

Introduction

In this chapter we explain the various theories of motivation and their implications for managers and organizations. We emphasize the difficulties of implementing and sustaining organizational change in pursuit of TQM and argue that culture change needs to be addressed as a long-term strategy.

Job Characteristics Model of Motivation

Hackman and Oldham (1976) have proposed a 'job characteristics model' that identifies five core job characteristics involved in job satisfaction and motivation (see figure 7.1) – skill variety, task identity, task significance, autonomy and feedback. According to the model, satisfaction and motivation are controlled by the critical psychological states (a) meaningfulness of the work, (b) responsibility for the outcomes of work and (c) knowledge of the results of work. Managers should note, in particular, this latter point with respect to response, feedback and communication of the results and progress of improvement initiatives and actions.

The critical psychological states are linked to the core job dimensions. 'Skill variety' or multi-skilling is concerned with the extent to which the activities of the job call for a selection of abilities and skills. 'Task identity' and 'task significance' concern the extent to which the activities of the job form an identifiable whole, and the extent to

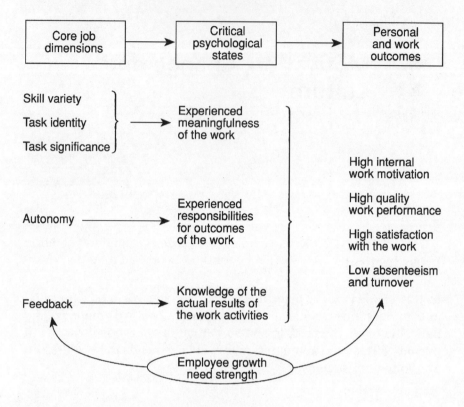

Figure 7.1   The job characteristic model
Source: Hackman and Oldham (1976).

which the job has an impact on the lives or work of other people. 'Autonomy' relates to the freedom and independence that the job holder has, and 'feedback' to the extent to which knowledge of results concerning individual effectiveness is provided.

For example:

- The learning and practising of 'problem solving skills' used in improvement projects, either individually and/or through team-work, the use of tools and techniques, and ownership of the process help to enhance these three core job dimensions.

- Statistical process control gives control over processes to the process owner.

- The internal audit and management review requirements in the ISO 9000 series should give control over the working procedures in a formalized way to the process owner.

Effort, Performance and Outcomes

PROCESS THEORIES

An alternative approach to motivation involves examining the cognitive processes that are involved. The most important process approaches to motivation make use of ideas about the expectations that people have about the consequences of their behaviour (Lawler, 1973). Put simply, the theory suggests that the amount of effort people are prepared to invest in a task depends on three factors:

1 Expectancy: whether the effort involved will produce better performance.
2 Instrumentality: whether the performance will pay off in terms of outcomes, e.g. promotion, job security.
3 Whether the possible outcomes are attractive for the concerned individual and/or working group.

As figure 7.2 suggests, peoples' motivation is reflected in the amount of effort they put into their jobs. Theories involving the concepts of expectancy, instrumentality and valence (usually called expectancy theory or expectancy/valence theory) form the basis of much of the current research on motivation and work behaviour (Steers and Porter, 1979). According to expectancy theory, the following factors are involved in determining motivation, effort and, eventually job satisfaction:

1 The perceived relationship between effort (E) and performance (P). This concerns the belief that extra effort will lead to better performance.
2 The perceived relationship between performance and outcomes (O). This concerns the belief that improved job performance will lead to outcomes such as promotion, extra pay, bonuses, more responsibility, increased job autonomy, job security, recognition etc.

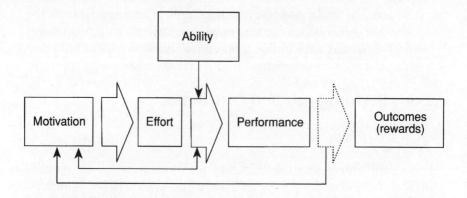

Figure 7.2 The basic motivation-behaviour sequence according to expectancy theory. A person's motivator is a function of (a) effort-to-performance expectancies, (b) performance-to-outcome expectancies and (c) perceived valence of outcomes
Source: Hackman et al. (1977). The material is reproduced with permission of McGraw-Hill Inc.

3   The attractiveness or valence (V) of the possible outcomes. This concerns the value of the possible outcomes for the person concerned, such as the elimination of dangerous and dirty aspects of the job, the job being made easier, more interesting etc.

Other points worthy of note are:

1   Even if motivation is high, this may not be reflected in performance, perhaps because of barriers such as a lack of ability, lack of training, inadequate materials, machinery, aids and tools, an inappropriate strategy for doing the job, a system and organizational environment that is not conducive to continuous improvement etc.

2   The beliefs that the person holds about links between effort, performance and outcomes are modified as a result of experience – hence the feedback loop. For example, an initial belief that good performance will lead to positive outcomes, such as promotion, recognition, improved working conditions and higher salary may not be borne out by experience, and this may result in a reassessment of the performance–outcome relationship; this includes suggestions put forward for some form of improvement

that are not taken up by management without any form of adequate explanation, the key issues identified from an improvement team or key issues conference that are not followed through, and some perceived useful quality-related initiative (e.g. training) that is cancelled as part of a cost-cutting drive.

ATTRACTIVENESS AND PAYOFFS

Two points are worth mentioning in connection with such theories. Firstly, they emphasize the fact that the attractiveness of specific outcomes or rewards is a very individualistic matter. What is important and attractive for one person may be irrelevant for another. Thus, although expectancy theories seek to provide a general model of the factors involved in determining effort and performance for all employees, the individual differences between people are an integral part of the theory. The recognition of employees' achievements and celebrating successes are key features in a process of continuous improvement, and organizations need to work out which are the best methods for them; a change is required from highlighting problems to celebrating successes. The second and related point is that although expectancy theories concentrate on the common processes involved, the contents of each individual's motivational system (e.g. whether increased pay, flexibility of working arrangements, more involvement in decision making or increased participation has higher valence) are also important.

IMPLICATIONS FOR INDIVIDUAL MANAGERS

The following points, put forward by Nadler and Lawler (1979), are among the chief implications for managers and warrant serious consideration in the development of a process of continuous quality improvement:

> Find out what particular outcomes or rewards are valued for each employee.

The theory proposes that different people will value different rewards.

> Be specific about the precise behaviours that constitute good levels of performance.

Make sure that the desired levels of performance are attainable.

According to the theory, people are prepared to put the effort in if they feel they can achieve their objectives. If employees feel that it is not possible for them to reach the performance level, even with high effort, their motivation will be low.

Deming's 'point ten' – 'eliminate slogans, exhortations, and targets for the workforce asking for zero defects and new levels of productivity' – should be noted. He also examines in his 'point eleven', – 'eliminate numerical quotas for the workforce and numerical goals for management' – the implications of management setting numerical targets without providing the means to achieve them (e.g. from objectives through strategies to action plans). Deming (1982) is of the view that if targets are too low, employees will achieve them easily and will not be encouraged to improve. On the other hand, if targets are too high employees will become disillusioned when they fail to achieve them. This may attract losses and lost opportunities. However, it is interesting that in Japan, improvement targets are set deliberately high in order to motivate employees. Although the targets are not imposed on employees they are set in conjunction with them as part of the policy deployment process (see chapter 9).

Ensure that there is a direct, clear and explicit link between performance at the desired level and outcomes and rewards.

In order words, employees must be able to observe and experience the performance–outcome connection. If this is not clear or is seen not to work, the motivation will not be created in employees' minds and this is likely to restrict their efforts to improve the processes for which they are responsible. An example of this type of problem is related to the way in which organizations appraise performance. The appraisal methods employed often need to be rethought and revised, particularly, in large organizations, where the methods are often decided by headquarters personnel and imposed on local management.

Check that there are no conflicting expectations.

Once the motivation expectancies have been set up and employees have a clear grasp of the effort–performance and performance–outcome relationships, it is important to check that other people, processes, systems and procedures within the organization are not encouraging alternative expectancies and employees are not getting mixed messages. For example:

- In multinational companies, management sometimes receive mixed messages from headquarters and top management; a case in point is safety and environment improvement concepts. A common complaint among middle management is that in order to understand the message they have to read between the lines.

- Some managers might put all the effort into meeting the production schedule, with the process of continuous improvement taking second place; this is typically the situation in a traditional fire-fighting environment and where the approach to quality management is based on detection.

- Middle managers are often frustrated about how they should commit their time, energy and resources to the key corporate strategies of quality, manufacturing, logistics, technology etc. and as a result are often likely to pursue their own 'pet' projects. This produces conflicting messages to their subordinates and is detrimental to the improvement process. TQM is long term and all embracing, and sustained senior management commitment and leadership in TQM with well thought out objectives and strategies can eventually lead to middle management taking ownership for the process, with improvement leaders and champions emerging from various parts of the organizational hierarchy. Executive commitment to TQM usually surfaces in the form of their understanding of the subject, it being their number one consideration in decision making, and their practising the principles in their day-to-day work activities.

Ensure changes in outcomes are large enough to justify the effort.

As Nadler and Lawler (1979) put it, 'trivial rewards will result in trivial amounts of effort and thus trivial improvements in performance'. However, rewards may be trivial in a financial sense but significant in terms of recognition and satisfaction. Managers should not always go for quantum leaps in improvement as encouraged by BPR; small incremental steps can produce attainable targets and should warrant recognition and reward.

Check that the system is treating everyone fairly.

The theory is based on the idea that people are different and therefore different rewards will need to be used for different people. Nevertheless, 'good performers should see that they get more of the desired rewards than do poor performers, and others in the system should see that also' (Nadler and Lawler, 1979). In other words, despite the use of different rewards, the system should seem to be fair and equitable to those involved.

In the pursuit of continuous improvement in manufacturing, great emphasis is placed upon the manufacturing and producing part of the business yet a large percentage of 'indirect' labour is employed ostensibly to aid these departments. It is therefore important that efforts and systems, tools and technique should be embraced by *all managers* and all employees in every function of the business.

IMPLICATIONS FOR ORGANIZATIONS

Below are some of the main implication for organizations, proposed by Nadler and Lawler. Like those for managers, they need to be considered in planning for continuous improvement:

1   Design pay and reward systems so that:
    (a)   desirable performance is rewarded (e.g. do not reward mere 'membership' by linking pay with years of service); and
    (b)   the relationship between performance and reward is clear. Whatever the rewards in terms of pay, promotion, learning new skills, education and training, job flexibility, involvement in improvement activities etc. that result from good performance, these should be made clear and explicit rather than kept ambiguous or secret.

2   Design tasks, jobs and roles so that people have an opportunity to satisfy their own needs through their work, but do not assume that everyone wants the same things. Some people may want 'enriched' jobs with greater autonomy, feedback etc. but some will not.

3   'Individualize' the organization. Expectancy theory proposes that people have different needs, values etc. Because of these

individual differences, it is important to allow people some opportunity to influence not only the type of work they do, but many other aspects of organizational life, such as reward systems, the format of the suggestion scheme or the fringe benefits offered by the business.

TQM provides opportunities to make and influence behaviour and attitudes that have real effects on internal and external relationships and the way the organization conducts its business. Any changes and restructuring will have to be achieved by a process of continuous and ongoing change. To build culture change into all of an organization's processes is a time-consuming task and not a part-time activity. It is also not 'one-off', but must continue in the spirit of continuous improvement. It is also important to note that making and sustaining the necessary change in company culture, at the same time as running a day-to-day business operation, is far from easy.

Changing people's behaviour and attitude is one of the most difficult tasks facing management. 'Resistance to change' is a term often used by managers to describe the situation when the improvement process goes into one of its troughs. However, many managers frequently use the excuse that it is the workers' attitude that is the main stumbling block to improvement and that it is not possible to change workers' behaviour, attitudes and approaches. Unfortunately, many of the managers making these claims have themselves not given the necessary long-term commitment to continuous improvement, and have failed to show the necessary leadership in this area. They sometimes forget the very simple lesson of 'seeing is believing'. They should be prepared to accept the more participative approach that TQM most certainly requires. As already discussed, TQM is about making incremental as well as step improvements.

Today, many managements have set themselves the objective of developing their organization towards a 'Total Quality Culture'. Unfortunately, this is capable of wide-ranging interpretation within the organization. To fully appreciate the task and implications of organizational change to such a culture, managers and organizations must understand not only assumptions about individual motivations and learning, but also the process itself, various strategies for change and individual resistance to change. The rest of this chapter deals with these issues.

Organizational Change

In order to deal with the introduction of TQM in an organization, it is important to understand the process of organizational change. This is frequently referred to as organizational development (OD), which usually refers to changing the total organization. Richard Beckhard (1969) suggested that OD interventions usually have the following five characteristics:

- they are planned
- they are organization-wide
- they are managed from the top
- they are attempting to increase the organization's effectiveness
- they are usually involved in changing not only the structure but also the organization's processes and attitudes

All of these five characteristics are relevant, and can be observed in the development of a total approach to the management of quality. For senior managers to understand organizational change, they must be aware of the process of change, the strategies that are available for change and the resistance to change.

The Change Process

BREAKING DOWN BARRIERS

Whatever type of change strategy is being used, change takes energy, time and resources since there is always inertia in the system that has to be overcome. Organizations by their very nature are not meant to change. They are social structures intended to make employees' behaviour more predictable and efficient by rationalizing it in the form of a bureaucracy. In relation to TQM, Lascelles and Dale (1989) identify six forces or triggers;

- the chief executive officer
- demanding customers
- competition

- the need to reduce costs
- a restart situation venture
- a greenfield venture

They go on to make the point that demanding customers are the key external change agent and the chief executive the key internal one.

Kurt Lewin (1951) suggested that change is a three-stage process, whether it be at an individual, group or organizational level. These three stages he refers to as *unfreezing*, *change* and *re-freezing*. He describes them as follows:

Unfreezing. Before any change can take place, the established methods and patterns of behaviour have to be broken down. People may be unaware of these established procedures until their attention is directed to them. Only when attention is drawn to them may their effectiveness be challenged. This demonstration of current ineffectiveness is essential for change to take place. People will only willingly become involved in a change process once they have accepted the need for change. The early activities of an organizational change programme are usually designed to bring about this unfreezing.

Change. Once current behaviours and attitudes are unfrozen it is possible to work on the change process. This can be done using any of the following interventions: strategic planning activities, goal setting, coaching and counselling, team building (including the development of cross-functional teams), techno-structural changes, a formal programme of education and training etc.

Re-freezing. For people to operate effectively, their behaviour must be reasonably stable. An individual or organization in a state of constant change will achieve little. This means that the new behaviour must be allowed to stabilize. Usually people are very good at doing this for themselves. All that is needed is time for re-freezing to occur naturally. Sometimes activities are included towards the end of a change programme that are designed to enable participants to look forward and review the effects of the planned changes. If these are perceived as beneficial, this review will aid the change process.

A key issue for European organizations in a difficult trading environment is how TQM can be introduced or maintained in organizations that are engaged in downsizing and delayering. One hypothesis would be that a context of rationalization with an associated fear factor is likely to provide a hostile climate in which to make change. TQM demands a high-trust set of relations, and in such a context a low-trust dynamic is more likely to be operating. On the other hand, a crisis situation is often thought to be a key factor in helping overcome organizational inertia and getting staff to see the necessity for change (Pettigrew, 1985), as indeed was the case at Xerox when it embarked on TQM using the 'Quality Through Leadership' approach in the early 1980s. However, it may be such that a reaction to crisis brings about compliance (or temporary cooperation) rather than real commitment (Hill and Wilkinson, 1995, pp. 21–2). Moreover, while it may be one thing for employees to accept that a crisis calls for radical action, they may be less willing to accept management action in downsizing once smoother waters are reached and the survival of the organization is not at risk. In such circumstances 'working for the good of the company' may seem a hollow phrase.

TOP-DOWN CHANGE

An important point to note is that change does not happen by itself. As Makin et al. (1989) suggest, there must be some source that initiates the change. This source must have sufficient power to be able to influence others in the direction of the desired change. In organizational change programmes, the source is usually located somewhere in the management hierarchy. There is, in fact, a view that any organizational change will only be successful if it is initiated by top management as they are the only group with sufficient power to make the change programme happen.

This is certainly true in the case of TQM. However, there are a few successful organizational change projects that have started at the bottom and worked up; the introduction of quality circles and the use of tools and techniques such as statistical process control (SPC) and failure mode and effects analysis (FMEA) are examples of this. This bottom-up approach in relation to TQM, while easier to start and involving little risk, may be difficult to sustain. It is only top management who have the authority to initiate, standardize and institutionalize real, irreversible change. However, in some organizations this approach has worked and has succeeded in changing the management style and behaviour. Some organizations in their approach to TQM have used both top-down and bottom-up methodologies and, through this pincer movement, have involved middle management and brought them into the process at a much quicker rate.

Strategies for Change

While 'openness', 'trust', 'truth' and 'care' remain the ideals of many change agents, there is a recognition that most organizations do not operate on these principles. Change strategies have to be adapted to suit the prevailing circumstances. Chin and Benne (1976) have defined what they call 'general strategies for effecting change in human systems'. They suggest that there are three of these, which provide a good framework for defining change strategies, both in organizations and, more widely, in society as a whole:

Empirical–rational strategies. Such strategies assume that people are basically rational. Change can be effected, therefore, by showing that it is in the individual's own interest to change. This is sometimes referred to as 'enlightened self-interest'. Change is achieved by the use of data and rational persuasion. The assumptions underlying this strategy lie deep in traditional education, and include a belief in the benefit of research and the general dissemination of knowledge. The communication and discussion of the quality requirements of customers can help to facilitate this change, including presentations by customer representatives, and also by participation in the improvement teams of both customers and suppliers.

Normative/re-educative strategies. Such strategies do not deny the rationality of human beings. They place more emphasis, however, on the belief that behaviour is largely determined by the social and cultural norms of the group or society to which people belong. Individuals have a strong commitment to conforming to, and maintaining, these norms. Successful change is therefore accomplished by changing these norms. This is achieved by a mixture of education, training, persuasion and peer pressure.

Power–coercive strategies. These strategies involve the use of physical, resource, or position power to coerce individuals into changing. The use of physical power is widely used by governments when adopting this strategy. At the organizational level, resource or position power is the more usual source. Chin and Benne (1976) point

⌐ut that passive resistance, along the lines used by Ghandi, is also an example of the power–coercive approach.

To aid understanding of the use of these strategies, the attempts of the British government to get both drivers and front-seat passengers to wear the seatbelts provided in cars is described, followed by some examples from the continuous improvement field.

The seatbelt case A considerable amount of time and money was spent using empirical–rational strategies. These involved advertising campaigns giving information on safety factors – 'you know it makes sense'. All of this had little effect. The government then switched to a power–coercive strategy. Not wearing a seatbelt became an offence, punishable by fines. The result was that seatbelt usage leapt overnight to in excess of ninety per cent. The maintenance of this high level of seatbelt wearing is now most probably due to normative/re-educative influences. Wearing seatbelts has become the norm. While the threat of fines is still in the background, it is suspected that most people would, even without this, continue with the new behaviour. In Kurt Lewin's terms, power–coercive strategies were necessary for the unfreezing and change processes. Normative/re-educative strategies produced the re-freezing.

CONTINUOUS IMPROVEMENT EXAMPLES

Several examples of these strategies are evident in the process of continuous improvement. In the majority of cases, the process has had to be started by the power–coercive strategy, the reason for this being that many companies have not adopted an aggressive or positive stance in improving the quality of their products and service without outside pressure.

Lascelles and Dale (1989) stress the importance of a demanding customer as a major external change agent; for example, a contractual requirement of a customer that its suppliers should use SPC and provide it with process capability data.

Another example is that of the quality system having to meet the requirements of the ISO 9000 series of quality standards in order for an organization to bid for business from particular customers.

Three automotive companies, Chrysler Corporation, Ford Motor Company and General Motors Corporation, have developed the

QS 9000 Quality System Requirements, which applies to their supplier base, internal and external, worldwide. The foundation for
QS 9000 is ISO 9001 (1994). In addition to the twenty requirements of
this standard there are supplemental quality system requirements.
Sector-specific requirements and customer-specific requirements
form the remaining sections of QS 9000.

All production and service part suppliers to Chrysler must be third-
party registered to QS 9000 by 31 July 1997 and to General Motors by
31 December 1997. The Ford Motor Company, in addition to
QS 9000, still requires its suppliers, internal and external to achieve
Q1 status; this is a preferred supplier award system that has been in
existence for many years. In July 1995 Ford's suppliers were told to
'begin the implementation of the new QS 9000' but the dates for
compliance were less specific than with Chrysler and General
Motors.

Motorola requires that all of its eligible suppliers sign a statement
of their intent to apply for the Malcolm Baldrige National Quality
Award. Any supplier that does not wish to compete is disqualified as
a supplier. This initiative by Motorola to coerce participation stimu-
lated considerable debate (see the letters column of *Quality Progress*,
November 1989).

The president of Aeroquip required all of the company's sites to
achieve the AQ+ award by 1996. AQ+ is an internal Quality Award
modelled on the MBNQA criteria. A score of a minimum of
700 points is required from a total of 1000 points. A score of at least
60 per cent is required for each of the eight categories. The assessment is carried out on site by eight internally trained examiners from
different Aeroquip locations and each formal assessment includes the
vice prescient of Quality Performance. Re-qualification is required
every two years. This, in addition to the minimum points requirements of 60 per cent in each category, requires an increase in the
results score.

Certain minimum criteria such as these have now become the
order qualifying criterion in many markets and customer–supplier
situations: normative/re-educative strategies. In many cases, the
results achieved and the stimulus of prestigious quality awards such
as the Deming Application Prize in Japan, the Malcolm Baldrige
National Quality Award and the European Quality Award have
caused some organizations to undertake continuous improvement
activities out of their own self-interest–empirical–rational strategies.

Individual Adaptation

So far change strategies have been considered from the point of view of someone trying to change others. To complete the picture, *how* change takes place within the individual needs to be considered. Kelman (1985) has provided a social influence model for this. He suggests that there are three mechanisms for change, which can be seen as responses to the attempted influence of others, as Makin et al. (1989), outline:

Compliance. Individuals change simply because they are unable to resist the pressure being placed upon them. This is a common response to physical, resource or position power. In some cases, if there are rewards, or at least no costs, for the individual, the change may become internalized and hence relatively permanent. Often, however, this is not a good way to create change, since the response is, at best, relatively passive. When the pressure is removed, the original behaviour and attitudes are likely to recur. At worst, it results in counter-dependence, and individuals may expend considerable energy and ingenuity in finding ways to avoid changing.

Identification. This is a frequent response to personal power. The person being influenced changes because of his or her desire to resemble the source of power. This may be because of admiration or being inspired by the individual concerned. The lifetime of change by identification may be long, with the change becoming internalized. It may equally be quite short lived, particularly if less admirable aspects of the source of influence suddenly become apparent. A charismatic chief executive officer who has made a personal commitment to TQM has been known to have considerable influence on his or her people; in some cases, problems have been experienced with sustaining the momentum when the CEO has changed companies (see Bunney and Dale, 1996).

Internalisation. This is the most effective form of change, since the individual accepts the change and adopts it as part of his or her own self-image. Inevitably, this form of change is likely to take longer than compliance and identification, hence time must be allowed for it to occur. It is likely to be slowed down even further if there are strong pressures for change. Individuals must be allowed to develop commitment in their own time. However, once this commitment has developed, the change is relatively permanent.

Unintended Consequences

It is also important continually to evaluate actions taken to analyze unintended consequences. Most actions taken to solve problems in turn create further unforeseen problems. For example, systems set up to ensure that things run smoothly gradually become more bureaucratic and become ends in themselves. Similarly, senior management who plan to get middle management to take quality seriously, by incorporating appraisal criteria relating to the number of improvement teams established, control charts in use etc. should not be surprised when the middle managers can point to a vast array of teams running and control charts established for a number of product characteristics although they may produce little in terms of results and improvements. Payment systems introduced to motivate staff by providing an incentive element, e.g. payment by results (PBR), can lead to the tendency to increase output at the expense of conforming product. Thus, management need to be very careful in setting performance indicators. If senior management focus on these indicators to the extent that employees feel they *must* meet these targets, it may be that they will focus their energies on 'improving' the indicators without overall performance being improved, i.e. against the spirit of the initiative. Moreover, the effect may be that 'data' is lost through being unreported or hidden and thus the chance to make improvement is also lost. If employees are fearful of what the results may show, the temptation must be to cover up and in this way reinforce the 'them and us' situation.

Resistance to Change

Finally, we need to look at resistance to change, particularly as there are two popular myths concerning it. The first myth is that people universally dislike change, and will attempt to avoid it. While it is

certainly true that change programmes (including TQM) often pro-
voke resistance, this is by no means a universal reaction. Indeed, on
many occasions people accept change and may look forward to it. If
this were not so, the rapid rate of change in relation to product and
service improvement that has happened in many European organizations would not have taken place. The reality is that the majority of
the population of the developed world has adapted to enormous
changes, both in technology and way of life, over the last few
decades. Rogers and Shoemaker (1971) have suggested that people
fall into five different types: *innovators, early adopters, majority*
(early), *majority* (late) and *laggards*:

* Innovators are quick to adapt to new ideas and to change accordingly. They are also risk takers, as some of the new ideas may
  prove to be mistaken and/or difficult to adopt and put into
  place.

* Early adopters follow closely behind the innovators, but are
  rather more respectable and tend to conform with societal norms.
  They are not seen by the rest of society to be as non-conformist
  as the innovators.

* The early majority take on change once it has started to become
  accepted.

* The more conservative late majority wait to see all of the effects
  before adopting change.

* Finally, the laggards are very suspicious of change and are slow
  to adapt.

Rogers and Shoemaker (1971) suggest that the largest number of
people fall into two 'majority' classifications, with far fewer occupy-
ing the extreme 'innovator' and 'laggard' positions. It might also be
the case that individuals vary according to the nature of the
change.

The other myth is that resistance to change is necessarily a 'bad'
thing. Sometimes such resistance may be healthy. Both people and
organizations need periods of stability to re-freeze and absorb the
changes that have already taken place. Also, the existence of resistance may be an indicator that, for some reason, a particular change
is not considered desirable. In such cases a closer look is needed at

the root causes of the resistance, and this in itself may produce an improvement.

REASONS FOR RESISTANCE

Where change is resisted it may be for a number of reasons. Sometimes people believe that the change is likely to be to their disadvantage and even to that of the organization itself. On occasions this may indeed be true. It can hardly be a surprise if people's jobs are at risk or if they have worries about whether or not they can cope with the new concepts, procedures, systems, skills, practices etc. that they will resist the related change. A good example of this is the worry among some shop-floor operatives that SPC would expose their lack of numeracy and literacy, and that they do not have the time in their day-to-day production routines to measure process parameters and/or product characteristics, carry out calculations and plot the data on control charts. Another example is that engineers often believe that they do not have the time in their jobs to contribute to the preparation of FMEA and the subsequent use of the results. Sometimes, it is felt by employees that changes are being made by a manager to establish his or her own personal mark as a form of 'impression management', and that it is unlikely to last for very long as new managers in turn do the same. The fear of change is often enhanced by the secretive manner in which change programmes are planned and implemented; fortunately this is not usually the case with the introduction of TQM into an organization! In some cases, the outcomes of improvement projects may not be actioned and as well publicized if there is any doubt about the successful outcome of the activity. This failure to communicate is often done, of course, because management fear that people will find ways of blocking the changes if they are aware of them in advance, and also because they themselves are unsure at the early planning stage of the likely outcomes of the change. Paradoxically, the secrecy itself makes people suspicious and often leads to the very behaviour that management had hoped to avoid. Secrecy, therefore, becomes a self-fulfilling prophecy.

Change will always involve some effort, as new ways of doing things have to be learnt. For some people the fear of the unknown will be a major factor, especially if there are high levels of insecurity and dependency. Again, using the example of SPC, when it is being introduced on a particular process as part of a pilot programme, there is a tendency for operators and first-line supervisors to react with the comment 'why us and not them?' and sometimes 'why them and not us?'

Other sources of resistance, may lie in the social system. The existing norms of the group of organization will usually be very powerful. These are necessary, of course, as they provide the rules within which people relate to each other and work together. Change may require that these norms are changed in some way. Problems may also arise if change programmes are instituted in only one part of an organization. This may cause imbalance elsewhere, which will be resisted as a means of restoring the balance. Other resistances, of a social nature, may be due to the change agent threatening vested interest or 'sacred cows'. If change programmes are carried out by outside consultants, there may also be an element of suspicion of outsiders and the view of 'what can they teach us?', 'all talk and no action', 'what do they know about the industry?', 'clever dicks from outside' and 'we are teaching them whereas it should be the other way around'. The use of a package from a management consultancy is employed by many organizations to start a process of quality improvement and this suggestion of suspicion needs to be recognized.

OVERCOMING RESISTANCE TO CHANGE

There is overwhelming evidence that the best way to reduce resistance to change is to involve those whom it is going to affect in the decision making process. Individuals who have been involved in the diagnosis, planning, devising and implementation of change are far more likely to feel positively about it. In general, they will feel more committed, which will lead to speedier and improved implementation. When managing a process of change the human trait of people wanting to support their own ideas should never be forgotten. Natural leaders within a business can also assist with breaking through the barriers of resistance to change.

The ideal situation is where all the necessary information is freely available, and decisions are then taken by consensus. There will, however, be occasions when it is not possible to be totally open (for example if some of the information is commercially sensitive). As Makin et al. (1989) continually emphasize, the general rule should be

that good communication and feedback channels should be established between the source of change and those who will be affected.
Even where there are short-term costs, such as a need for retraining,
it is necessary to show that there will be long-term benefits, such as
improved pay, improved job security, better working conditions,
avoidance of a takeover, achievement of a prestigious quality award,
the award of customer contracts etc. Obviously, it will be easier to
effect change if there is a general climate of trust in the organization
where people feel that their fears will be listened to, and their
problems recognized and dealt with in a sympathetic manner.
Ideally, the programme itself should be open to change in the light of
such feedback.

Cultural Change

Changing culture has become one of the most hyped and written
about areas of management and it is a relatively new phenomenon.
Management had historically been seen as concerned with planning,
organizing and controlling, largely an administrative function. A
number of books written in the USA in the 1980s suggested that
culture was a primary weapon for management in the battle for
competitive advantage. Ouchi (1981), Pascale and Athos (1981), Deal
and Kennedy (1982) and Peters and Waterman (1982) argued that
strong cultures could lead to better performance and that one of the
main responsibilities of senior management was to manage corporate culture. There is little doubt that the notion of culture has flooded
rather than seeped into management thinking and there has been a
burgeoning interest in initiatives such as customer care, BPR, team
building and organizational change initiatives, as well as TQM, which
have sought to change culture or 'mindsets'.

The assumption is that managers with a vision can use various
tools and techniques to manipulate culture. This takes a particular
stance on culture. For 'purists' culture is something an organization
is: 'culture is a socially constructed system of shared beliefs, mean-
ings and values. It emerges from the social values of organisational
members and is the product of shared symbols and meaning' (Bright
and Cooper, 1993, p. 22). In contrast, cultural 'pragmatists' define
culture as something an organization *has*: 'a set of variables to be
managed in the pursuit of organisational objectives' (p. 23). The term

culture is used very loosely in management today. It originates from studies of 'primitive' societies in the nineteenth century. The term has now been used to look at smaller social groups such as organizations.

Corporate culture is a somewhat ambiguous concept and is difficult to define. Schein's (1985, p. 9) definition encompasses the most key aspects of culture:

> a pattern of basic assumptions – invented, discovered, or developed by a given group as it learns to cope with its problems of external adaptation and internal integration – that has worked well enough to be considered valid and, therefore, to be taught to new members as the correct way to perceive, think, and feel in relation to those problems.

Corporate culture, then, is not easily observable, and it is not the same as the behaviour one can observe when studying organizations. It can be seen as existing on several levels, with different features attached to each level. (Huse and Cummings, 1985; Kotter and Heskett, 1992; Schein, 1985). The basic idea is that corporate culture's deeper levels, the basic assumptions and the values – what Schein (1985) refers to as the 'essence of culture' – exist on an invisible level. These assumptions and values are seen as extremely difficult to change, hence any attempt to change them will require a long-term effort by senior management. In contrast, we have what Kotter and Heskett (1992) term the 'group behaviour norms', and Schein (1985) and Huse and Cummings (1985) call the 'cultural artifacts' which one can observe when visiting an organization. These are typically easier to change and are the manifestations of culture (e.g. office layout, dress code, architecture).

In recent years managing culture change has become one of the most debated issues in management literature. Because organizations are faced with an environment where change is almost a part of the daily routine, organizations must adapt and change accordingly. However, Huse and Cummings (1985) suggest that organizations should always try other solutions before attempting cultural changes. Similarly, Kotter and Heskett (1992) argue that the difficulties involved in managing these processes are often underestimated. Not only are such changes disruptive to the organizational processes and procedures, they are also disruptive to the members of the organization. It should also be said that some changes in culture (eg. elimination of reserved car parking spaces) are relatively easy to make but the benefits are short-term, whereas others are more difficult (e.g. managers become coaches rather than supervisors) but the effects are longer term.

The role played by leaders is an integral part of most texts on culture and change (see Kotter and Heskett, 1992; Peters and Waterman, 1982; Schein, 1985). Leaders have been found to play an instrumental role in guiding the organization through cultural change, as well as other organizational change processes (Huse and Cummings, 1985). As Kotter and Heskett (1992, p. 92) note, 'Leadership from one or two people at the very top of an organization seems to be an absolute essential ingredient when major cultural change occurs'. Moreover, this process has to come from the top, because to change cultures one needs power at the level only found at the top of organizations, and usually the scope of change is of such magnitude that only top management are in a position to carry it through (see Brubakk and Wilkinson, 1996).

Learning that is embodied within culture arises through the process of dealing with threats or by the positive reinforcement of successful behaviour, with the resulting assumptions eventually leading to habitual behaviour. Moreover, as Morgan (1986, pp. 126–7) observes:

> Culture is not something that is imposed on a social setting. Rather, it develops during the course of social interaction. In organizations there are often many different and competing value systems that create a mosaic of organizational realities rather than a uniform corporate culture.

Furthermore, the role and influence of middle managers and supervisors receive little attention in the corporate culture literature. However, according to Kotter and Heskett (1992, p. 93), middle managers play an important part in major culture change – 'Ultimately, it is their actions that produce the changes' – although they are not seen as being able to initiate such changes.

Organizational Culture

If TQM, as Oakland (1989) maintains, is 'a way of managing the whole business organization to ensure complete customer satisfaction at every stage, internally and externally', then it could be a way of changing corporate culture to manage change in a more customer-responsive manner. Achieving cultural change is central to what TQM is about. Deming (1982) does not mention the term TQM but his fourteen points encourage managers to change the way in which the organization is managed (i.e. cultural change).

However, cultural change is problematic. While TQM may be seen as an answer to the problem of large companies suffering from 'rigid hierarchies which isolate top management, confine middle management to administrative roles and frustrate operational and supervisory management in their decision making' (Thurley and Wirdenius, 1989), TQM alone may not be able to overcome all these problems. The corporate culture of the organization and existing ways of doing things might be too strong for TQM. Indeed, existing ways of doing things constitute the main barriers to TQM's successful adoption in the first place; that is, quality management is often introduced so as to operate within existing structures and cultures rather than being used as a vehicle to transform them (Wilkinson and Witcher, 1993). Thus, the emphasis is on how to make existing processes work better rather than on altering those processes in the first place. This is particularly true when it is considered as an evolutionary process from a base of quality assurance. As Burack (1991) notes, 'established organization cultures are not easily modified because their very reason for existence often rests in preserving stable relationships and behaviour patterns'. Thus, it may be that rather than viewing TQM as a process for changing organizations, conversely organizations must change to accommodate TQM (Wilkinson and Witcher, 1993). In reality it is a mix of both.

Mechanisms of Culture Change

According to Schein (1985), there are five primary mechanisms for the culture change:

- what leaders pay most attention to

- how leaders react to crises and critical incidents

- role modelling and teaching by leaders

- criteria for allocating rewards and determining status

- criteria for selection, promotion, and termination

Schein's secondary mechanisms for the articulation and reinforcement of culture are:

- the organizational structure

- systems and procedures

- space, buildings and facades

- stories and legends about important events and people

- formal statements of philosophy and policy

The central message arising from the work of Schein is that organizations devote too much time and attention to changing mission statements and changing organizational structure. What is far more important are the roles of leadership and the use of the full range of the organization's 'rewards and punishment' levers such as pay, appraisal and promotion. Mission statements and company values need to be underpinned by changes in senior management attitudes, which are likely to be reflected by new appraisal or pay criteria. In terms of TQM this means promoting those managers and employees who practise the principles of continuous improvement.

Programmatic change which starts with a 'big splash' educational approach intended to change the behaviour of individuals by changing their attitudes has been criticized as ignoring the fact that the change process in fact works in the exact reverse way, i.e. changed behaviour leads to changed attitudes and the most effective way to change behaviour is by changing the context in which people work by creating new responsibilities and relationships (Beer et al., 1990).

Summary

In this chapter we have examined various theories of motivation and their implication for managers and organizations. By examining these theories in the context of TQM, managers might better understand some of the road blocks typically encountered in the introduction and development of the concept. While the links between culture change and total quality ideas have attracted much attention in the popular management literature, there is little detailed guidance available which pays attention to the practical issues of managing culture in organizations. In the long term, there is a necessity for the introduction of both quality systems and a quality culture to facilitate a company-wide improvement process.

References

Beckhard, R. 1969: *Organizational Development; strategies and models.* Reading, Mass.: Addison-Wesley.

Beer, M., Esienstat, R. and Spector, B, 1990: *The Critical Path.* Boston Harvard Business School.

Bright, K. and Cooper, C. 1993: Organisational culture and the management of quality. *Journal of Managerial Psychology*, 8(6), 21–27.

Brubakk, B. and Wilkinson, A. 1996: Agents of change? Bank branch management and the management of corporate culture change. *International Journal of Service Industries Management*, 17(2), 22–44.

Bunney, H. S. and Dale, B. G. 1996: The effects of organisational change on sustaining a process of continuous improvement. *Quality Engineer*, 8(4), 649–57.

Burack, E. H. 1991: Changing the company culture. *Long Range Planning*, 24(1), 88–95.

Chin, R. and Benne, K. 1976: General strategies for affecting changes in human systems in W. Bennis, K. Benne, R. Chin and K. Carey, (eds), *The Planning of Change*, 3rd edn. New York: Rinehart and Winston.

Deal, T. and Kennedy, A, 1982: *Corporate Cultures.* Reading, Mass.: Addison-Wesley.

Deming, W. E. 1982: Quality, productivity and competitive position, Massachusetts Institute of Technology, Centre of Advanced Engineering Study, Cambridge, Mass.

Hackman, J. R. and Oldman, G. R. 1975: Development of the job diagnostic survey. *Journal of Applied Psychology*, 6, 159–70.

—— 1976: Motivation through the design of work: test of a theory. In *Organizational Behaviour and Human Performance.* Florida, Academic Press.

Hackman, J. R., Lawler, E. E. and Porter, L. W. 1977: *Perspectives on Behaviour in Organisations.* New York: McGraw-Hill.

Hill, S. and Wilkinson, A. 1995: In search of TQM. *Employee Relations*, 17(3), 8–25.

Huse, E. and Cummings, T. 1989: *Organisation Development and Change*. St Paul, Minn.: West Publishing.

Kelman, H. 1985: Compliance, internalization and identification: three processes of attitude change. *Journal of Conflict Resolution*, 2, 51–60.

Kotter, J. and Heskett, J. 1992: *Corporate Culture and Performance*, New York: Free Press.

Lascelles, D. M. and Dale, B. G. 1989: What improvement: what is the motivation? *Proceedings of the Institute of Mechanical Engineers*, 203(B1), 43–50.

Lawler, E. 1973: *Motivation in Work Organisations*. Belmont, Calif.: Brooks/Cole.

Lewin, K. 1951: *Field Theory in Social Science*. New York: Harper and Row.

Makin, P., Cooper, C. and Cox, C. 1989: *Managing People at Work*. London: Routledge.

Morgan, G. 1986: *Images of Organizations*. London: Sage.

Nadler, D. and Lawler, E. 1979: Motivation: a diagnostic approach. In R. Steers and L. Porter (eds), *Motivation and Work Behaviour*. New York: McGraw-Hill.

Oakland, J. 1989: *Total Quality Management*. London: Heinemann.

Ouchi, W. 1981: *Theory Z*. Reading, Mass.: Addison-Wesley.

Pascale. R. and Athos A. 1981: *The Art of Japanese Management*. New York: Simon & Schuster.

Peters, T. and Waterman, R. 1982: *In Search of Excellence*, New York: Harper-Row.

Pettigrew, A. 1985: *The Awakening Giant*. Oxford: Blackwell.

Rogers, E. and Shoemaker, F. 1971: *Communication and Innovation*. New York: Free Press.

Schein, R. 1985: *Organisation Culture and Leadership*. New York: Jossey-Bass.

Steers, R. and Porter, L. (eds) 1979: *Motivation and Work Behaviour*. New York: McGraw-Hill.

Thurley, K. and Wirdenius, H. 1989: *Towards European Management*. London: Pitman.

Wilkinson, A. and Witcher, B. 1993: Holistic TQM must take account of political processes. *Total Quality Management*, 4(I), 47–56.

8 Involvement at Work

Introduction

The development of people and their involvement in improvement activities, individually and through group activity, is a key feature of TQM and represents a rejection of the ideas of Taylorism. Several of the TQM experts advocate Employee Involvement (EI) and participation in decision making (see in particular Deming, 1982; Feigenbaum, 1991; Ishikawa, 1985) and this is reflected in the standard texts. Oakland (1989) writes of 'total involvement':

> everyone in the organization from top to bottom, from offices to technical service, from headquarters to local sites must be involved. People are the source of ideas and innovation and their expertise, experience, knowledge and co-operation have to be harnessed to get these ideas implemented.

A number of assumptions lie behind the view that EI is a key contributor to quality. Firstly, each employee has knowledge and experience to contribute to the organization's effectiveness. Secondly, the traditional management approach based on Taylorism provides little opportunity to become involved. Finally, if people do have an input then they are more likely to become committed to 'quality' (Hill, 1992).

Employee involvement is thus a cornerstone of modern TQM ideas, in terms of both an educational process and more direct involvement in quality issues and how it relates to the job. The TQM philosophy emphasizes that those doing the job should have the tools and resources to improve the process. This introduces elements of 'bottom-up' issue identification, decision making and problem solving, which contrast with traditional 'top-down' management style. Moreover, if there are areas to address that require collecting information or change elsewhere in the organization, the scope of jobs can be enhanced by introducing a horizonal dimension. In this way TQM may, 'empower' employees by delegating functions that were previously carried out by managers. However, empowerment is set within certain boundaries. Juran (1974), for example, felt that operators could use their tacit knowledge of work processes to achieve substantially higher levels of quality, and the task of management was to create the conditions that would facilitate their efforts, but employee activity would tend to be confined to diagnosing improvements in their own areas of work. Depending on the nature of the approach within the organization, (e.g. semi-autonomous working which combines authority with the responsibility for work), they might implement these themselves (Hill and Wilkinson, 1995).

Thus, management needs to be careful how it goes about 'empowering' workers, because unless the systems (which managers control) are changed, involvement offers few benefits to employees or to the organization as a whole. Deming (1986, p. 78) for example, is scathing of managers who establish 'employee involvement, employee participation, quality of working life as smoke screens' and sees hope soon withering away when managers show themselves to be unwilling or unable to take action on the suggestions for improvement. He points out that little will change until they remove the *fundamental* barriers to workmanship (Hill and Wilkinson, 1995).

A typical example of the type of empowerment that managers have in mind is illustrated by this quotation from a CEO in the USA: 'We're moving from an environment where the supervisor says "This is the way it is going to be done and if you don't like it go someplace else" to an environment where the supervisor can grow with the changes, get his troops together and say "Look, you guys are operating the equipment, what do *you* think we ought to do?" ' (cited by Evans and Lindsay, 1995, p. 403). But in many cases the employees only *suggest* what ought to be done, rather than *decide* what should be done.

In addition while much of the language of TQM is about increased involvement, there is also a strong emphasis on reinforcing management control through systems and procedures. In theory, TQM shifts the focus of responsibility for quality to the people who actually do the job and makes use of participative groups such as teams. The emphasis, in some types of improvement teams, is on mixing up people and functions to create empathy, to tackle the road blocks that arise in the implementation of planning and the service to the customer (Wilkinson and Witcher, 1991). In a plant of some 150 employees manufacturing corrugated products, the plan formulated by the senior management team was that every employee should visit a customer. The formulation of a number of the groups going about such visits was of a cross-functional nature to stress the importance of the internal customer–supplier concept and to break down departmental barriers.

In theory, TQM could represent a transformation from traditional authoritarian 'top-down decision making' to more task-oriented ideals premised on worker commitment and where there are flatter structures and a participative culture. However, if done properly, this requires a degree of participation that represents a major adjustment to the corporate culture and style of managing for most UK-based organizations (Wilkinson and Witcher, 1991).

Introduction and Maintenance of Employee Involvement

In research undertaken at UMIST a variety of reasons appeared to be important in influencing management to introduce employee involvement. These relate to:

1 Information and Education. Establishing direct lines of communication with all employees, and ensuring they are aware of the business position of the organization, recognize the importance of the customer, and understand organizational policy and values.

2 Commitment. A similar rationale to point 1, with the encouragement of employees to identify with the organization and exercise discretionary skills towards its success.

3 Securing enhanced employee contributions. Tapping into employee knowledge and ideas through problem solving approaches

and techniques (such as quality circles) and the encouragement to seek opportunities for improvement.

4   Recruitment and retention of labour. Employee involvement was seen as a vehicle for the attraction and retention of staff. Financial participation schemes linked with service criteria (e.g. minimum of two years service) are an obvious example, but other schemes were also seen to promote a favourable impression of the organization in both the product and labour markets.

5   Conflict handling and stability. This was often a less direct objective, and is associated with a better informed labour force having an improved understanding of management policies and decisions. It can include introducing consultative committees, in part as a 'safety valve'.

6   External forces. These include legislation, although the 1980s legislation on employee involvement was of the 'facilitative' kind in terms of encouraging financial participation rather than laying down mandatory schemes. They also include the adoption of 'best practice' from other companies and initiatives originating elsewhere in the organization, for example, corporate personnel policies or via consultants (Marchington et al., 1992).

There are a number of ways in which involvement and group participation through teamworking can be facilitated. These ways include quality circles, yield improvement teams, quality improvement teams, problem elimination teams, process improvement groups, corrective action teams, kaizen teams and cross-functional teams in areas such as design, quality assurance, costs, standardization, delivery and supply, plus natural groups or cells, which may be hybrids between quality circles and quality improvement teams. Some teams are formed from members of one functional area and have a narrow focus, while others, which are cross-functionally based, have a much wider focus and deal with some of the more deep-rooted problems, including internal customers and suppliers.

The effective solution of problems through any of these types of group activities facilitates the process of team building, and this, along with improved communication and understanding and people involvement and development, can often be as important as the actual outcome. Team building is a primary building block in the development of TQM. The Japanese appear to be much more comfortable with the use of teams as part of their continuous improvement efforts than is usually the case in European companies, where there is often a lack of attention to team activity and team building. This may be because of the divisive nature of Western industry – 'them and us', 'management and unions' etc. It is often the case in European organizations that management will decide on some form of team activity as part of an improvement initiative, throw the members together and expect the team to work in an effective manner without any form of coaching, direction, counselling or team building. Central to TQM is the involvement of people in a more focused way.

Methods of Involving People

A wide variety of methods can be used to help establish involvement in the workplace and create an environment conducive to everyone participating in continuous improvement.

JOB ENRICHMENT, JOB ENLARGEMENT AND JOB ROTATION

Job enrichment   This was derived from Herzberg's theory of motivation, in which he emphasized the importance of 'motivators' at work – characteristics such as recognition, advancement and responsibility. This theory was extended by Hackman and Oldham's (1976) 'job characteristics model', which suggested that if you want to motivate or involve people in their work, it is essential that there is task variety, task significance, autonomy in the job and a feedback mechanism. Job enrichment, therefore, involves developing the job so that the individual has variety, perceives the job to be significant, has significant room for action or autonomy, and is given recognition and feedback on a regular basis.

Job enlargement   This, on the other hand, might include a number of the characteristics mentioned above, but tend to emphasize task variety – that is, extending the number of activities in which an individual worker is involved. It does not necessarily enrich the job in terms of the job characteristics model. The Japanese concept of total productive maintenance (TPM) is a good example of this. In natural and autonomous work groups machine operators can take on initial cleaning, eliminate sources of contamination and inaccessible areas, basic first-time servicing and maintenance, setting, self-checking etc. In this way a sense of 'plant ownership' is developed by the operators. TPM is discussed in chapter 9.

Job rotation   A variation on the theme would be job rotation, where employees are rotated from one job to another and perform all or most of the tasks that are involved in a process, whether in an office or factory environment. This can present a problem because it can generate 'Jacks of all trades and masters of none'. For it to be effective it needs very good initial and refresher training, plus clear, non-ambiguous procedures and working instructions.

The question arises, of course, as to which of these different approaches to use to develop the effectiveness of quality improvement group type activity. This will depend upon a number of factors, such as:

- the type of team
- the constituents of the team
- the objectives of the team
- how long the team has been in operation
- the type and degree of training that the team members have received
- the situation
- the projects to be tackled
- whether a consultant/facilitator is to be used
- the skills and preferences of the consultant/facilitator
- the assumptions about how change takes place
- existing organizational culture

The success of these schemes is well documented (Wall and Martin, 1987). For example, in a Dallas plant of Texas Instruments, maintenance workers were organized into nineteen-member cleaning teams, with each member having a say in planning, problem solving, goal setting and scheduling. It was found that this form of job enrichment decreased employee turnover from 100 to 10 per cent, with significant cost savings.

Although job rotation, enlargement and enrichment can produce benefits, the reorganization of the whole work environment, from top to bottom, is likely to be more successful and long lasting. This was shown in the job restructuring process called 'autonomous work groups' in both manufacturing and administration, which was much discussed if not widely implemented, in the 1970s.

AUTONOMOUS WORK GROUPS

As Wall and Martin (1987) describe them, ' a key feature of autonomous work groups is that they provide for a high degree of self determination by employees in the management of their everyday work. Typically, this involves collective control over the pace of work, distribution of tasks within the group, and the timing and organization of breaks; also participation in the training and recruiting of new members'. This differs from rotation, enlargement and enrichment in that the work group itself decides details of production, distribution and work group norms to a much larger extent than in the former job restructuring schemes.

Interesting examples of work redesign and participation programmes in Europe come from Philips, the manufacturers of electrical appliances and other equipment, mainly in their assembly operations. Most of these experiments took place during the 1960s in different assembly departments. For instance, autonomous work groups were set up in the bulb assembly and finishing departments, where thirty individual jobs were combined into groups of four, with a certain amount of job rotation. It was found that production costs were reduced by 20 per cent, defect levels were halved and output increased; worker satisfaction was no higher, but workers indicated a strong preference for the current job design in contrast to the old. In the black and white television factory, the same sort of results were attained with the autonomous work groups introduced there in the 1970s. Seven-person work groups were formed with twenty-minute work cycles and multiple job tasks (e.g. quality control, work distribution, material ordering etc). The evaluation programme in this department revealed that there was significantly lower absenteeism, lower waiting times for materials, better coordination and improved training, and component costs were reduced by 10 per cent; unlike the bulb department, greater satisfaction was expressed as well (den Hertog, 1977).

It can be seen from the above that some of the sources and manifestations of stress for the individual at work can be minimized (e.g. alienation), and many of the organizational objectives can be achieved (e.g. lower absenteeism, high productivity etc.), when conditions for improving the quality of working life through involvement and participation at the work site are introduced.

Autonomous work groups have found more recent expression in the growth of teamworking and the development of new forms of work organization such as cells. In these flexible work groups, as one writer calls them, 'work is assigned to the group rather than to particular individuals or roles' (Kelly, 1982). Others prefer the term 'high performance', but the definition is similar: 'a work group is allocated an overall task and given discretion over how the work is to be done, the groups are "self-regulating" ' and work without direct supervision' (Buchanan and McCalam, 1989). Many of the examples of teamworking come from the motor vehicle and chemical industries. At Scotchem, the contrast between old and new was clear. The old units were manually controlled, with workers changing the machines, manhandling drums and standing at filling points. The newer units are computer-driven and the unit is controlled by operators who input information to the computer from a terminal within the control room via local operator panels within the plant. In the new plants, operators rotate tasks among themselves and complete their own worksheets rather than have work allocated by a supervisor. The new management style is described as moving from being 'cops' to 'coaches', with the supervisor being a facilitator rather than a director of operations. The new approach requires less manual work but more knowledge of processes and greater teamwork, thus requiring social skills and creating opportunities for involvement (Wilkinson et al., 1993). Process and craft work have merged, and maintenance has become the responsibility of the team rather than a specialist department. Tacit skills are needed to override computer messages, as appropriate.

Similar findings are reported for the team-based high performance systems at Digital described by Buchanan and McCalam (1989). The teams, ten to twelve in number, had full 'front to back' responsibility for product assembly and testing, fault finding, and problem solving and maintenance. The research done at Digital pointed to two key factors that were important in explaining success. Firstly, the move behind this new approach was quite different to that behind the quality of working life movement in the 1960s and 1970s, being more business-oriented (to create competitive advantage) and much wider in its approach. Secondly, the context within which the teams operated was critical to their success. Management had a clear vision of how the teams fitted in with the broader business strategy and this was shared with all employees. Moreover, the teams were supported by a whole raft of other initiatives such as an open management style, open plan layout, flexitime, the removal of clocking and a payment system based on skills acquisition. This was vital to the full operation of teamworking in that it needed to be nurtured by the whole work environment within which it operated. Teamworking is unlikely, for example, to be very successful with an individualized payment system which cuts across the group ideal.

The extent to which these are typical examples is open to question. Teamworking appeared to be the goal of all the companies in recent UMIST research (Godfrey et al., 1996), but there was considerable variation in the degree to which teams existed and in the autonomy they were given. It appeared to be the norm to develop teamworking on the shop-floor and then to extend the practice into the support areas. The shop floor teams are sometimes aimed specifically at process improvements or alternatively they are workgroup teams whose role is wider than searching for process improvement and problem solving, acting as the basis of shop-floor organization and structure. At one company, Southco, teamworking was viewed as the normal mode of working, with the teams having considerable autonomy, controlling task allocation, monitoring of attendance, health and safety issues, and to a lesser extent the flow of production. The teams were responsible for choosing the areas that were measured (within certain guidelines) and setting their own year-on-year improvement targets. Some of the more advanced teams were allowed to set their own levels of overtime and also to recruit and train temporary workers when they felt it appropriate. However, in many of the other companies, teamworking was the ideal but movements towards it had been piecemeal in their adoption (Godfrey et al., 1996).

PROBLEMS ASSOCIATED WITH EI

Despite the fact that we have reason to believe that EI experiments have many beneficial outcomes, there are a number of problems and difficulties associated with their implementation. The following are some of the common potential problem areas:

1 Difficulties associated with the consequent changing roles of management and workers occasioned by these interventions.

2 Problems of designing and re-creating programmes to meet the specific needs of the different varieties of EI projects. In short, training is a problem in many Western business situations and needs improving.

3 Coping with the fears of first-line supervisors and middle management. The involvement from the outset of supervisors and middle managers, and discussion with them on redefinition of roles, is important. Placing responsibility for implementation in the hands of those whose future is threatened by EI is likely to shape the manner and enthusiasm with which they perform and is clearly a major issue. The concerns of supervisors have been well documented. Fears of job security, job definition and additional workload may lead to them withholding their support and damaging the initiative. Bradley and Hill (1987) have argued that the burdens involved in operating participative management are usually ignored by its advocates, so while the language of teamwork may be widespread, the reality is that in practice it can be little more than exhortation.

4 Dealing with the concerns of the unions, who may feel threatened that some of these approaches may affect the number of jobs, staffing levels and traditional communication channels. This is very much dependent upon the skills of management, a positive work environment and the opportunity to redeploy, with suitable training, 'excess' personnel.

5 Increasing costs during the initial phase of these interventions.

6 Organizations may have to change their systems to reflect the new culture. They may also need to examine the supporting infrastructure (e.g. management style, work layout, single status etc.).

In addition to these sequential implementation stages, and something that permeates the whole process of change in the worker participation and quality of working life fields are four underlying principles which, according to French and Caplan (1973), must be adhered to throughout:

1   The participation or change programme is not illusory, that is, it is not used as a manipulation tool (for example, when management asks employees for advice and then ignores it).

2   The decisions on which participation are based are not trivial to the people concerned (for example, management asking workers to decide on the colour of the paper to be used for the company's newsletter).

3   Those aspects of the work environment on which participation is based are relevant to the needs of the workers.

4   The decisions which people participate in are perceived as being legitimately theirs to make.

These conditions are critical guidelines in designing and developing processes that encourage involvement and work sharing, as major steps towards total quality management.

QUALITY CIRCLES

Quality circles are a direct form of employee participation in the business of any organization. A typical quality circle is a *voluntary* group of between six and eight employees from the same work areas (smaller and larger circles exist, but this is the average size). They meet usually in company time, for one hour every week or fortnight, under the leadership of their work supervisor, to solve problems relating to improving their work activities and environment. Quality circles are a means of providing employees with the opportunity to solve problems, and implement and monitor their solutions.

Dale and Oakland (1994) outline the typical operating characteristics of a quality circle as:

● the members join in a Circle voluntarily and can opt out as and when they wish.

● the members select the problems and projects which they wish to tackle.

- the seven basic quality control tools – Pareto diagrams, cause and effect diagram, quality control chart, check sheet, histogram, scatter diagram and graphs, are employed by the Circle members to find potential solutions to the problem being considered.

- the solutions are evaluated in terms of their cost-effectiveness.

- the findings, solutions and recommendations of the Quality Circle are presented to senior management for comment and approval.

- the Circle implements, where practicable, their recommendations. If this is not possible, the departments responsible for putting the recommendations into place should maintain a dialogue with the Circle concerning the progress being made and the likely date of implementation.

- Once implemented, the Circle monitors the effects of the solution and considers future improvements.

- the Circle carries out a critical review of all activities related to the completed project. This enables the members to identify ways by which they might improve their problem-solving activities.

A number of these features give quality circles a special character quite different from those of other methods of group working and group problem-solving.

While the experience with quality circles suggests that employees may decide not to participate in such bodies, Hill (1992) attributes this to inappropriate structures and argues that creating the right framework is the real obstacle to participation rather than employee resistance. Furthermore, involvement in such processes is said to benefit staff, improving their motivation, morale, work environment and skills, with the promotion of people building (Hill, 1992).

In Japanese plants, the line workers are involved with their foreman in making day-to-day improvements in their routine work and zone activities; and they do not appear to separate out, as is the case in the West, quality circle activities and day-to-day work activities. It is a more unified effort at shop-floor level, to meet the important targets of the section as established through the process of policy deployment and circle activities, which tend to be well managed by section managers. This is partly due to company organization around natural working groups or zone cells. In the West, quality circles are operated in an almost mechanistic way as part of a rigid system, whereas the Japanese establish a framework which allows for considerable autonomy and improvement activities to take place. In Japanese companies there is a clear relationship between quality circles and the suggestion scheme: circles can submit suggestions and their projects through the scheme, for which they are rewarded. These two initiatives are, in general, kept separate in Western organizations.

CHARACTERISTICS OF OTHER TYPES OF QUALITY IMPROVEMENT GROUPS

Superior performing companies operate a variety of teamwork related to quality improvement activity. Companies will often define the characteristics of their different forms of team activity, in particular, to separate out quality circle type activity from that of their other teams. The following two examples from Betz Dearborn (manufacturers of speciality chemicals) and Gould Corporation (electronics) are typical.

Betz Dearborn (Dale, 1994)

In deciding which quality improvement approach to use, the following three major factors should be taken into account:

- Where the idea for the improvement originated.
- The strategic significance of the improvement.
- Whether the improvement affects more than one major area of the company's operation.

These approaches, coupled with those improvements brought about by individual employees, provide the basis of continuous quality improvements.

1 *Management Action*
   The characteristics of quality improvement which is driven through by management action are as follows:

   - The need for change may have been identified at any level in the company.
   - The improvement objective has been defined by management.

- The process of quality improvement is management led.

- The objective can address both improvement and strategic issues.

- The process to be improved is owned by one department.

2 *Quality Project Teams*
The characteristic of project teams are:

- The need for change can have been identified at any level within the company.

- The objective has been defined by senior management.

- The project team is management led.

- The project team addresses strategic change.

- Achievement of the objective requires that a number of different functions within the company be represented in the team.

- The process to be improved is owned by more than one department.

3 *Quality Improvement Teams*
Characteristics of quality improvement teams are:

- The improvement need has been identified at a non-managerial level.

- The improvement objective has been defined and agreed with senior management.

- The process of quality improvement is employee led within the objective agreed above.

- The objective addresses improvement issues rather than strategic changes.

- The process to be improved is owned by more than one department.

Gould Corporation: involving employees in TQM The Gould Corporation is part of a Japanese-owned multidivisional company. The factory is the sole producer of the company's portable digital oscilloscopes. TQM was introduced in the late 1980s when it was clear that the company had a very departmentalized approach to its manufacturing process and that this was causing problems in terms of product quality. One central problem was that the company had a high proportion of long-serving staff which had grown cynical over the years, having experienced a number of short-lived initiatives (including quality circles) introduced by a number of different managers. Hence, it was important to mark out the initiative as something different, and the Managing Director, to show his commitment, interviewed all staff (then over 300) on a one-to-one basis, with meetings ranging from half an hour to over two hours. It was at this stage that the MD decided to appoint the Human Resources director to champion TQM. This was for three main reasons. Firstly, given that the company was stressing communication it made sense to place responsibility within the HR function. Secondly, it was felt that the wrong message (i.e. that quality is a manufacturing concern only) would be given if the quality department were given the responsibility for introduction. Thirdly, given some conflict and friction between different departments, it was important to have 'quality' steered by what was perceived to be a neutral body.

TQM was introduced and overseen by a Central Steering Committee (the Quality Improvement Team) comprising senior management and chaired by the HR director. At the centre of Gould's approach to facilitating employee involvement is an Error Identification Form (EIF). This report sheet, which can be filled in by any employee, starts with the statement, 'the following is preventing me from performing error-free work'. The EIF is filed with the coordinator (the HR director), who approaches either the supervisor or the Quality Improvement Team to address the issue, and the report stays in existence until the problem has been dealt with, whereupon the document is signed off by the employee who originated the enquiry. A list of outstanding EIFs is displayed on the notice-board to provide some peer pressure for those responsible for addressing the problems. There have been over 200 EIFs in less than two years, addressing problems ranging from poor lighting to product design.

The main benefits of TQM are seen as flatter structures and improved teamworking, particularly with the development of project teams. Before TQM was introduced design and production were organized around product families, but support functions were not. As departments grew this led to greater complexity, and departmental goals came to be seen as superior to project goals. Under the new approach half of the site's workforce and equipment was moved to facilitate a greater cross-fertilization of ideas.

In the early days – when it was important to demonstrate good faith and when a high proportion of the EIFs related to the physical condition of the building – the HR department was responsible for a variety of work, including the installation of new floors, ceilings and air conditioning. HR issues have been at the forefront of the TQM approach: all staff have attended a two-day quality seminar, with full union cooperation. Improvement, personal responsibility, involvement and self-development are all implicit in the approach. Staff are now less likely to 'go on living with problems' and the EIF provides a mechanism to address this, although there has been some middle management concern that this undermines their role. Communications have also been improved, with a TQ newsletter and noticeboards (updated every two weeks) to go alongside team briefing. Finally, performance appraisal now gives greater emphasis to quality and employees' willingness to change, and a recognition team is responsible for a variety of prizes, badges and certificates (Wilkinson, 1996).

While the Gould example dealt with a range of EI issues, the key issue from both this and the Betz Dearborn case studies is that it is not the name of the team activity that is important, but the structure of the team, its operating characteristics, remit, accountability and ability to facilitate improvements. If management initiate any form of improvement activity – be it quality control circles, quality improvement teams or suggestions schemes – they have an implicit responsibility to investigate and evaluate all recommendations for improvement, otherwise there is demotivation.

The emphasis on teamwork pervades literature. According to Hill (1991), teamwork offers real opportunities to bring about more collegial relationships within the managerial group, a decline in resistance to change due to sectional interests and less organizational rigidity. Oakland (1989) argues that 'much of what has been taught previously in management had led to a culture in the west of independence, with little sharing of ideas and information. Knowledge is very much like organic manure, if it is spread around, it will fertilize and encourage growth, if it is kept covered, it will eventually fester and rot'. He further argues that teamwork devoted to quality improvement changes the independence to interdependence through improved communications, trust and free exchange of ideas, knowledge, data and information.

Juran's (1988) notion of self-control suggests that responsibility for quality be assigned to those who control the quality of what they do. This is said to improve motivation by encouraging employees to find satisfaction in their own work. Furthermore, the supervisory climate is meant to support this, with fear of failure discouraged in favour of a search for failure. As Deming (1982) has argued, a drive through fear is counterproductive. It is felt that individuals who are blamed for mistakes are unlikely to search for them to put them right, and thus key systems failures will not be addressed. Thus, teams take responsibility, alleviating the strain on individuals. Working through teams also makes TQM seem less like a form of management brainwashing (Wilkinson and Witcher, 1991). Individuals and teams should have the power to improve their quality, and this must represent real authority and the ability to regulate what they do. They must not take responsibility for something that is beyond their control. Semi-autonomous work groups can help create the conditions for self-control, as advocated by Juran (1988).

TEAM BUILDING

According to Porras and Berg (1978), 40 per cent of all organizational change interventions involved team building. As already mentioned, teams are an essential part of organizations and, in particular, are valuable in helping to foster and develop TQM. They exist wherever several people need to cooperate to complete a task and/or to seek improvements. The emphasis in team building is usually on the manager or first-line supervisor and his or her immediate group of subordinates, and focuses upon improving the way the teams operate together. It may also be used at a more casual level, for example, with people who work together occasionally, but are not part of a formal team (e.g. in the internal customer–supplier relationship as part of a Departmental Purpose Analysis, or as part of joint problem solving between external customers and suppliers).

The origins of team building go back to the work of Elton Mayo, who built upon the early work of the Hawthorne studies to demonstrate the importance of social relationships at work. Other influences are the work of Kurt Lewin at the National Training Laboratories, and the development of the 'T-group' movement. In order to improve a team's effectiveness, it is common, in practice, to concentrate on one or more of a number of themes:

● Increasing mutual trust among team members.

● Increasing awareness of both your own and other people's behaviour.

● Developing interpersonal skills, such as listening, giving feed-back and bringing others into the discussion.

Deciding which themes are to be developed will depend upon a number of factors, in particular, the theoretical orientation of the consultant, trainer or facilitator who may be working with the team, together with the diagnosis of weaknesses in the team. Ideally, this diagnosis should be made in cooperation with the team members.

Role negotiation was developed by Harrison (1987) in order to take account of the issue of 'power' in organizations. In preparation for the negotiations implied in the technique's name, each team member considers each of the other members and prepares a list of items under the following three headings:

It would help me increase my effectiveness if you would:

● Do more of, or do better, the following . . . .

● Do less of, or stop doing, the following . . . .

● Keep on doing (i.e. maintain unchanged) the following . . . .

Members then meet in pairs to negotiate the changes that they would like to see and those that they are themselves willing to make. The negotiations are 'genuine' ones, in the form of 'I will agree to do X if you stop doing Y', or 'I will do A if you do B'. Negotiations continue until both parties are happy and agreement has been reached. The agreements are then written down and signed by both parties. It is part of the agreement that if one of the parties does not keep to the bargain, the other can use the sanction of withdrawing his or her half. The intention is that the negotiations should be done in such a way that there is an incentive to keep to the agreement, so as to gain the benefits promised by the other. Harrison makes the point that it is not legitimate, or necessary, to probe into individual feelings. What is required, however, is honesty. Threats and pressures, on the other hand, may be used, but it should be remembered that their use may lead to defensiveness. The role of the consultant/trainer/facilitator/ is to help the negotiators understand and keep to the guidelines, and to help them clarify the requirements for change. It is, of course, important that they do not actually influence the terms, but simply help the individuals to clarify their own ideas.

STRUCTURED APPROACH

This is based upon assumptions that change is best brought about by providing information so as to understand the processes within groups – a cognitivist approach. The core of this approach is a team building workshop or training course. This comprises a series of exercises, each designed to focus on some aspect of team working. The exercises are usually of a type known as 'substitute task exercise'. These are tasks that are not related in any way to the normal work of the group, but are designed to highlight some aspect of group process, such as competitiveness, goal clarity, use of tools and techniques, decision making etc. The fact that the task is unrelated to normal work makes it easier for the group to focus on the process, and avoids undue attention being focused on the particular task being undertaken. On the other hand, there could be a lack of motivation due to the non-reality or artificial nature of the tasks. It is common to use short questionnaires and other measures to bring out key aspects of team processes. These activities, assisted by interventions from the consultant/trainer/facilitator, help the group and individuals to gain a better understanding of how their present methods of working could be improved.

'Interaction process analysis' is an approach that enables participants to analyze what type of contribution each person is making to the group, and what the implications are for group effectiveness. It is based on the work of Robert Bales of Harvard, who designed a rather complex classification of the types of interaction that take place between individuals in groups (Makin et al., 1996).

One way in which this is used is for teams to take it in turns to observe the group, either when it is working normally or in special training sessions, and classify and count the types of contribution made by each team member. Alternatively, the consultant can undertake this task. The results are fed back to the group members, who consider their implications, both for individuals and for the group as a whole. It is not uncommon to find that certain individuals' contributions tend to be predominantly of one or two types. They are often surprised to discover this. Sometimes this is true for the group as a whole. There may, for example, be a great deal of giving of opinions and suggestions, but not asking. Sometimes categories such as 'gives support' are noticeably lacking. If this is the case, it is necessary for group members to widen the range of contributions they are making.

Summary

While employee involvement initiatives have spread widely in the UK organizations, the implementation in practice has been ad hoc and piecemeal, and the impact has often been limited. Employee involvement should not be seen as a bolt-on activity which is separate from the management of the organization as a whole. Senior managers should be clear about what the objectives are and should agree them with the management team as a whole. This may mean significant changes in existing management style, and this should be recognized at the outset. The methods of employee involvement used by an organization should be monitored and reviewed at regular intervals in order to assess their effectiveness and identify means of improvement.

References

Bradley, K. and Hill, S. 1987: Quality circles and managerial issues. *Industrial Relations*, 26, 68–82.

Buchanan, D. and McCalam, J. 1989: *High Performance Work Systems: The Digital Experience*. London: Routledge.

Dale, B. G. and Oakland, J. S. 1994: *Quality Improvement through Standards*, Cheltenham: Stanley Thornes.

Deming, W. E. 1982: Quality, Productivity and Competitive Position, Massachusetts Institute of Technology, Centre of Advanced Engineers Study, Cambridge, Mass.:

—— 1986: *Out of the Crisis*. Cambridge, Mass.: MIT Press.

den Hertog, J. F. 1977: The search for new leads in job design: the Philips case, *Journal of Contemporary Business*, 6, 49–67.

Evans, J. and Lindsay, W. 1995: *The Management and Control of Quality*, 3rd edn, St Paul, Minn.: West.

Feigenbaum, A. V. 1991: *Total Quality Control*. New York: McGraw-Hill.

French, J. R. P. and Caplan, R. D. 1973: Organizational stress and individual strain. In A. J. Marrow (ed.), *The Failure of Success*. New York: Amacom, p. 52.

Godfrey, G., Wilkinson, A. and Marchington, M. 1997: Competitive advantage through people? UMIST Working Paper.

Hackman, J. R. and Oldham, G. R. 1975: Motivation through the design of work: test of a theory. *Organisational Behaviour and Human Performance*, 16, 250–79.

Harrison, R. 1987: *Organizational Culture and Quality of Service*. London: Association for Management Education and Development.

Hill, S. 1991: Why quality circles failed but total quality might succeed. *British Journal of Industrial Relations*, 29, 541–66.

—— 1992: People and quality. In K. Bradley (ed.), *People and Performance*, Aldershot: Dartmouth.

Ishikawa, K. 1985: *What is Total Quality Control? The Japanese Way*. Englewood Cliffs, NJ: Prentice Hall.

Juran, J. M. (ed.) 1974: *Quality Control Handbook*, 2nd edn. New York: McGraw-Hill.

—— 1988: *Quality Control Handbook*, 3rd edn. New York: McGraw-Hill.

Kelly, J. 1982: *Scientific Management, Job Redesign and Work Performance*. London: Academic Press.

Makin, P., Cooper, C. L. and Cox, C. 1996: *Organisations and the Psychological Contract* London: Routledge.

Marchington, M., Goodman, J., Wilkinson, A, and Ackers, P. 1992: New developments in employee involvement, Department of Employment Working Paper, London.

Oakland, J. 1989: *Total Quality Management*. London: Heinemann.

Porras, J. I. and Berg, P. O. 1978: The impact of organizational development. *Academy of Management Review*, 3, 249–66.

Wall, T. and Martin, R. 1987: Job and Work design. In C. L. Cooper and I. T. Robertson (eds), *International Review of Industrial and Organizational Psychology, 1987*. New York: John Wiley & Sons.

Wilkinson, A. 1994: Managing human resources for quality. In Dale, B. G. (ed.), *Managing Quality*, 2nd edn. London: Prentice Hall, 273–91.

Wilkinson, A. 1996: Variations in total quality management. In J. Storey (ed.), *Cases in Human Resource and Change Management*, Oxford: Blackwell, 171–89.

Wilkinson, A. and Witcher, B. 1991: Fitness for use? Barriers to full TQM in the UK. *Management Decision*, 29(8), 46–51.

Wilkinson, A., Marchington, M. and Ackers, P. 1993: Strategies for human resource management: issues in larger and international firms. In R. Harrison (ed.), *Human Resource Management*, Wokingham: Addison-Wesley.

9 The Japanese Approach to Total Quality Management

Introduction

Many experts believe that quality, in its widest sense, is a key factor in the success of Japanese companies in world markets, and much has been written on this during the past decade or so.

In describing the development of quality control in Japan (Deming Prize Committee, 1996) the point is made:

> It is well known both inside and outside Japan that Company-Wide Quality Control (CWQC) or Total Quality Management (TQM), through the use of statistical methods has been widely practised in Japanese industry and has produced remarkable results, such as improved product and service quality, enhanced productivity and reduced costs.

In any text dealing with the subject of TQM, it would be a serious omission not to discuss the ways in which Japanese companies manage continuous improvement. There is also considerable benefit in learning from best practice, and in this way it is possible to discover pointers to the future strategic directions along which Western organizations should move if they are to gain competitive advantage.

Total quality control (TQC) and CWQC are the terms usually used in Japan to refer to TQM. It is the integrative strategic framework of the Japanese company and it is the qualifying criterion in their home market-place, with new product development being the order winner.

In the view of the authors there is no fundamental difference between TQC, CWQC and TQM in theory.

CWQC is defined by the Deming Prize Committee (1996) as:

> a set of systematic activities carried out by the entire organization to effectively and efficiently achieve company objectives and provide products and services with a level of quality that satisfies customers, at the appropriate time and price.

TQM is not merely perceived as desirable; it is considered essential by Japanese companies for their continued survival. A number of Japanese companies, through their considerable efforts over the past 25 to 30 years, have put the principles of TQM firmly in place and are totally committed to sustaining and advancing a process of continuous and company-wide improvement.

The chapter is structured under a number of broad headings: customer satisfaction, long-term planning, research and development, the motivation for starting TQM, organizing and planning for quality management and improvement, visible management systems, involvement of people, education and training, total productive maintenance (TPM) and just-in-time (JIT).

The data on which the chapter is based was collected by Barrie Dale, who led four study missions of European manufacturing executives to Japan to examine the Japanese approach to TQM in a selection of major manufacturing companies. At relevant points in the text comparisons are made between Japanese and European approaches to managing continuous improvement.

Customer Satisfaction

In Japan, the internal market-place is dominant and competition is fierce in manufacturing. This means that organizations need to be totally dedicated to satisfying customers. This effort must be long-term and continuous, otherwise they will be overtaken by the competition. Their internal market is saturated and demands ever-increasing product diversification and attractiveness, speedy response to market needs, rigorous reliability and quality of conformance. Japanese companies believe that bringing new products to the market-place quickly is the means by which they can sustain their competitive edge. 'The customer always comes first' and 'the customer is king' are terms used by organizations to describe their market-place spirit. Organizations are forever looking at the needs of the market. Japanese managers also comment that their customers' requirements for quality are becoming increasingly rigorous, and that these requirements are a moving target. Japanese companies concentrate on increasing market share and net sales, and not simply on the rate of return on investment.

There is a belief that business operations and efficiency can always be improved by reflecting customer needs and requirements. Japanese organizations have a variety of systems, procedures and mechanisms by which they can properly identify these needs and keep focused on the market. They go to considerable lengths to collect information (through talking and listening) on the wants and needs of customers, to obtain their opinions, better understand their expectations, and assess their satisfaction with products and services. For example, a manufacturer of ceramic products has a 4500 fixed points of observation from which data is collected.

Japanese companies believe that it is important for the engineers who are involved in the development of new products to go to the customers and locations where the equipment is being used and ask users (including field operators):

- what they feel about the product

- what bothers them

- what features new products should have

- what is required to satisfy customer needs, expectations, thinking and ideas

This knowledge, together with that accumulated through various means at the company and other means of listening to 'customer voices', is used in new product development in order to pinpoint the technical gaps of the competition. It also helps to identify product features and characteristics that the customer finds attractive and charming and which differentiate the product from those of competitors.

In Japan there is an implied expectation that customer expectations will be beaten. It is also common practice for Japanese organizations to use quality function deployment (QFD) in conjunction with the seven management tools (relations diagrams, affinity diagram, systematic diagram, matrix diagram, matrix data analysis method, process decision program chart and arrow diagram; see Mizuno, 1988) as the mechanisms for coordinating this type of data. These methods are also employed to clarify the required quality (objective and subjective) from the customer to translate customer wants into design requirements and build in quality at source. Detailed information is also developed on customer profiles, their current needs and future expectations. The databanks that Japanese organizations have built up on this are far in advance of anything encountered in European companies.

Long-Term Planning

Quality (including service), cost and delivery (accuracy and lead time) (QCD) are the main organizational objectives as a company strives to become the best in class in relation to QCD. This is a prime consideration in company vision, mission, policy and values statements. The evidence collected indicates that this has been the case in most Japanese companies for the past thirty or so years. Extensive use is made of mottoes expressing some appropriate message on QCD. This assists in keeping the theme in the forefront of employees' minds.

Japanese companies believe that their corporate strength is built up through TQM, and customer-oriented quality is foremost in every aspect of organizational corporate policy. This view is encapsulated in the point made by one organization that even if only one out of ten thousand products failed, the failure rate for that customer would be 100 per cent.

Planning, feedback and decision making on TQM is long-term, often extending at least ten years into the future. A series of middle-range plans of between three and five years are formulated to assist in meeting the long-term business plan and strategic themes.

One of the main TQM planning activities is the deployment of the President's annual management policy plan (developed from the company's long-range and mid-term plans) to all levels of organizational hierarchy (i.e. policy deployment). This process provides the skeleton for TQM and helps to turn strategic intent into an annual operating plan. This plan is made available to group companies at the beginning of a fiscal year. The deployment is carried out in the first place by the plant managers in their respective manufacturing divisions, and the plant manager's policy is successively deployed by each section/department manager to his or her area of responsibility through to foreman and line operators. The deployments are usually in terms of QCD. Figure 9.1 is an illustration of the policy deployment system from a manufacturer of ceramic products.

Each plant manager develops his or her annual policies, improvement targets and plans for every section and department of the plant(s) within his or her remit of responsibility to meet the president's policy. He or she decides the annual policy for the plant, and what key problems need to be tackled in relation to the president's policy. The policy is based on: the long-range business plan, the long-range plan for the plant's operation, the improvements that need to be made (taking into account an evaluation of the previous year's activities and performance). This policy is fully discussed and debated with each manager in relation to the annual policies and plans for departmental activities until a final target is agreed along with the methods and means to reach the goal. For example, the plant manager may suggest to a section manager a target of 5 per cent improvement and the section manager may reply with a suggestion of 2 per cent; this process continues until a target is agreed that all parties consider feasible within the time frame of the plan. The assessment of capability, setting and agreeing of targets and establishing the means is conducted through discussion and consensus – what the Japanese term 'Play Catch' or 'Catch Ball'. It is usual to set yearly and half yearly improvement plans and targets. The section manager then agrees with all of his or her foremen the activities, plans and targets for their groups, who in turn agree roles, targets, methods and improvement activities with each operator. Each division keeps a register of the improvement action agreed with staff.

In this way the improvement activities of an organization are focused on carrying out projects to meet these policies. This ensures integration and the internalization of objectives. Every employee understand his or her manager's policy and therefore knows what to do and understand that everyone is working in a common and unified direction to achieve the goals of the business. In addition, employees understand the issues that are important to the company, helping to facilitate relations between the different sections of the business.

There is a set timescale (usually six to eight weeks) for this policy management deployment activity to be cascaded down through all organizational levels. In each company, the policy deployment commences at a set time in the calendar year. The long negotiations that are involved in the deployment help to ensure consensus and that there is a genuine commitment at all levels to meet the agreed targets.

The control and review of policies are necessary to compare actual to planned performance, to identify gaps, problems and root causes, to determine countermeasures, to recognize and reward achievement. The regular reviews are generally made through:

- The president's diagnosis

- Plant manager and section manager diagnosis and monthly review of plant activities

- Discussion of achievements and improvement at plant and conferences on QCD

- For each section the daily management and records in terms of clarity of the section's function in the organization and the role of each person, clear points of control activities for improvement, standardization and taking corrective action.

The 'Plan–Do–Check–Act' cycle is extensively used in all these diagnoses (see figure 9.2). The results of these activities are reflected in the following year's policy and assist in improving the process of deployment.

It is usual for the plant manager to audit on a quarterly basis the progress being made by each section to achieve its improvement objectives, and for section managers to undertake a diagnosis of their sections at quarterly and monthly intervals. It is usual for the line operators to carry out a self-assessment of their achievements on a one-to-five scale against the agreed target. This written assessment is commented upon by the foreman and is followed up by a personal interview and, where appropriate, methods and plans are revised. The foreman then reports to the section manager on his achievement, the outstanding problems and the priority actions to be taken. This reporting procedure is continued up through the organizational structure. If there is low achievement against the target, a full and frank discussion will take place with all concerned to determine the

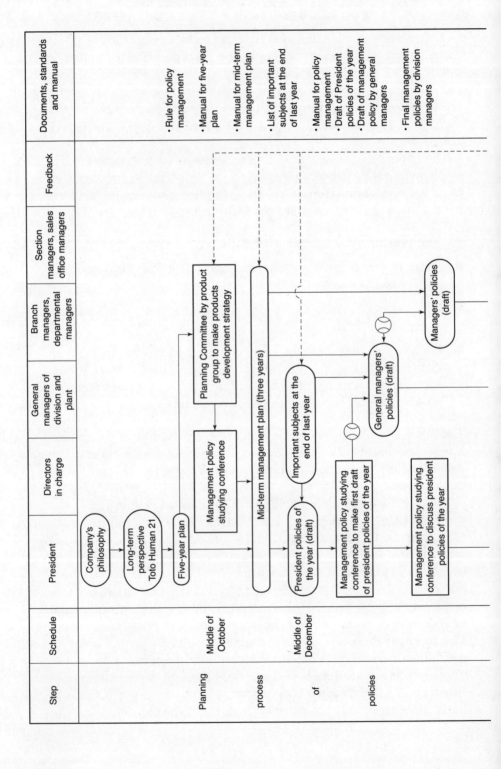

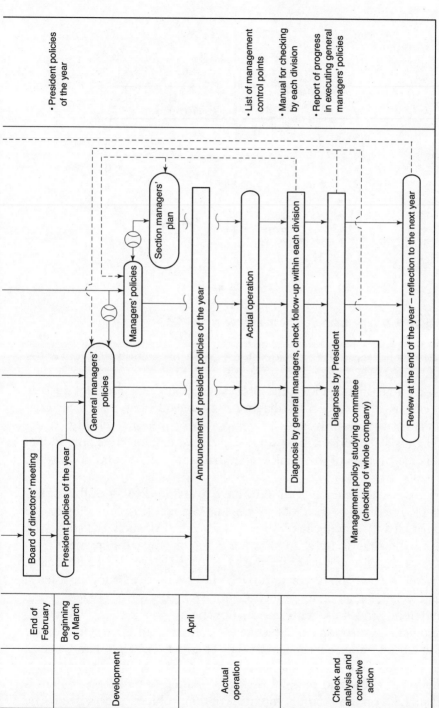

Figure 9.1 An example of the policy management system
Source: Toto Ltd, Chigasaki Works, Chigasaki City, Japan.

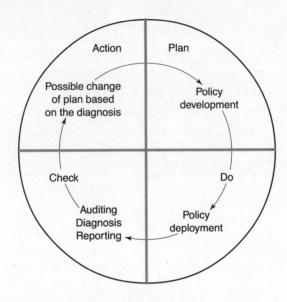

Figure 9.2 The plan-do-check-act cycle

reasons for this and to decide on the corrective actions to recover the situation.

In some organizations, the process of policy management deployments is also subject to diagnosis by outside experts (JUSE consultants and/or university professors). Any reports relating to the diagnosis are subjected to an in-depth examination. It is argued that it is the process of the deployment that is important, and not just the results.

It is usual for each section to have a visible display of this policy deployment as part of its visible management system. Figure 9.3 illustrates the key points of the typical format of such a display. The left-hand side of the chart shows the tree of policy deployment from the plant manager down to the level of each section. Each section makes its own plans for improvement based on existing problems. The overall rate of imperfection for each section is related to the different processes, with information being provided on individual problems. A proportion defective (p) control chart is used to monitor the rate of imperfection against the set target. The right-hand side of the chart displays annual improvement targets, for quality, cost, delivery, safety and morale. A slogan relating to the improvement is displayed on the board at the head of the problem to be solved. The

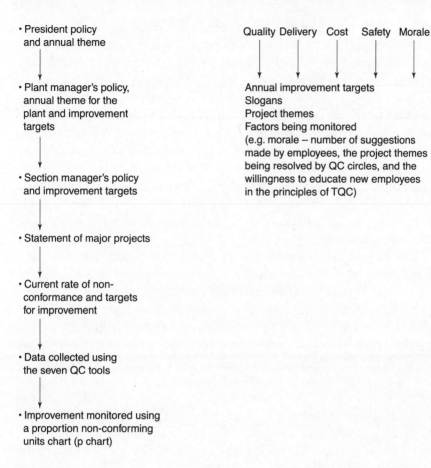

Figure 9.3 Key points of the visual display of policy deployment for a section

names of the workers who are responsible for the various activities relating to the policy deployment are also displayed. All of these plans include a number of provisions for the involvement of employees in the improvement process. Positioned at right angles to the board and completing the policy deployment 'corner' are pictures of typical imperfections in the section together with an improvement book. The book logs each improvement that has been made and helps to promote standardization. It also helps to serve as a point of reference for people on what type of improvements has been made in the past. For the manufacturing departments some organizations keep the specific details of deployment within the relevant offices, posting only the specific key actions, responsibilities and measures on the shop-floor policy deployment; in this way employees' attention is focused on the specifics rather than on the elaborate details.

Within each section there is an effort to solve at least two major projects each year; these projects are registered as themes and are derived from the policy deployment. This is in addition to activities of quality circles (QCs) (i.e. small voluntary groups of employees from the same work areas who meet on a regular basis under the leadership of their supervisor to solve problems relating to the work activities of their departments). In European companies there is a tendency by departments to try to solve too many problems at the same time, and as a consequence the improvement effort tends to be too thinly spread.

In European companies the job of the chief executive office is a lonely one. It is often the case that managing directors, plant managers and middle managers filter out information to the CEO. In Japan, the policy deployment and its visible display at shop-floor level not only ensures that the president has a window on what is happening in each section of each division under his or her control, but that all people are clear on the details of the president's policy and what is required by both their section and themselves to make the necessary contribution to the achievement of overall policy. This discipline of policy deployment and the agreement at each organizational level of achievable targets ensure that the energies of line operators and section managers are directed towards the same ends, and likewise up to the level of the president – a spiral upward movement.

In this way the policy deployment method facilitates the attainment of corporate goals and the operation of the organization in a systematic manner. It also assists in integrating the improvement process with organizational long-term strategic plans and actions arising from challenging for the Deming Application Prize. It is clear that with the attention and resources being committed to policy deployment in Japan, European companies have much to gain by studying how best they may use this method. See Akao (1991) for further details of policy deployment.

The commitment and leadership of senior management on a long-term basis is always stressed by the Japanese as being the key point for successful TQM activities. The role of senior management includes:

- Ensuring that the entire organization is committed to TQM and establishing corporate quality systems
- Continuously promoting TQM activities
- Involvement in quality-related education and training
- Participating in activities such as:
  - membership of the committee for quality planning
  - quality assurance meetings for design and manufacture of quality into the product
  - quality audit, improvement and corrective action meetings, and diagnosis of the improvement activities of site locations. In relation to these audits and diagnoses, senior managers study, prior to the actual visits, information on factors such as the quality improvement plans, targets, achievements and problems. This data is provided by the TQM promotions office (the role of this department is discussed later)

Research and Development

In a situation in which product life cycles are shortening while competition is intensifying Japanese companies believe that research and development (R&D) is the main means for helping them to sustain their competitive edge, and this is the major focus of their efforts. They invest heavily in R&D and vigorously pursue new product development, with the aim of achieving maximum products from new products before competitors enter the market. They typically have a focused strategy to develop products that will feed into company performance and profitability within a prescribed time frame. Japanese companies are engaged in short-term, and long-term R&D. The long-term R&D tends to relate to materials development, and how to combine different types of technologies. The less innovative short-term R&D is geared to the development of new product features and process development (i.e. incremental product improvement). It is also interesting to note that in what European companies may regard as the maintenance department, it is not unusual to witness R&D being undertaken in machine technology using in-house expertise and/or through collaboration with external specialists. Japanese companies also tend to engage in pure research as opposed to leaving this to universities.

Their aim is the bring an increasing number of attractive high value added products to the market in the shortest possible time. This is seen to be a key and is one to which they commit considerable time and resources. Product life cycles in Japanese markets are becoming shorter and shorter, and there is an ever increasing demand from the market-place for new products. The Japanese market is forever concentrated on reducing the cycle time for product development and looking for more unique features, and there is a never-ending demand for new products. Japanese companies believe that if they produce standard products with only a minimum of diversification they will not survive in the market-place. Some Japanese companies have combined the functions of R&D and marketing to facilitate the creation of new market demands, develop their present market share and exploit technological know-how.

Japanese companies have a systematic approach to R&D, which helps to reduce the time from conception of an idea to market launch. They have a huge R&D database in their accumulated experiences from product development to full-scale production, which their designers can draw on to satisfy customer needs. This typically contains a variety of information on aspects such as: design features, QCD carried out on previous products, product development concepts, design for manufacturability, failure mode and effects analysis (FMEA), fault tree analysis (FTA), success tree analysis (STA), reliability, and the product shapes and features that appeal to customers. The database provides them with a competitive advantage by enabling them to produce new designs and products at a faster and faster rate. This is something that European companies will find hard to emulate. Japanese companies thrive on their reputation for leading-edge technology, and corporate prestige is measured in terms of the R&D activity.

The R&D project team steers the product concept through the various stages, from R&D through development to trial and ultimately full-scale production. The process for new product introduction is usually well developed and clearly outlined. Therefore, the R&D team ensures that the design intent is being planned into the product and helps the production areas understand the product. In addition, the team assists with operator training and deals with problems as and when they arise during each stage of the manufacturing process. The attention to detail in this type of activity and the closeness of interfunctional communication is particularly impressive. A common view is that the research laboratory is the teacher and the factories are the students. The R&D centres tend to select and prove the equipment before it is used by the factory in full-scale production.

At one research centre, it was clear that, as a supplier of components to the automotive industry, advanced electronics for use in automotive components were being developed, and that these developments were in turn driving design developments in the major motor manufacturers. In general, the reverse is true in the European motor industry, with the supplier manufacturing to an original equipment manufacturer's design and carrying out little development work of its own.

The Motivation for Starting Total Quality Management

A general view among European industrialists is that all Japanese companies have been operating to the principles of TQM since the early 1960s; this is a popular misconception. A number of Japanese companies have only introduced TQM within the past ten years or so. This reflects, to some degree, the priorities of the Ministry of International Trade and Industry (MITI) in developing Japanese industry.

The major motivations and associated problem points include:

- Environmental, national and business factors and changing circumstances such as: the second oil crisis, the exchange rate of the yen, slow economic growth and severe competition.

- A lack of effective long-range planning.

- An organizational emphasis on defensive mechanisms.

- The new products that were launched did not achieve their sales target values.

- A need to develop new products that are attractive to the marketplace. In the past, the tendency was to carry out formal and technological development rather than listening to the real needs of customers.

- Slow growth in sales and market, leading to stagnation of the business.

- Concerns about how to achieve the long-term plan of the organization and the president's plan on QCD.

- Complacency with current profits and a failure to recognize the seriousness of the situation.

- The written and verbal experiences of companies who were already practising TQM, in particular, those companies who had received the Deming Application Prize and are major customers of the company in question.

- Organizational, conceptual and business weaknesses such as:
  - lack of advanced planning for quality,
  - lack of liaison between development, design and manufacturing departments,
  - emphasis on manufacturing for quantity without sufficient regard for quality,
  - the management policies were not universally understood throughout the organization,
  - there was a poor approach to the solution of problems,
  - the morale of workers was poor,
  - only stop-gap measures were employed to cope with cutomer claims,
  - there were chronic defects in the manufacturing process, and
  - problems at production start-up due to insufficient pre-production planning.

It is worthy of mention that the reasons are similar to those found in European companies, as outlined in chapter 1. TQM has often been introduced as a response to a crisis to act as a principal organizing pillar for management activities.

The priority actions in the introduction of TQM include:

- Promotion of policy management,

- Planning the introduction of new products in a more effective manner,

- Building in QCD at source and putting in place a company structure for quality assurance and daily control, and

- Developing stable processes.

The introduction of TQM in Japanese companies has not been problem-free, and they have encountered similar problems to their Western counterparts in the introduction and advancement of TQM. For example:

- Committing the requisite time and resources required to bring improvement activities to a satisfactory level,

- Involvement of senior management in the improvement process, and

- Making effective use of quality management tools and techniques.

The following are the factors that Japanese companies consider as the key for success in the introduction of TQM:

- The president and senior management executes strong leadership. These top managers must find out what their middle managers' views are on TQM and obtain their ideas on improvement projects and targets.

- Starting with the president, a good level of TQM education and training must be given at all levels of the organization and this must be put into practice and repeated using the PDCA cycle.

- Top and middle management must take the responsibility for training their subordinates in TQM.

- It is important that middle managers are committed to TQM and provide effective leadership. The role of middle management includes:
  - maintaining close relationships between different divisions in the organization,
  - communicating concepts and ideas vertically down the organization,
  - educating employees about making quality their first priority, and
  - spreading the concept of continuous improvement throughout the organization.

- There is a need to develop effective quality assurance procedures.

Organizing and Planning for Quality

Japanese companies take a holistic approach to the assurance of quality from product panning through to sales and services. They usually have a TQM promotions office at their head office and sometimes at each plant. As the name suggests, it is used to promote TQM though a variety of activities, such as:

- Establishing a TQM policy,

- Education and training (inside and outside the organization),

- Promoting standardization,

- Facilitating QCs and cross-functional teams,

- Involvement in steering committees,

- Ensuring that all company employees, suppliers and distributors achieve the same TQM aims,

- Analyzing and coordinating improvement activities, and

- Communicating and exchanging data with suppliers.

The Japanese are great advocates of the lateral management of major functions, and typically have committees dealing with quality assurance, development, cost, delivery supply, policy and standardization. For example, a typical improvement committee will meet three or four times each year and will establish improvement policies and deal with issues such as the organizational activities of QCs and how you develop the skills of employees. A quality assurance committee will analyze, catalogue and discuss any day-to-day problems and non-conformance problems in the field and make decisions on how to resolve them.

The manufacturing department is responsible for maintaining quality, and in this respect, it is usual to find inspectors reporting to the manufacturing manager. The quality assurance department is responsible for:

- Providing guidance to manufacturing and other sections in terms of problem analysis and developing improvement plans,

- Evaluation of product quality performance,

- Audits of the manufacturing division,

- Product and audit inspections,

- Quality-related training, and

- Ensuring that people follow up the plans that have been decided by the TQM promotion office or TQM committee and assisting in cascading these plans down to all levels in the organizational hierarchy.

In large organizations, there is usually a corporate quality assurance department (CQAD). For example, the role of the CQAD at a major manufacturer of electronic products is to:

- Give guidance on TQM to all companies within the group,

- Set a long-term and medium-term policy for the manufacturing divisions,

- Give quality education and training,

- Give quality auditing,

- Maintain a quality performance system for each division and to grade them according to performance,

- Assess that the product is easy to use,

- Determine if the product is safe if used correctly,

- Carry out inspections of their own products on a component by component basis,

- Examine packaging,

- Carry out endurance tests,

- Undertake comparative studies and evaluation of their own and competitors' products and other tests to anticipate problems before they occur,

- Undertake lifestyle research, and

- Study how to produce readable instructions manuals.

In order to reach a consensus on the promotion of TQM activities, increase the level of corporate awareness of TQM and exchange quality-related information, regular meetings are held between corporate and plant quality assurance departments.

The general manager of each division is responsible for TQM, and the TQM promotion office and quality assurance department work together to facilitate continuous and company-wide improvement. Each section and division is responsible for QCD planning at source. They all submit a report on their improvement activities to the quality assurance department; the department then compiles a report for the TQM promotion office, which in turn is passed to the president for consideration in the annual audit of the division. This report typically covers specific improvements, goals and achievements, explanation of achievements and/or shortfalls, projects undertaken, feedback data, state of health of cross-functional teams and customer satisfaction. The annual audit involves the president going around the offices and plants to evaluate their TQM activities. The purposes of the audit include:

- Checking that improvements are being made against the plan,

- Demonstrating to employees that the president is committed to TQM,

- Sharing ideas and future plans with employees and obtaining their thoughts,

- Assessing the use of statistical methods, and

- Enabling employees to report their achievements to senior management.

The Japanese hold the view that quality assurance in all aspects of their business is the central core of TQM, and without effective quality assurance procedures to support the communication of company requirements, TQM is difficult. Quality assurance is part of the Japanese style of thinking. Consequently, intensive effort is devoted to the assurance of quality on a day-to-day basis. All of the companies visited had charts and diagrams that outlined, in considerable detail, their basic quality assurance system and procedures.

When problems occur they are analyzed in detail using a defect analysis sheet. Everything is itemized in considerable depth and incredible attention is paid to the smallest of details. The Japanese place a lot of emphasis on finding out exactly where and why they are doing things wrong. The usual procedure is to put into place some temporary countermeasures to gain control of the situation while investigation is made into the root cause of the concern. This is followed by individual and then systematic recurrence prevention measures. They are very careful not to repeat any failures made in the past, and make continual reference to various failure recurrence prevention checklists. When anything unsatisfactory is detected, it is fed back to the appropriate upstream stage and preventive actions are taken to counteract the trouble.

The emphasis is on source control and discipline. For example, in a transformer manufacturer they emphasize the theme of: 'if you do not observe such and such a factor, mistakes will happen' (with graphical details of the mistakes being displayed). Other typical activities employed for source control include:

- Quality assurance tables (e.g. control plans) for in-company and subcontractors work,
- Design and review to prevent any failure on the part of designers,
- The production of operating procedures by the foreman and line operators, and
- Standards and instructions for daily control.

A variety of aids are provided to ensure that operators have all the help required to get it right first time and prevent errors from occurring. These include:

- Check sheets,
- Operating instructions,
- Product identification cards,
- Mistake-proof devices.
- Process operation sheets,
- Defect analysis sheets,
- Features and parameters to which attention is required,
- Quality assurance tables, and
- Machine vision systems.

At a furniture manufacturer, to promote process management and control at source, every line worker produces a working instruction entitled 'what I know about my job – the knack of doing my job'; these are displayed at appropriate prominent places. In a transformer manufacturer, white boards are available at strategic places in the factory and are used by employees to develop quality improvement ideas.

Japanese companies tend to use all of the seven quality control tools – cause and effect diagram, histogram, check sheet, Pareto diagram, control chart, scatter diagram and graphs (see Ishikawa, 1976) – and visibly display the results on a quality control notice-board (termed an MQ station). In this way they are not only listening to the process but taking action to improve it, and this combined use of seven quality control tools facilitates problem resolution and improvement action. Each section in a Japanese company has an MQ station, which is a base point for TQM activities. It is usual for workers together at the station to consider quality issues and exchange information on the PDCA cycle.

In recent times considerable use has been made of SPC by Western companies. However, it is rare to see quality control charts used in conjunction with the other six quality control tools. This is a lesson to be learnt from the Japanese.

In planning for quality from the R&D and design stages, consider-able attention is given to listening to the voice of the customer and a variety of means are employed for this purpose. In the stages of planning and production preparation, trial production and full-scale production and field experience, detailed notes are kept of any problems encountered and the countermeasures that have been put into place. In addition a detailed report is produced at the end of the new product introduction process. These detailed notes of knowledge are collected and filed to provide an extensive database. These notes are always referred to and used in the planing of new products and during various investigations. All of the necessary preparations are made in advance of actual production and consider-able resources are committed to this activity. In European organiza-tions, production preparation is often rushed in the hope that any problems can be corrected later. Even if notes are made they are often not analyzed and used to prevent recurrence of concerns in future products.

In the development and design stage, engineers from the quality assurance and inspection department take up residency in the development and design department. This is termed the 'resident engineer system' and is what is termed in Europe concurrent engineering or simultaneous engineering. The designs are evaluated for potential difficulties at the volume production stage. Consideration is given to the preventive measures used for troubles experienced in the past, and an efficient means of production to ensure design quality. In the production preparation stage, engineers from the development and design department take up residency in the manufacturing and quality assurance departments. This is to ensure that design intent is fully translated into the following process, to feed in know-how obtained during the design and development stage and promote the implementation of countermeasures against troubles, including mistake-proofing (for details of mistake-proofing, see Shingo 1986). These cross-functional teams facilitate the process of simultaneous/ concurrent engineering, encourage a problem solving orientation, develop diversified skills and improve communication, which not only reduces the time for product development and production preparation, but also ensures that the designs are suitable for manufacture and reduces the number of late and costly engineering changes.

Major suppliers also join in at the design stage (they are called 'guest designers'). This activity recognizes that suppliers are the product specialists and helps to ensure that their expertise is used to identify improvements early in the design cycle.

To help assure product quality, there is a feedback and/or feed forward of quality information in production planning, product design, evaluation of prototype products, pre-production planning, purchasing, quality audit, evaluation of pre-production products, volume production, inspection, evaluation of the products from volume production, and sales and field service operations. The objective is to build in quality at each step before sending work to the next process. There is full collaboration and cooperation between R&D, technical, quality assurance and manufacturing departments to eliminate problems and ensure that processes are mistake-proof. This is facilitated through the use of cross-functional teams.

In order to identify defects early on in the design process and to assure the quality design, it is usual to use techniques such as design reviews, design of experiments, quality assurance meetings, QFD,

FMEA, FTA, quality audits and reliability tests. In the production preparation phase the production engineers endeavour to predict failures for the process and to take collective action before machine and process sequences are finalized. FMEA and process capability studies are employed to assist with this. It is usual to carry out a process capability study every time new production facilities are used, when a new design is produced on existing facilities and in the mass production of established products.

In all of the companies visited, the housekeeping was immaculate and factories and offices were clinically clean. For example, a visit around a steel mill involved the mission members wearing white gloves, which when discarded were hardly discoloured. When touring the photosetting department of a printing company, members had to tie plastic covers over their shoes. Little dust was found on window ledges in any of the organizations visited. Japanese companies believe in clear gangways. Any necessary equipment relating to the process is put onto racking which is located on an outside wall. It is not uncommon to see the space between the gangway and the outside wall painted green to represent grass and potted plants placed on the painted areas. The discipline of cleanliness and housekeeping is a prerequisite for effective quality assurance, and this should be pursued more vigorously by European companies. However, many European companies do not spend sufficient effort on defining and quantifying their housekeeping requirements and do not appear to recognize the impact they have on business performance. It is accepted the condition of housekeeping is the responsibility of the employees local to the area and is maintained by them. A variety of aids and evaluation methods are used to promote housekeeping under what are termed the 'five Ss'. These are Japanese words (seiri, seiton, seiso, seiketsu and shitsuke), which when translated relate approximately to:

- Seiri: sort – separating what is required from that which is not.

- Seiton: Neatness – arranging the required items in a tidy manner and in a clearly defined place.

- Seiso: Cleaning – keeping the equipment, surrounding area and environment clean and tidy.

- Seiketsu: Standardization – eliminating causes of dirt, leaks and spills, developing systems to keep things organized and developing standard methods for cleaning and maintaining.

- Shitsuke: Sustaining – following the procedures that have been laid down, practising until it is a way of life and sharing best practices.

Management of Improvement

It was clear from the presentations made by the Japanese managers and technical specialists that they form part of a committed management team who are enthusiastic, enjoy work and are vigorously working on continuous improvement. They also have a long-term vision of where their respective companies are heading. The Japanese companies visited exhibit the typical profile for growth. For example, one company during the past three years had experienced an increase in sales of 21 per cent, the new products to sales ratio had increased by 25 per cent, and labour productivity had improved by 50 per cent. Most companies were planning to increase sales by 20–25 per cent over a period of three years.

Japanese managers articulate very effectively what they are doing and have considerable confidence that the strategy and course of action they are pursuing are right. This confidence is based on a detailed understanding of the actual situation, based on statistical data from extensive ongoing monitoring activities. The aim of each company is to be the market leader and best in class. Japanese improvement activities tend to have a single title, banner of umbrella, e.g. total productive maintenance (TPM) (for details see Nakajima, 1988a,b), TQM or JIT, under which various initiatives are brought together as an integral part of the company's business plans and translated into a company-wide effort. This helps to give their improvement activities and teams a clear focus. In European companies the initiatives being pursued often tend to be segmented and somewhat fragmented, and are the responsibility of individual departments and people; there is also a tendency for people to be on the lookout for the next concept to replace the one which is current.

The Japanese have developed an organizational culture and management style which, based on the evidence of their investments and success in worldwide production facilities, can operate successfully anywhere. The key to their success lies in their ability to create an organizational culture within an environment that is conducive to continuous improvement. The saturation of the Japanese markets, the strength of the yen, high labour costs and aggressive sales drive of individual companies with expectations of higher and higher sales will cause Japanese companies to seek an increasing number of offshore manufacturing bases.

In many European manufacturing companies if a small number of key people leave, there is a danger that the improvement process will first stagnate and then finally degenerate. In contrast, the Japanese appear to have moved to a situation of what might be classed as autonomous improvement. All employees manage for themselves the improvement effort, which proceeds in a common direction with each person accepting ownership of the improvement. They appear to have developed a standardized method of managing companies and the improvement process, a method that can be applied to most cultures. They are expanding on a worldwide basis in order to maintain their high sales growth and most have made a series of moves to internationalize their base of operation.

Through their involvement with individual initiatives, quality circles and/or the suggestions scheme, supervisors and operators are constantly engaged in problem prevention and improvement activities. They also pay keen attention to machinery and equipment quality through the application of TPM. In Japanese companies operators can stop the production line, using what is known as a helpline, if they are experiencing any kind of quality problem or if they cannot keep up with the production rate. When problems arise emergency teams assist the operator to rectify the situation. There are regular meetings between operators, supervisors and technical specialists to discuss problems and improvement actions. In Western companies when problems occur there are usually a number of organizational layers between spotting the problem, its solution and recovery of the situation. It is worth pointing out that Japanese manufacturing managers operate in a more favourable environment than their Western counterparts. Japanese companies have a bias towards manufacturing in general and engineering in particular. Companies employ huge numbers of engineers. The majority of European manufacturing companies employ insufficient numbers of engineers and consequently do not have the resources to solve problems. Every Japanese manager with whom discussions have been held realizes that manufacturing is the key to the national economy. Work occupies the collective consciousness of the Japanese people and there is a general realization that their future depends in it.

Japanese managers and technical specialists exhibit a caring attitude towards production and what is happening on the factory shop floor. Senior and middle managers spend a considerable amount of time on the shop floor to see what is happening. They ask about results and problems, they give advice and they help to create good habits through leadership (management by walking about). There is a tendency in European companies for senior managers to isolate themselves in their offices and fail to have regular contact with those involved with the production of products and delivery of services. Senior European managers should ask themselves the question – what is the purpose of my office?

The Japanese invest in equipment, technology and process improvement, without having to worry about short-term, payback periods; they know that this will be beneficial over the longer-term. This also applies to investing in a period of recession. This willingness to invest must be a considerable feature in the motivation of their managers and engineers. In the main, the investment is to reduce production costs. Over the last thirty or so years the Japanese have amassed considerable proof of the wisdom of this policy. The typical payback period for equipment is three to five years, compared to the one year that is typical in European companies; interest rates for borrowing money are also lower. In European companies the production personnel are usually required to specify a breakeven production volume, and in relation to the investment in new equipment, it is a common requirement to make the justification over a three-shift operation.

European manufacturing management frequently complain that their engineers always want sophisticated computer equipment and software for their projects. By contrast, while they make extensive use of computer-aided design and manufacturing systems, Japanese engineers concentrate a considerable amount of their improvement effort on doing the simple things well. A considerable amount of the equipment employed by Japanese companies is relatively basic. The key factor is not the equipment itself but how it is used to improve manufacturing efficiency. It is always remembered that the equipment

Table 9.1 Results of improvement activities in two Japanese companies

Semiconductor manufacturer		Temperature controller manufacturer		
Goals	Achievements in three years	Function	Before JUMP	After JUMP
Equipment	85% utilization	Production lead time	3 days	2 days
Manufacturing cost	50% reduction	Inventory: parts	30 days	3 days
Failure rate	10% reduction	WIP	12 days	8 days
Production	Twofold improvement	finished product	5 days	2 days
Suggestions	Four per person per month	Workforce	13	6
Accidents	Zero	Space	20 m^2	12 m^2

JUMP, Just-in-Time, Upgrade, Manufacturing Process.

is only required to support manufacturing and improve efficiency. All of the Japanese companies visited had their own internal machinery manufacturing division and a considerable amount of the equipment seen in their plants was customized. The proprietary equipment is often employed to eliminate waste and transportation between process and to facilitate good internal logistics.

The Japanese are never shy in sharing the results of their improvement activities with Western visitors (see table 9.1).

Visible Management Systems

Japanese companies place considerable emphasis on ensuring that their operating data is visible on the factory shop floor. They believe that everyone in the company benefits from an open information system. A complete range of information, in a variety of formats, is displayed, usually in simple, locally developed formats. This data assists managers, technical specialists, engineers and operators to manage their processes more effectively, facilitates the process of continuous incremental improvement, and identifies and publicizes the improvements. It is a common communication mechanism which keeps employees in touch with what is happening, provides a focus to help concentrate efforts, indicates to people when events are not going to plan, and provides warning signals for all kinds of different events. Display devices are often created by operators and first-line supervision. In some cases, the display is related to a specific manufacturing section (e.g. who is responsible for specific activities, TPM achievements, QC members and projects, and a skill matrix, including photographs of operators), and in others it is related to a particular topic (e.g. policy deployment, mistake-proofing, QCs, education and safety). The following are examples of this visible management system:

- A display of the activities of QCs in terms of where they are located in the factory, current projects, achievements and membership.

- One company, as part of a campaign to improve the plant safety performance, displayed on a notice-board the safety actions to which each operator had committed him or herself together with the operator's photograph.

- In a software engineering department a board displayed against each workstation the name of the software engineer and the job on which he or she was currently working.

- In a metal part punching department, the process instructions of jobs that were scheduled to be started at various times during the day were hung on a rack against a time scale from 0830 to 1930.

- A schematic layout in the sub-assembly and assembly areas of one organization indicated the flow of work and, using different colours, the zone position of full-time employees, brown – casual employees, blue – operators responsible for the supply of parts; yellow – employees who are used to assist sections that have fallen behind their scheduled production targets.

- The main steps of a JIT system in terms of its purpose, targets, activities and achieved improvements was displayed on a notice-board.

- A complete wall of one plant was covered in charts relating to a variety of issues, including details and pictures of improvements that had been made, safety achievements and performance, attendance statistics, quality issues, suggestions, production targets, QC activities and TPM activities.

- Another company hung on racks at the side of machines a series of large cards that operators had produced to train their peers on specific aspects of TPM.

- In a refrigeration unit assembly line, quality control check-sheets were displayed at each workstation indicating the product characteristics that required attention, the important processes in terms of quality, and the self inspections and tests to be carried out.

- In one organization, a number of sub-assembly areas were supplying assembly lines, across a gangway. Each sub-assembly area and line had scheduled production targets for specific times of the shift along with actual production achieved. If production was going according to schedule a grey card was displayed across the gangway, if production was two units behind schedule a red card was used.

- In a staff room at the Corporate Quality Assurance Division of a major electronics company various data was displayed on the walls relating to product performance in comparison to that of the competitors and the problems currently being experienced by users of their products.

This sharing and diffusion of information helps to facilitate a common purpose for the company, and can help to reduce organizational conflict. Concepts such as TQM, TPM and JIT are closely understood by employees and they also know why a particular concept is being used, the strategies and objectives, the techniques employed, and successes and failures. In a number of companies, the information displayed indicated that the improvement objective was to reduce the number of operating staff in a production section. Any staff affected in this way are transferred to other sections and to subsidiaries. For example, in one company, operators are sometimes transferred to the sales function.

The pump manufacturing division of a mechanical engineering company suffers considerable seasonal fluctuation, with some 65 per cent of production output scheduled between October and March. Middle and first-line management, together with the company union, make plans on how to adjust the workload of people in the manufacturing, assembly and engineering areas in both the slack and busy periods. A matrix showing the movement and activities of people in these periods is communicated and displayed. For example, during the slack period employees are moved between manufacturing, assembly and engineering to improve their skill and knowledge, maintenance, mistake-proofing, standardization and improvement activities are carried out, jigs are produced and trial manufacture is conducted on parts currently purchased. Employees also go to customers and dealers to assist with the selling of the product and to listen to what they have to say about the product and service.

These two examples emphasize the flexibility of the system and of the Japanese worker. All of the companies visited stressed this point and said that workers accepted job rotation and movement from one job or another very readily. Job flexibility and job rotation help to eliminate departmental boundaries, which are often a major stumbling block to improvement activities, and diffuse new technologies, approaches and systems to every corner of an organization. Most workers are in multi-skilled groups and are able to do all jobs in the area. There are no detailed job descriptions and the salary is paid for the person and not for the job. Japanese companies firmly believe in developing generalists and not specialists. The system of lifetime employment and single company labour unions obviously facilitates flexibility, job rotation and long-term education and training programmes.

Involvement of People

There is a clear recognition in Japanese companies that their key asset is human resources, and all employees are encouraged to participate in continuous improvement activities. In more than one company visited, it was said that because of the lifetime employment situation they were always searching for ways to motivate and revitalize their staff. The usual means was through QCs, suggestion schemes, other small group activities, a variety of presentations, job rotations, and continuous education and training.

Quality circles and suggestions schemes provide the main mechanisms and motivation for involving everyone in an organization in continuous improvement. Considerable importance is attached to these two activities; they are viewed as complementary activities and it is claimed that there is no friction. Quality circles can submit suggestions and also have their projects evaluated by the scheme. A variety of recognition and award schemes, contests and prizes are in place for recognizing employees efforts and to provide direct rewards. Great kudos is attached to these awards. The quantity and quality of suggestions are seen to be important and reflect the department manager's ability to create an environment that is conducive to improvement.

SUGGESTION SCHEMES

The following is typical of the operating characteristics of Japanese suggestion schemes:

> A suggestion is submitted and evaluated the same day by the foreman of the section, the person making the suggestion gets a sum of 100–300 yen. If the suggestion is considered to have potential it is evaluated by the assistant section manager and section manager or the QC committee, who evaluate how many points it is worth. Alternatively, more data can be requested from the proposer, and the second proposal is evaluated in the same way. The formal acceptance and

Table 9.2 The performance of corporate suggestions schemes in the US and Japan

	US	Japan
Number of suggestions per 100 employees	21	2530
Adoption	35%	86.1%
Participation	8%	68.3%
Average reward	$461.22	$3.50

payment are, in general, made within one month of a suggestion being presented. The suggestions can be spiralled up to receive monthly, six monthly and annual commendations; this involves a presentation by the proposer to explain his or her idea. The following are the values of the awards given to suggestions by one company.

1st grade: 10 000 Yen
2nd grade: 5000 Yen
3rd grade: 3000 Yen
4th grade: 2000 Yen
5th grade: 1000 Yen

Robinson and Robinson (1994), drawing on comparative data produced by the Japan Human Relations Association on the performance of corporate suggestions schemes in the US and Japan, quote the statistics shown in table 9.2. The success of the Japanese style suggestions scheme in terms of participation and number of suggestions produced is clear from these statistics. It indicates the value of fast feedback to the suggestions that are raised and the importance of small rewards to the vast majority of the workforce.

QUALITY CIRCLES

Without exception, all of the organizations visited had thriving QC programmes involving a large proportion of the total workforce. According to JUSE, some 5.5 million workers are members of QCs, equating to 10 per cent of the Japanese workforce. QCs are applied as follows:

- Production areas
- Non-production areas: high level, managed
- Non-production areas: low level, supervised

In general, QCs are employed for reasons of education, communication, improving the environment, changing attitudes etc. and not to reduce costs.

QCs can be considered as a natural part of Japanese working life, and in this respect it is perhaps not advisable to compare them with the use of QCs by Western organizations. Within each section the line workers are involved with their foreman in making day-to-day improvements in their routine work activities. They do not appear to separate out, as is the case in the West, QC activities and day-to-day work activities; it is one unified improvement effort. QCs generally tackle projects related to their section's improvement objectives of meeting the president's, plant manager's and section manager's policies and they tend to be managed by the section manager. The organizations did stress that QCs, while essential, are but a small part of the quality improvement process. In discussions with Dr Noguchi (executive director, JUSE) on this matter, he reported that the quality management experts have differing views as to the effectiveness of QCs in solving an organization's quality problems: Ishikawa claimed 30–35 per cent, Juran 15–20 per cent and Deming 5 per cent.

In most Japanese companies all non-managerial employees belong to a QC. There is some suggestion that membership is not voluntary, with considerable peer pressure to be involved. The effectiveness of QCs is usually assessed at annual or six monthly intervals, at which time good performance is recognized.

During the past few years Japanese companies have been making changes to the way in which QCs are operated. These changes have come about as the popularity of QCs has spread out within the country and as a result of pressure from the labour union. The changes identified are:

- If QCs meet outside work time they are paid.

- A project carried out by a QC can be submitted through the suggestion system and a monetary reward made to each circle member. The money received is usually allocated for recreational facilities, education and training, social activities etc. for the general development of the group. There appears to be little difficulty in acknowledging the ownership of a suggestion either by an individual or a group.

- In the manufacturing areas it is expected that each working zone has a QC.

- Each QC is expected to complete a set number of themes, usually two, each year.

- While the circle members can select their own themes, it is expected that they submit their choices to the section manager for approval.

- The QCs are managed. The section manager will check the progress of the themes undertaken by QCs and if they are behind schedule with their projects will step in and assist them. The QCs have themes related to their section's improvement activities derived from the policy deployment process.

- Each circle is required to submit a written report to the section manager when they have completed a project. The manager comments on the report and signs to say that it has been competed satisfactorily along with suggestions to improve the future efficiency of the Circle.

- The way that QCs are operated by the Japanese companies is more akin to the quality improvement team concept followed by Western companies and not to the typical textbook definition. In most cases, an engineer is available to assist QCs with difficult projects.

Typical objectives of QCs and suggestions schemes in the organizations visited are as follows:

Quality Circles

- To provide opportunities for self-improvement of knowledge and skills through cooperative team efforts,

- To create a rewarding work environment, and

- To create a workplace where total participation in quality control is a reality.

Suggestion schemes

- To improve employees' ability to do their jobs in an effective manner and to develop individual abilities,

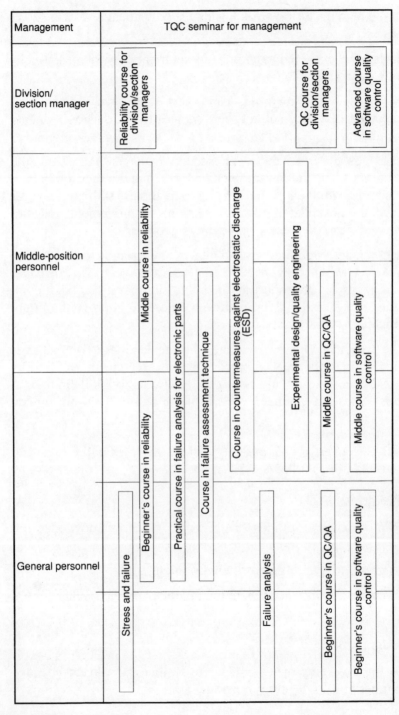

Figure 9.4 Education system for TQC
Source: Omon Corporation, Kusatsu City, Japan.

- To promote friendly and healthy human relations among all employees and to vitalize activities, and

- To improve the company structure and operations.

There is a considerable effort to create a work environment in which staff are active participants. Employees are treated as human beings and not as tools, and companies go to considerable lengths to promote harmony between personnel and technology.

Education and Training

Japanese companies believe that everyone in an organization must understand TQM and that this can only be achieved by education and training. They take a long-range view of quality education and training and tend to have a master training schedule and curriculum to develop the skills of all their employees. The schedule recognizes the different training requirements of people in different functions and levels in the organizational hierarchy (see figure 9.4 for an example of such a matrix). Senior managers take a personal interest in the content of the training programme of their organization.

Most of the TQM training is aimed at engineers (for example a thirty-day course – for five days each month for six months) and the general view in a Japanese company is that 'if an engineer does not understand TQM then he or she is not an engineer'.

Education and training programmes are developed to promote an awareness of TQM and increase each person's knowledge and skills. Japanese companies take the view that the most important factor in TQM is the education of people, and the point is made that education and training act as key motivators for the pursuance of improvement. The majority of companies encourage their employees to suggest the professional training they wish to undertake. The Japanese firmly believe that better education makes for an improved worker. In one company's training programme two machine operators were undertaking CAD/CAM training and the plant director had enrolled for a course on gas welding techniques.

The Japanese companies do not develop specialists such as quality engineers. Their aim is to give everyone a knowledge of the principles of techniques of TQM, and consequently there is a clarity of understanding, with everyone being involved in improvement activities. It should also be noted that new employees receive formal TQM training within a short time of joining a company.

The following is an outline of the training given at supervisory level by a mechanical engineering organization:

- Self-development

- Effective use of time

- Education of subordinates

- Labour and personnel management

- Safety and health management

- Enhancement of production efficiency

- Understanding costs

- Quality consciousness/tools and techniques

- Process control

- Maintenance

- Environmental control

Both the breadth and depth of this company's supervisor training programme are worthy of comment. For example, in the section on 'understanding costs', the supervisors are given detailed information on both fixed and variable costs in their area, plus an understanding generally of everything in a production operation that influences costs (e.g. assembly line balancing). This depth of knowledge would be unusual at much more senior levels in European organizations. The breadth of training is illustrated by the information given on what would generally be regarded as other people's jobs. In this way the supervisors are given a total picture of business operations. The majority of the training material is in the form of checklists that the supervisors is expected to go through before and after taking action.

In general, European companies give little real training at supervisor level. By contrast, Japanese companies regard supervisors as the first level of management and given them the skills to match this responsibility. All senior managers have been through the same training and so have shared knowledge and beliefs, providing a common platform for understanding and action.

Everyone in a Japanese organization is trained to use the seven quality control tools, and there was ample evidence (as displayed on the quality notice-boards discussed earlier) that these tools were well developed during all stages of production. A variety of training is given in techniques, and presentation and leadership skills to deepen TQM consciousness among employees and to improve their problem solving ability. The most intensive training is given to design and production engineers.

In European companies, people are usually trained by one company, often then moving on to another company, which benefits from the training and development already done. European companies may need to adopt a broader approach to expect to gain as much as they lose from this turnover of people skills, otherwise there is a danger that investment in education and training will be inhibited. This also frequently results in a failure to develop training strategies; rarely do European companies set improvement objectives for training programmes.

In Japan the quality training programme is typically carried out by staff from corporate and divisional quality departments, engineers, invited lecturers from outside the company and by institutions such as JUSE. For example, JUSE offers 25 different courses which deal with TQM and these are attended by a range of people, from presidents and top management to line workers. Between 600 and 800 people are undergoing TQM training in any one day at JUSE and currently some 40 000 take their courses. There has been a fourfold increase in the number of delegates since 1980 following the second oil crisis and a tenfold increase since 1960. Currently some 300 courses are held each year and they are updated annually. Almost without exception the instructors carry out an audit to assess the effective use of newly acquired skills by people they have trained.

Because of the lifetime employment practices of large Japanese organizations, it is possible for them to invest heavily in a long-term programme of education and training and retraining to develop their employees' capabilities. A programme of initial training prepares them for work with the organization in terms of mission, philosophy, systems, procedures and job skills. The fact that all new employees, whether they are from junior or senior high school or university, begin employment in an organization at the same time each year helps the organization of the training and forms the basis for relationships which will last for a very long time.

Total Productive Maintenance

The concept of TPM is now very much in evidence in Japanese companies. Nippondenso (a subsidiary of the Toyota Motor Group) has achieved considerable success with TPM, which every company in Japan is now trying to emulate.

Japanese companies are very much motivated by national prizes. They have the Deming Prize, which recognizes outstanding achievement in quality strategy, management and execution, the Japan Quality Medal for companies who have won the Deming Application Prize and can thereafter demonstrate five or more years of continuous improvement, the Ishikawa Prize for new methods of new systems for the modernization of management and achievement by their application, and the Japan Institute of Plant Maintenance Award for TPM. These awards are perceived as being extremely prestigious. More than one company commented that the TPM award was the hardest of all awards in Japan to achieve.

There was a range of different views among the companies visited on the meaning of TPM. The widest definition was total productive maintenance, which encompassed the more narrow term of total prevention maintenance. Therefore, TPM is seen as a total method of management. Full details of TPM can be found in Nakajima (1988a,b). It was Nakajima who developed TPM by combining the key features of preventive, productive and predictive maintenance with TQM, QCs and employee involvement. However, in terms of actual maintenance procedures and systems, TPM contains nothing new.

It is clear that TQM and TPM are similar concepts, with the common goal of improving product quality. TPM is considered as an additional driver, which is complementary to TQM. At one company it was suggested that TQM is about 'how to' and TPM is concerned with 'why'. However, while a number of Japanese companies started TQM some twenty-five to thirty years ago, the majority of them have only become involved with TPM during the past decade. The consensus view among the companies is that, in their experience, TQM has only a limited influence on machine performance and so they have introduced TPM to focus on the machines. The condition of the equipment has a considerable influence on the quality of production output and is a key element in manufacturing a quality product. The machine needs the input of people to keep it clean and to improve its efficiency and operation, thereby promoting a sense of 'plant ownership' by the operators.

TPM is a scientific company-wide approach in which every employee is concerned about the maintenance and the quality and efficiency of the equipment. The objective is to reduce the whole life cost of machinery and equipment through more efficient maintenance management, and, as far as possible, to integrate the maintenance and manufacturing departments. Teamwork is a key element of TPM. By analysis of each piece of equipment it focuses on reducing manufacturing losses and costs (i.e. the six major losses – breakdown, set-up/adjustment, speed, idling and minor stoppages, quality defects and start-up) and establishes a system of preventive maintenance over a machine's working life. The emphasis of TPM is on improving the skills of operators in relation to machine technology and training and educating them to clean, maintain and make adjustments to their machines. The training and education of operators is carried out by maintenance and engineering staff. In this way machinery is kept at optimal operating efficiency. The 'five Ss' are essential activities in TPM and they also promote visible management.

In addition to QCs, Japanese companies operate TPM circles made up of operators and maintenance staff, which tend to focus on the production facility.

In a battery manufacturing company, the three-year TPM programme has the usual seven key steps of:

- Step 1: initial cleaning
- Step 2: countermeasures at the source of problems, to minimize accumulation of dirt and other contaminants
- Step 3: set maintenance, cleaning and lubrication standards
- Step 4: general inspection procedures and schedules
- Step 5: autonomous inspection procedures and schedules
- Step 6: orderliness and tidiness
- Step 7: full autonomous maintenance

After each TPM step has been achieved a TPM sticker is issued and placed on a machine. The company started TPM to improve efficiency, quality, control and the ability of supervisors. Each employee is given the twenty-hour education programme on TPM. The operating personnel devote some eight to ten hours of paid overtime each month to TPM activities and produce TPM study sheets to educate and involve their peers. Twice a year the best ideas are selected for an award. Silver stars are put on machines that have operated at one hundred per cent efficiency during a period of two shift operation. Examples of TPM efficiency improvements are a 20 per cent increase in machine performance for the battery plate making line and a 100 per cent increase on the battery assembly line.

Just-in-Time

JIT is typically considered by Japanese companies as a key feature of TQM, so it is worth mentioning how JIT is being developed. Most companies said that their systems were still being developed and each day they try to make progress to one-by-one production. The aim in all cases is to eliminate the 'seven mudas' (wastefulness, or non-value added aspects):

- Excess production
- Waiting
- Conveyance
- Motion
- The process itself
- Inventory
- Defects

This is to ensure that all actions carried out are adding value to the product. The typical cycle employed to eliminate waste is: identify waste, find the cause of waste, make improvements and standardize the improvement to hold the gains.

The main factors currently surrounding the deployment of JIT by Japanese companies are outlined in the following subsections.

Customer service   The main purpose of JIT is not inventory reduction but improved delivery of products to customers. The first aim is to reduce waste and the second is to reduce lead times.

Selective use   JIT is not applied universally to all products and components. The Japanese investigate each manufactured item and determine if JIT can be used. For example, the view was formed that the Japanese were finding that JIT was difficult to apply in the case of semiconductor manufacture. To cater for fluctuating demand they kept stocks of diffused wafers which were then customized.

TPM essential   TPM is crucial to the effective operation of JIT.

Pilot projects   When JIT is initially applied a production/assembly line is chosen as a pilot, where it is developed and refined before being extended to other production/assembly areas.

Reduced set-up times   Reductions in machine and process setting up times. For example, on the lead oxide grid pasting line of a battery manufacturer it previously took two operators thirty minutes to change the dies; this has now been reduced to one minute for one person.

Selective use of Kanbans   A variety of Kanbans are used – cards, small boxes, Kanban squares and lights. Kanbans are used in only certain parts of the production system; they are also used to order some parts from suppliers.

Flexible supply chains   A feature of the production system is that if operator A is being supplied with product by operator B and if A is not meeting the production schedule, B stops supplying the product and comes to A's assistance. Some operators are dedicated to the supply of parts to manufacturing and assembly line personnel, and others are responsible for coming to the production line and assisting with emergencies as and when they occur.

Logistics   At one company, most suppliers are located within fifty to sixty kilometres of the factory, some within twenty kilometres and others at a much greater distance. The delivery frequency is dependent upon the quantity and varies between daily, every two days and every three days. Another company said that it delivers three times a day to original equipment manufacturers and that on average its own suppliers deliver twice a day to it. One company provides a three-month forecast to its suppliers and each day picks from suppliers' production lines and/or stores the parts it requires. It is interesting to note that at a wire harness manufacturer the comment was made that 'like it or not, we have to be JIT supplier to Honda, Nissan and Toyota'. This comment is typical of that heard in European automotive component suppliers.

The suppliers tend to work to a specific delivery time on the day in question and the supply is made in small lorries, which make trackside deliveries. There is often a mix of parts from different suppliers on the same truck. This is also the case in the delivery of finished product to the customer. There is serious traffic congestion in Japan's principal cities and this has no doubt been exacerbated by the transportation of small amounts of goods at frequent intervals. Koshi (1989) claims that 43 per cent of motor vehicle traffic in Japan carries freight, and proposes an underground network for the distribution of goods.

Supplier audits Some parts are supplied directly to the line without inspection, while others are inspected. This decision is related to previous quality performance of the parts and the supplier's quality system. An audit to assess a suppler's quality system, manufacturing processes and parts quality is usually carried out. There are three types of audit – new supply audit, periodical audit and emergency audit. Their results of incoming inspections and of non-conformances found on the line are evaluated each month and fed back to suppliers. Information between customer and suppliers is exchanged regularly using computer-aided quality information systems. Quality improvement meetings are usually held once a month with the aim of improving the quality of supplied product. It is interesting to note that, in general, control charts and process capability data are only requested from suppliers when non-conformances occur. The considerable attention to the use of SPC by European companies is not seen in Japan. Japanese companies only tend to use SPC when proving capability and when they are experiencing problems. The absence of 'visible' SPC is indicative of the progress made in continuous improvement. If an organization has very capable processes (a process capability index (Cpk) value greater than 3) the ongoing use of charting may be considered superfluous.

Dual sourcing   A mix of single and dual sourcing is employed by the companies visited and in both cases the relationships with suppliers are long-term. Among the reasons for dual sourcing are to keep some flexibility in a customer's dealings with its suppliers, competition in terms of QCD, maintaining a competitive edge, and the capacity of suppliers. It is usual to ensure that the largest volume of business goes to the supplier who performs best in terms of QCD. One manager, when questioned about the sourcing of wire harnesses by major Japanese motor manufacturers, said, 'of course Honda, Nissan and Toyota employ dual sourcing'. These three motor manufacturers divide their requirements between the company and its competitor depending on capacity, demand and schedule. At regular intervals the company confirms its capacity to these three major customers.

Manufacturing technology   The Japanese are employing the same machinery and technology as their European counterparts. However, because of activities such as TPM, reduced setting up time by use of single minute exchange of dies (SMED) (for details see Shingo, 1985) and integrated materials handling, their machine efficiency and effectiveness are much higher. None of their machinery and equipment is new. For example, one company had die casting machinery that was over fifteen years old. Several of its production system improvements have come from developing and applying small inexpensive customized equipment for the handling and transfer of parts between processes, processing itself and the application of mistake-proofing devices. In general, it employs modern production layouts within huge visible investments, apart from computer-aided design, manufacturing and simulation systems.

Production system development   Examples of some of the means employed by Japanese companies in developing their production systems include:

● Product and cellular layout. They tend to change the layout to reflect changes in product mix.

● The use of mixed model production and assembly lines.

- The employment of cycle time conveyors.

- To facilitate easy movement and production flow, operators stand at workstations.

- Considerable efforts are made to smooth production in relation to volume, variety and capacity. They carry out a number of iterations if the sales and production plan to achieve this. Most organizations give their annual or six monthly production programme to suppliers. They are then issued with a more precise schedule three months before delivery, and with one month to the build programme they are issued with the exact delivery schedule.

- When human operation is more efficient and effective than machines, the Japanese will employ human effort. On a number of occasions it was said that on some tasks people can work faster than machines.

- In assembly situations jobs are kept together in kit form.

Summary

A number of simple facts can be learnt from the Japanese experience of TQM:

- Total quality management depends on a systematic approach, which is applied consistently throughout the entire organization.

- There are no quick fixes for the TQM success of Japanese companies. Western executives are always on the lookout for the universal panacea; unfortunately, there is none. This search for the quick fix is often an irritation to the Japanese. Their success is the result of the application of a combination of procedures, systems, tools, improvement actions and considerable hard work and education from all employees.

- Senior and middle managers must believe in TQM as a key business strategy and be prepared to stick with it over the long term and ensure that it is integrated with other strategies.

- There must be a permanent managed process that examines all products, service process and procedures for the elimination of costs on a continuous basis and develops the mindset in all employees that there is no ideal state. Self-assessment against criteria such as the Deming Application Prize, Malcolm Baldrige National Quality Award and the EFQM Model is an invaluable means of assessing progress in order to ensure that an organization continues to win customers.

- Each person should take personal responsibility for the quality assurance activities within his or her area of control, and quality assurance must be integrated into every process and every function of an organization.

- Planning for improvement must be thorough.

- Improvement is a slow, incremental process. Companies should not expect quick and major benefits from the application of any single method, system, procedure and/or tool and technique. To be effective the quality management tools and techniques must be used together, in particular the seven original quality control tools.

- The concept of TQM is simple; however, defining, introducing and fostering the process is a considerable task and requires commitment from all employees.

- TQM is all about common sense. The Japanese put common sense into practice. They manage and apply common sense in a disciplined manner. In European companies a typical saying is 'you cannot teach common sense' – the Japanese have done just that.

References

Akao, Y. (ed.) 1991: *Hoshin Kanri: Deployment for Successful TQM*. Cambridge, Mass.: Productivity Press.

The Deming Prize Committee 1996: *The Deming Prize Guide for Overseas Companies*. Tokyo: Union of Japanese Scientists and Engineers.

Ishikawa, K. 1976: *Guide to Quality Control*. Tokyo: Japanese Productivity Association.

Koshi, M. 1989: Tokyo's traffic congestion can be unravelled. *The Japan Times*, 14 November, 5.

Mizuno, S. (ed.) 1988: *Management for Quality Improvement: The Seven QC Tools*. Cambridge, Mass.: Productivity Press.

Nakajima, S. 1988a: *Introduction to Total Productive Maintenance*. Cambridge, Mass.: Productivity Press.

—— 1988b: *TPM Development Program*. Cambridge, Mass.: Productivity Press.

Robinson, A. G. and Robinson, M. M. 1994: On the tabletop improvement experiments of Japan, *Production and Operations Management*, 3(3), 201–16.

Shingo, S. 1985: *A Revolution in Manufacturing; The SMED System*. Cambridge, Mass.: Productivity Press.

—— 1986: *Zero Quality Control: Source Inspection and the Poka-Yoke System*. Cambridge, Mass.: Productivity Press.

Bibliography

The following material was used in the preparation of this chapter.

Asher, J. M. and Dale, B. G. 1989: The Japanese approach to quality. *The TQM Magazine*, November, 275–8.

Dale, B. G. 1990: Japanese manufacturing efficiency: a study in the electronics industry. *IEE Proceedings*, 137A(5), 293–301.

—— 1993: The key features of Japanese total quality control. *Quality and Reliability Engineering International* 9(3), 169–78.

Dale, B. G. and Asher, J. M. 1989: Total quality control: lessons European executives can learn from Japanese companies. *European Management Journal*, 7(4), 493–503.

Dale, B. G. and Tidd, J. 1991: Japanese total quality control: a study of best practice. *Proceedings of the Institutions of Mechanical Engineers*, 204(B6), 221–32.

10 Epilogue

As we have seen throughout this book, total quality management is not just meeting the requirements of a quality system standard such as the ISO 9000 series or using some tool or technique to retain the business of a key customer. It is about continually searching for improvements and better ways of doing things, having the right attitude, creating a sense of improvement, pride in products and services and the progress made in their performance, recognizing how dependent others are on our actions, being a part of a team that really cares about what they do, and providing products and services that customers want. In other words, it is a practical approach to running a business with the involvement of employees at all levels, in terms of their own development, participation in the business and helping to eliminate problems. The focus is directed on understanding and anticipating customer requirements through creative thinking, meeting these requirements, giving complete customer satisfaction and, in this way, building customer loyalty.

To achieve these goals, it is essential that senior executives give adequate attention to creating an organizational climate that is conducive to continuous improvement. This means that large-scale change is inevitable, because nothing stays still, with all the attendant problems, as Machiavelli suggested in *The Prince*: 'It should be borne in mind that there is nothing more difficult to arrange, more doubtful of success and more dangerous to carry though than initiating changes . . . the innovator makes enemies of all those who prospered under the old order, and only lukewarm support is forthcoming from those who would prosper under the new'. Senior management need to recognize that the responsibility for change belongs to them.

Quality that delights the customer and guarantees loyalty does not come easily, neither is it free from problems. It costs in time, energy and resources, but the pay-offs in terms of business efficiency can be significant. On the other hand, the failure to continuously provide customers with what they need can be disastrous. It takes a dedicated team of top management to push TQM to its limits, but there are a number of general guiding principles that can be followed to ensure some degree of success.

The following are some of the principles and activities that senior executives should engage in to encourage the development of TQM. In producing this listing we are mindful that executives might be tempted to skip this Epilogue chapter and fail to read through the book; we strongly advise against this.

Principles to Be Adopted

1 Everyone in the organization is involved in continually improving the processes under his or her control and takes responsibility for his or her own quality assurance.

2 Each person is committed to satisfying his or her customers (internal or external).

3 Teamwork is practised in a number of forms.

4 There is a commitment to the development of employees through involvement.

5 A formal programme of education and training is in place and this is viewed as an investment in developing people's ability and knowledge and helping them to realize their potential.

6 Suppliers and customers are integrated into the improvement process.

7 Honesty, sincerity and care are integral parts of daily business life.

8 Simplicity in processes, systems, procedures and work instructions is pursued.

9 Regular and consistent care of the plan-do-check-act cycle.

Senior Management Activities to Encourage TQM

1   Allocate time to understand the concept, principles and practices of TQM.

2   Make sure that TQM becomes integrated and aligned with the organization's business strategies.

3   Take responsibility for providing key inputs into the improvement process and become a role model.

4   Ensure that everybody in the organization knows the reasons for the adoption of TQM and understands their role in the improvement process.

5   Provide guidance and encouragement for your managers, so that they can manage in a manner that is conducive to TQM. This will usually mean redefining leadership behaviours in terms of specific actions, such as positively addressing issues and problems as opportunities, expanding individual knowledge of quality management practices, applying what has been learnt and encouraging others to do the same.

6   Commit resources to TQM.

7   Listen patiently and completely to people and practise what you preach. As Roger Milliken of Milliken and Company says, 'Walk the talk' and 'Our people must believe that we mean what we say'.

8   Encourage flexibility and creativity.

9   Establish a relevant infrastructure for the continuous improvement process.

10   Identify key internal and external performance measures and agree improvement objectives.

11   Devote some part of every day to improvement activities.

12   Deal with customer complaints yourself at random times.

13   Visit, on a regular basis areas, units and divisions.

14   Communicate as never before.

15   Measure the progress being made with TQM.

Introduce Organizational Changes to Support and Develop TQM

1 Put into place a process of policy deployment as part of the business planning cycle.

2 Develop a strategic quality plan to meet the business objectives.

3 Set up and chair a TQM Steering Committee or Quality Council.

4 Ensure that quality features on the agenda of all meetings.

5 Aim to create a continuous improvement environment, which permeates all departments.

6 Encourage participation, trust and people development and ensure that you listen carefully to what your people are saying. As Roy Polson of Manchester Circuits Ltd puts it, 'Build quality into people'.

7 Facilitate teamwork.

8 Institute advanced quality planning, audit and improvement meetings and organizational housekeeping.

9 Ensure that the organization listens to all of the views through the barriers of sectionalism.

10 Promote and encourage cross-functional management to break through the barriers of sectionalism.

11 Establish a formal TQM education and training programme for all employees.

12 Recognize accomplishments and celebrate success.

13 Employ benchmarking to help change attitudes and identify and build upon best practice.

14 Conduct feedback sessions to assess the progress and effectiveness of improvement plans that have been developed to address weaknesses.

Total quality management is about changing the climate within the organization, involving everybody, and, for top management, doing jobs formerly never considered, at least, in the majority of Western organizations (e.g. talking to customers, dealing personally with customer complaints, frequent visits to the producing and delivering areas, 'hands-on' management, auditing and assessment of improvement activities, involvement in advanced quality planning and improvement meetings, visiting superior performing companies to swap and share improvement ideas). The area of interpersonal communication is crucial for the success of TQM, and nobody can do this better than the CEO and his or her top team. As Saul Gellerman once said, 'Nothing is more central to an organization's effectiveness than its ability to transmit accurate, relevant, understandable information among its members. All the advantages of organizations – economy of scale, financial and technical resources, diverse talents, and contacts – are of no practical value if the organization's members are unaware of what other members require of them and why. Nevertheless, despite its overwhelming and acknowledged importance, the process of communication is frequently misunderstood and mismanaged'.

We have made a clear case in this book for the need for senior management to be committed to TQM and described why they need to demonstrate and exercise effective leadership and become immersed in the concept. We also believe that despite the developments going on in information technology, globalization of operations, increasing complexity of products and services etc. the need for quality will not diminish.

Are you ready to accept the challenge?

Index